I hear the question upon your lips: What is it to be a color?

Color is the touch of the eye, music to the deaf, a word out of the darkness. Because I've listened to souls whispering – like the susurrus of the wind – from book to book and object to object for tens of thousands of years, allow me to say that my touch resembles the touch of angels. Part of me, the serious half, calls out to your vision while the mirthful half soars through the air with your glances.

Orhan Pamuk
My Name Is Red

URBANISMS OF COLOR
GARETH DOHERTY

Gareth Doherty currently teaches Landscape Architecture and Urban Planning and Design at Harvard Graduate School of Design. He holds a Doctor of Design from Harvard University and an MLA and Certificate in Urban Design from the University of Pennsylvania. With Mohsen Mostafavi, he edited *Ecological Urbanism* published by Lars Müller Publishers in 2010. Doherty is a founding editor of *New Geographies* and editor-in-chief of "Urbanisms of Color."

Shlonek? Literally, "What's your color?" is a popular greeting in Arabic. Used as pervasively as "How are you?" or "How's it going?", the phrase implies that color is a measure of a person's wellbeing. Although color is clearly a sign, it generally remains so intangible or elusive as to be largely ignored in discussions of the world around us. It is telling that *Shlonek?* invariably brings the reply, "I am well, thank God," rather than the color the question literally asks for. Imagine, though, that we lived in a world where we did answer with a color: "I am blue!" "I am yellow!" "I am pink!" "I am chartreuse!" "I am green!" "I am turquoise!" The aim of this volume is to bring color more into our deliberations of the urban environment, and to help build a vocabulary of color.

Who can forget the red of London's buses and telephone boxes? The seasonal greens of Costa and Niemeyer's Brasilia? The rosy hues of Petra? The yellow of New York's taxicabs? The red brick of Rio's *favelas*? The color cacophonies of Times Square and Shinjuku? Colors have a presence over and beyond the buildings, people, spaces, and artifacts that make up the city: not alone does color give meaning to cities but cities give meaning to color. And they are signs of each other. Many commercial paint colors are named after cities: *Milano Red, Oxford White, Providence Olive, Salzburg Blue,* to name but a few shades from a recent Benjamin Moore paint catalog.[1] Colors take identity from cities. Cities take identity from color. Whether carefully coordinated, clashing, or an expression of the materiality of the city, color is a powerful social, economic, and political force.

Color is all around us, yet is at the neglected heart of urban planning and design. Is a green city the same as a pink one? A blue house the same as a yellow house? Red grass the same as green grass? Discussions on color are inherently discussions on design. Yet we design programs, forms, and policies, but color is much too often avoided, or taken for granted, or left to chance or personal whim. Color is critical when thinking of the city, but despite a few notable exceptions, somehow we have largely managed to avoid it in the urban literature.[2]

Artists seem more comfortable with color than urbanists. Perhaps urbanists do not usually focus much on color because colors are often seen as being beyond rationality, or any one authority, or taste. To be fair, urbanists rarely have the luxury of an empty canvas to paint on like Ellsworth Kelly or Jim Dine.[3] If the city were a paint-by-numbers picture, the most anyone can usually expect to ever paint is one number, if that. The city is not a place for overarching chromatic control, and in order to intervene with color, urbanists need to be very canny in the chromatic interventions that are

1 See Adobe Illustrator Plugins for color themes —http://kuler.adobe.com—and type in names of cities to see what colors are associated with them.

2 Notable exceptions include Lois Swirnoff's, *The Color of Cities: An International Perspective* (New York: McGraw Hill, 2000).

3 See Charles A. Riley II's essay in this volume.

made.[4] Olafur Eliasson's works, for example, are intended as very precise moves that inspire collective emotional and political reactions.

SPATIALITY

Some might say that color is the lipstick of the city, makeup used to make the city prettier.[5] The color theorist and artist David Batchelor, who contributed a series of white monochromes to this volume, tells us that the Latin *colorem* is related to *celare*, to hide or conceal. White, of course, is no color and all colors at the same time, hence the title of Batchelor's photo essay, "A Bit of Nothing."[6] Imagine a cityscape freshly covered in snow: highways, gardens, lawns become indistinguishable as they are blanketed in white. Buildings appear as objects on an otherwise monochromatic field. The spatiality of the urban landscape changes with the bright white color. The same landscape may have quite a different spatial reading during the autumn months with a tree canopy of fall colors casting long shadows with the low autumn light. As Alex Byrne and David Hilbert affirm in this volume, color and light are inseparable. They tell us that the distance from which one views a color affects the hue that we actually see. Color is more than a concealer. Color attracts. It also repels. Color creates space.[7] And because it is spatial, how can we design the built environment if we don't consider its color?

City blanketed in snow (© Simon Mills/Corbis).

4 Another reason that colors are not much considered in relation to the city may be that colors are simply dismissed as naïve, intangible, or irrational. "Color," says David Batchelor, "is routinely excluded from the higher concerns of the Mind." David Batchelor, *Chromophobia* (London: Reaktion Books, 2000), 23.

5 "Neon is the lipstick of the city" was the slogan that a neon lighting firm in Rotterdam painted on their vans, as seen by a friend in 2002.

6 See, for instance, Kanya Hara, White (Baden: Lars Müller Publishers, 2007) and Mark Wigley, *White Walls, Designer Dresses: The Fashioning of Modern Architecture* (Cambridge, MA: MIT Press, 2001).

7 A local authority in the United Kingdom painted the town's litter bins pink to discourage vandalism—thugs, it seems, don't like pink and are reluctant to loiter adjacent to pink.

A cyclist rides through the snow in central London (© Toby Melville/Reuters/Corbis).

8 As mentionend by Charles R. Riley II in this volume. Riley says the London pavements are in contrast to the color world of Inishfree.

IDENTITY

Color is spatial, but it is not tied to scale. London, for instance, is often associated with the Royal Red of the UK's telephone boxes, mailboxes, and buses, rather than the gray pavements that proportionately make up much more of the city's color.[8] Jean Nouvel's 2010 summer pavilion at London's Serpentine Gallery was as red as the mailboxes and buses of the city, the urban red complementing the greens of Hyde Park. Not especially known for his use of color, Nouvel chose the red for its association with London. During the annual hajj pilgrimage, Mohja Kahf writes, the beiges and whites of Mecca are animated with the cheerful hues of women temporarily liberated from clothing restrictions, unlike their male counterparts, who must wear two pieces of white fabric. En masse, they represent a chromatic geography that originates with the body yet identifies with the city. From the body to cities, color lends identity.

RELATIVITY

The city consists of many colors, not just as a collection of objects that are colored and make up the city, but also the objects and colors in relationship to each other. The urban environment provides a multitude of chromatic juxtapositions, frequently fleeting and seldom static. Josef Albers touches on this urbanism in his famous exercise, "A Color Has Many Faces: The Interaction of Color." The aim of Albers's project is to emphasize the relativity of colors. Albers advises the reader to imagine three pots of water arranged from left to right. The water in one pot is warm, one is lukewarm, and one cold. If one puts one's hand into the cold pot first, followed by the lukewarm

4

Serpentine Gallery Pavilion 2010 (Photograph: John Offenbach).

pot, the lukewarm water will seem warmer than if your hand comes first from the hot pot and then to the lukewarm pot. So although the water in the lukewarm pot remains the same temperature, the perception of the temperature depends on the experience and memory of the perceiver. Color perception, Albers argues, is just as relative.[9] This relativity is central to any discussions of the urbanisms of color.

      Color also embodies collective values. Black, for instance, signifies sophistication among certain social groups. Among the Ndembu people of northwest Zambia, however, blackness may represent: 1. badness or evil; 2. to lack luck, purity, or whiteness; 3. to have suffering or misfortune; 4. to have diseases.[10] Yet color is neither black nor white in the sense that its interpretative possibilities depend to a large extent on the context (and some say the neurological wiring) of the perceiver.[11] As Petra Blaisse points out in an interview in this volume, "In Europe we interpret white as a sign of purity in the context of a wedding or a religious occasion, but in Korea white symbolizes death, even when it is in the form of a white-blooming tree." Color has different interpretations for different perceivers in different contexts. Color is relative.

INSTRUMENTALITY

While we can choose not to work with color, or to take it seriously, we really can't avoid color. It is everywhere. It is all-pervasive. Many designers are using color in very effective ways, and several such projects are included in this volume. A word of caution, however, because color doesn't have to be "colorful." Although color is mostly underused in terms of the design and

9 Josef Albers, *Interaction of Color*, revised and expanded edition (New Haven and London: Yale University Press, 2006), 8–11.

10 According to Victor Turner, the linguistic anthropologist. The remaining are; 5. Witchcraft or sorcery; 6. Death; 7. Sexual desire; 8. Night or darkness. See Victor Turner. *The Forest of Symbols* (Ithaca: Cornell University Press, 1967), 60.

11 For exampe, see Bevil Conway's work on neurology and color such as, Cleo M. Stoughton and Bevil R. Conway, "Neural basis for unique hues," *Current Biology* 18: R698-R699.

Maciachini, Milan, designed by Sauerbruch Hutton (Photograph: Jan Bitter).

12 At a lecture at the Harvard Graduate School of Design in April 2010, entitled "Color is more than Decoration," Claude Cormier, the Canadian landscape architect, showed a series of projects that demonstrated the thoughtful and compelling use of color. Cormier is one of a few practicing designers to openly engage with color.

representation of the built environment, it is sometimes overused to the point of becoming overbearing: we can all think of examples that we might consider distasteful because they are colorful. When we refer to color we often really are thinking of bright color, but colors can be subtle, pastel, light, and not necessarily bright.[12]

URBANISMS

One of the aims of *New Geographies* is to articulate the link between the social and the physical, the very large and the very small. A focus on color allows us to bridge such professional and spatial divides. The purpose of this volume was not to go into issues of race, color perception, optics, or even the philosophical issues of the relationship between language and color—all labyrinthine issues that have consumed many of the best minds in aesthetics, philosophy, art history, and physics, from Aristotle to Newton, Goethe and Wittgenstein, Albers and Rothko. The primary intent of this volume is to bring the issue of color into discussions on urbanism. With a concern for the interrelationships, spatiality, and geographies of color in the built urban environment such an exploration

Hamad Town, Bahrain (Photograph:
Camille Zakharia).

follows the physicalist argument that necessitates a discussion of the object, and its context, in order to discuss the color.[13] The red of a London telephone box takes part of its significance from being a phone box in London, as it does from the pigment of the color, and that is part of its urbanism. These multi-faceted relationships are among the reasons that color is so hard to pin down. In illustrating the spatiality, identity, relativity, and instrumentality of color in relation to the city, we hope the journal will open up discussions on the urbanisms, the interrelations and sensations and—most importantly—the possibilities for color across multiple geographies.

In going back to the question of *Shlonek?* in the case of *New Geographies* Volume 3, the answer, as illustrated by the cover and edges of the pages, is Honeysuckle, and some Turquoise. Honeysuckle is the Pantone 2011 Color of the Year, whereas Turquoise was the 2010 equivalent.[14] While Turquoise was seen as an "escape," from reality, Honeysuckle is aimed toward our testing economic times. "Honeysuckle is intended to encourage and uplift in a time of recession and financial insecurity," in the words of the executive director of the Pantone Color Institute®, Leatrice Eisenman. "In times of stress, we need something to lift our spirits. Honeysuckle is a captivating, stimulating color that gets the adrenaline going—perfect to ward off the blues."[15] Now, the question remains, "what's *your* color?"

13 For more on philosophical positions on color, see Alex Byrne and David Hilbert eds., *Readings on Color* Vol. 1 (Cambridge, MA: MIT Press, 1997).

14 See William W. Braham's essay in this volume where he writes about color prediction.

15 See: http://www.pantone.com/pages/pantone/pantone.aspx?pg=20821&ca=1 (accessed December 10, 2010).

COLOR COATING/CODING IN GHANA'S MOBILITY MARKETPLACE
YASMINE ABBAS AND DK OSSEO-ASARE

Yasmine Abbas has a Master of Science in Architecture Studies from MIT under an Aga Khan scholarship and a Doctor of Design from Harvard Graduate School of Design. She recently joined Zayed University in Abu Dhabi as a Professorial Research Fellow. Her publications include *Digital Technologies of the Self*, co-edited with Fred Dervin in 2009. http://blog.neo-nomad.net/

DK Osseo-Asare received A.B. in Engineering Design and MArch degrees from Harvard University. He is a principal of Low Design Office, co-founder of nonprofit design think tank DSGN AGNC and a TEDGlobal 2010 Fellow. His research recouples form-making with the social dimensions of global environment, situating sustainability between technology and geopolitics. osseo-asare.com

1 The competition among global telecom players (both foreign and "indigenous," such as Glo and MTN) echoes the historical "scramble for Africa," when colonial powers consolidated economic exploitation of the continent's material wealth through geopolitical conquest. African and Middle Eastern telecom companies such as MTN, Orascom, and Zain pioneered this latest contest for African terrain. For the first comprehensive survey of Africa's telecommunications market, see Ernst and Young, *Africa Connected: A Telecommunications Growth Story* (Norway: Ernst & Young, 2009). Downloadable here: http://www.ey.com/US/EN/home/library

2 While African markets are (stereo)typically represented as hypercolored if not chaotic transactional zones that self-organize around sites of economic density, mobile technology

POLYCHROMY

In Ghana the strategy of telecom companies to gain market share translates to an overwhelming effort to render brands visible by painting logos and brand colors on buildings: swathes of yellow for South African MTN, fuchsia or light green for Kuwaiti Zain (Zain Africa set to be acquired by Indian Bharti) and bright red for British Vodafone, relative to which blue Luxembourgian Tigo and dark green Nigerian Glo are near-invisible.[1] This practice of painting brand colors spilled first from billboards and signage to the array of informal micro-architectures such as sales kiosks and retrofitted containers that line city streets, before spreading to full-scale buildings. Brand colors complement logos to advertise service and signal the availability of a network's recharge cards for purchase at a given location. While critics say that this invasion of branded coloration compromises the image of the city, the color field of corporate branding ultimately blends with the already colorful fabric of the urban environment, as well as with the broader brand ecology. Some brands share similar colors: Pepsi is blue, as is the local Star beer; both Vodafone and Coca-Cola are the same shade of red. Further confusing the visual field, sometimes the artists contracted to paint on behalf of the brands intermix logos and colors.

Although this model of pervasive branding is clearly effective in labeling network coverage within both urban and rural environments, in the urban context the colors of global brands are absorbed by the intensity the color fields. The color of cities such as Accra-Tema and Kumasi comprise a pixelated field of vibrant colors; the prevailing image of the African city is polychromatic.[2] This relationship between individual colors and the field—which mutes the legibility of component colors—is similarly evidenced both in the colored patterns of traditional textiles such as *kente*, wax prints, batik, and tie-die, and in the work of Ghanaian artists such as El Anatsui and Ablade Glover, which resembles pointillism in its respective aggregation of points of metal and pigment to produce indivisible fields of material and color.[3] If Ghanaian visual culture is polychromatic, African culture more generally is about being multiple—simultaneously polyrhythmic, polyglot, and polyvalent.

ALLEGIANCE

In *Invisible Governance: the Art of African Micro-Politics*, David Hecht and Maliqalim Simone describe the fluidity of African identity and the creativity of using images, beliefs, and other constructions to assert individual micro-power. This hypertextual agency aligns with the politics of the hybrid and neo-nomad.[4]

Africans are accustomed to changing identities possibly because they are used to foreign domination: as the authors write, "The African continent is layered with multiple legacies from Europe and Asia."[5] In their analysis of doubly hybrid "Pan-African deity" Mami Wata, a reinvention of global mermaid (half-woman, half-fish), the authors observe: "Like technology, Mami Wata is international and multicultural, connecting diverse communities while not being restricted to one of them."[6] This aspect of Africa's chameleonic nature, together with the fact that African culture is oral, further suggests that the continent may be particularly well positioned to adopt, adapt, and appropriate digital tools because in the digital realm, and through social networking especially, people claim multiple allegiances.

The strategy of colorizing the architecture of African cities to build market share fails to understand the tactics by which Africans mobilize their micro-power as individuals in the world. Ubiquity of brand colors does not automatically produce brand loyalty. Because the barrier to joining a network is intentionally kept low (to build customer base), so too is the barrier to leave it. Changing mobile phone networks is trivial: a SIM card costs as much as two bottles of water. Thus many of Ghana's citizens switch back and forth between networks to modulate levels of privacy, in response to variations in quality of network coverage over time and geography, or to take advantage of special promotions. Branded buildings merely contribute to a backdrop of color against which the everyday performance of human activity plays out, without transferring any particular benefit to the telecom networks themselves. From

has radically transformed the market landscape, enabling everywhere to be a market. For an overview of Africa's mobile revolution, see N. Scott, S. Batchelor, J. Ridley, and B. Jorgensen, *The Impact of Mobile Phones in Africa* (Gamos, 2004). Downloadable here: http://www.gamos.org/icts/the-impact-of-mobile-phones-in-africa.html and Vodafone Group, *Africa: The Impact of Mobile Phones* (Vodafone Policy Papers Series No. 2, 2005). Downloadable here: http://www.vodafone.com/start/about_vodafone/eu/policy_papers.html

3 El Anatsui. Represented by October Gallery (London): http://www.octobergallery.co.uk/artists/anatsui/index.shtml. Last accessed May 10, 2010. Ablade Glover. Represented by October Gallery (London): http://www.octobergallery.co.uk/artists/glover/index.shtml. Last accessed May 10, 2010.

4 Yasmine Abbas, "Mobilization: an investigation of Barack Obama's Presidential Campaign and Peer-to-Peer Identity," in Yasmine Abbas and Fred Dervin, eds., *Digital Technologies of the Self* (Cambridge: Cambridge Scholars Publishing,

2009), 85–106.

5 David Hecht and Maliqalim Simone, Invisible Governance: The Art of African Micro-Politics (New York: Autonomedia, 1994), 11.

6 Ibid., 62.

7 DK Osseo-Asare, "Africentricity: From Kiosk Culture to Active Architecture," in *NOMA Magazine* Issue 06 (Spring 2010), 12–17.

this perspective, *citizens win*: corporations saturate the urban fabric, but architecture gains a coating against the elements and individual and collective agency is amplified.

COLOR-COATING/CODING

Color-coating architecture is, in the context of Africa, superficial. Alternatively, color-coding represents an enormous opportunity to restructure the relationship between telecom companies and citizens of the city. This demands new forms of design intervention that correspond to people's needs on the ground: despite ongoing improvements across the continent, many buildings and many people are still held hostage by unreliable or expensive delivery networks (water, electricity, telecommunications, etc.). As a countermeasure, the concept of *active architecture* seeks to augment delivery by embedding production within architecture—a shift from a project of creating buildings to creating buildings that *do* things.[7] Instead of providing color to paint buildings without securing brand loyalty, brand-color could highlight deeper forms of engagement between interested parties. For example, color-coding solar recharging stations or the mobile web supports both the growth of local information and lends it brand-association. Given that color is already used for coding land-use maps in urban planning, let color-coding convert telecommunications networks into social networks as part of the semantic of space. Delaminating brand from building opens up the related possibility of encoding brands within the operating system of the city itself, an alternate strategy that integrates aspirations across Africa's mobility marketplace by converting customers to users and actively leveraging networks on their behalf.

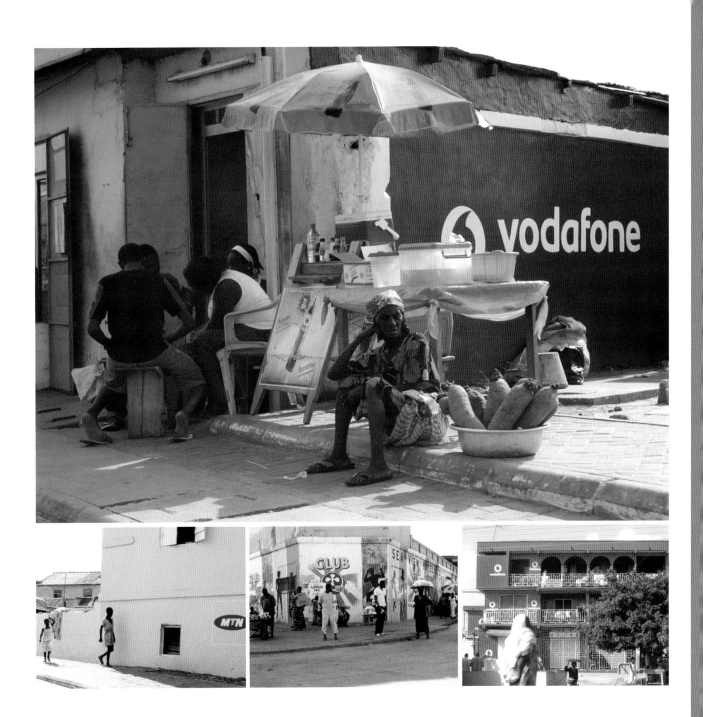

INDIGO, TO BE PRECISE
JOHNNY QUINN ALSTON

Johnny Quinn Alston is a graduate of New York University's Tisch School of the Arts, with a degree in filmmaking, having explored the design of urban environments in his studies with hopes of graduate pursuit in the field. He is currently one of two Silk Road Connect fellows working with 6th graders as a part of the Silk Road Connect pilot program in New York City.

1 A line from the poem "Coming from Elsewhere" by Glencairn Balfour-Paul, late husband of Indigo author Jenny Balfour-Paul. Glencairn Balfour-Paul, *A Kind of Kindness* (Crediton, Devon: Cervisian Press, 2000), 10.
2 The Silk Road Project is a nonprofit organization whose goals include educating about the world's cultures as they are continually relevant today. Consisting of artists and music representing traditions along the vast trade routes of the ancient Silk Road, the project incorporates hands-on, practical experience into its method of exposures and education.
3 Jenny Balfour-Paul, *Indigo* (London: Archetype Publications Ltd., 2006).

4 Ibid. Balfour-Paul, the renowned expert on indigo, also completed a dissertation on indigo in the Arab World at the University of Exeter and has informed the Silk Road Connect project extensively.

Slicing orange of construction sites, warning cones, scattered about scaffolding that's covering *this* sidewalk today (it was across the street last week). Masking the hodgepodge of red McDonald's signs, blinking orange and white walk/don't walk hands, multicolored advertisements for bands and brands, and neo-hued artwork from spray-paint cans. Flirting greenery. Silver, rust, no... gray; the metal the metal the metal of the subway, fire escapes, light poles, and sewer/pipe/chimney holes. There's a cool building in that neighborhood with pretty colors, but here there's a lot of brick, reflected in car bodies glued to asphalt, concrete. All the while some ongoing, contagious project (or its ghost) exposed, leaving behind the hues of industry, effort or "control"; dry to the eye, this palette is supreme among this borough's colors, altogether fleeting and ephemeral. Inconspicuous.

Where is the sky? Oh, up there, where it always is, woven over all! Only there's probably a wider, better view from up high, like on a roof; is it legal to go on yours? Probably unsafe. The view from down here is obstructed, though.

And here, we also find children. Children who have been asked to spend a whole year thinking about blue. *Indigo*, to be precise.

"Neatly folded in rainbow wrappings,"[1] the color, dye, plant, and common cultural fiber that is indigo serves as a focal thread within Silk Road Connect, a pilot education program under the guidance of the Silk Road Project.[2] As presented to roughly 450 New York City sixth graders across five middle schools, the program provides a cornucopia of cultural education opportunities inspired by the ancient Silk Road trading routes. From lush encounters with musical and artistic traditions, tactile dyeing exercises, immersive field trips, and interactive performances to learning geography, ancestry, and migration through one's own dna, indigo is woven through it all as the graceful shade of this cultural endeavor.

Relatable throughout and beyond the Silk Road, indigo colors ancient tales of "international" trade and travel, crop cultivation, ancient textile processes, and indigo gods.[3] Relatable to any classroom subject, indigo also colors science lessons on plant biology and chemistry. It expands math and art through pattern-making on cloths to be dipped into blue dye, or crafting notebooks from denim. History and humanities sessions coach synthesis via reflection in these notebooks regarding early trade of goods like indigo along the Silk Road, or an understanding of how one's blue jeans get their color. These escapades are recorded in numerous ways, including presentation on an "Indigo River Timeline," an imaginative blue bulletin board scrolling down the school hallway.

The aptly titled book *Indigo*[4] accompanies the project as a base resource (to be supplemented by the forthcoming issue of *Calliope* magazine, "Shades of Indigo," aimed at nine to fourteen-year-old students). Crafted by indigo guru Jenny Balfour-Paul, this work illuminates indigo as "a thread binding

diverse cultures together" as it explores the past, present, and future possibilities of this immortal dye through the histories of near every culture on earth.[5] Identified by Silk Road Project founder Yo-Yo Ma, the decision to embrace indigo echoes the virtue of a statement describing the Silk Road Project's aims: "If we want to preserve a tradition, the best way to preserve it is to let it evolve."[6]

Whether considering its practical uses worldwide in worker clothing, war paint, medicinal substances, and royal garments, its more tainted associations with forced labor on colonial plantations (e.g., the United States, Central America, the Caribbean, and India), or its spiritual qualities right down to mystic dye bath procedures, one thing is certain: the indigo color, seen by some as "loyal," has for centuries been significant to peoples of all classes, customs, and creeds.[7]

An organic reason for indigo's vivid posture within mankind's saga might reflect the color's likeness to the universally treasured rolling seas and starry skies: majestic expanses that have been faithful companions to human beings throughout time, offering transcendence and alive with boundless energy and splendor beyond one's immediate trappings. It is then conceivable that via clothing, artifact, and even lifestyle, indigo has for ages been intuitively used to make the essence of such inspiring natural magic portable, and thus present anywhere, within any landscape.

Forwarding the tradition of appreciation for this vastly significant hue in an education program suggests that illuminating a fact as simple as *distinction* can spark passionate curiosity about the world at large. Interpreting the integrity of such a concept, the urbanist is here invited to consider how this may be relevant, and perhaps transferable, in the realm of the city.

In one light, volume 0 of this publication entertains Alexander D'Hooghe's impressions on "defragmentation," the idea that urban elements can provide "vantage points" for the understanding of location and role within the context of a collective entity.[8] Within the geography of education, indigo could likewise be seen as a tool for defragmentation in a few respects.

5 Quote from a New York City school teacher within the Silk Road Connect program, from *A Good Day to Dye*, film piece for the Silk Road Project, 2010.

6 Yo-Yo Ma: The Rest Is Noise Interview, http://www.therestisnoise.com/2007/09/yo-yo-ma-the-re.html

7 Balfour-Paul, *Indigo*.

8 Alexander D'Hooghe, "Platforms for a Permanent Modernity," *New Geographies 0* (Cambridge, MA: Harvard Graduate School of Design, 2009).

9 In the 2009-2010 school year, students in the Silk Road Connect program participated in an indigo dyeing workshop with dyeing expert Linda Labelle, whose fiber arts studio, The Yarn Tree, is located in Brooklyn, New York City

10 Bassam Saba is a musician for the Silk Road Project who also participates as a teaching artist in the Silk Road Connect program. Accompanied by April Centrone, a percussionist, he displayed music and instruments of the Middle East to the pilot-program students. 11 Hybrid examples of reflections from Silk Road Connect students during the indigo dyeing experience.

12 Student interpretations of indigo.

As the centerpiece to several educative elements, indigo provides an orientation for synthesis of concepts as grand as the Silk Road or as simple as beauty. Students shape the connections via tactile explorations such as indigo dyeing: dipping one's resisted cloth into a thick, mysteriously oozing blue indigo vat.[9] The liquid itself undulates as if alive, shimmering a silvery-purple whenever hitting the light at *this* angle until "POP!", there goes an indigo-bubble. Excess dye is squeezed out revealing the blue-and-white pattern each student created by stitching, clamping, rubber-banding, or perhaps drawing with flour paste on cloth, yarn, or more—to the imagination's satisfaction. A connection sinks in as the student realizes: "this *ikat* technique is from the Middle East, where Bassam and his *Oud* are from... I know where that is on the map!"[10] Created with one's own hands, a personal product forms physically as a personal grasping of relationships between facts and forms *mentally*, all the while that "stinky!" substance turning from yellow to green to blue, *oxidizing* (the word just learned in class!) the dye, which just so happens to smell like, ahem, "organs!"[11] A magical process indeed.

Such experiences also "defragment" in another way, knitting the students into indigo's story as it entwines traditions into their "modern" lives, making history a part of the present and stitching this people's blue of the natural oceans and heavens into the fabric of their built and bricked urban lives. In these urban classrooms the color indigo is, in part, a darling ode to rekindling one's being with the aspects of natural and cultural beauty that have been fragmented by the obscuring tendencies of time, space, identity, and habitat itself.

Silk Road Connect students conceptualize experiences with indigo throughout the year. They say they've learned the value of looking at one color to see its deeper significance. Several students point out that although working with indigo has opened their eyes to the intrigue one color can have, often in their everyday environments color isn't necessarily used to spark curiosity, and if anything, specific colors such as indigo (blue, denim) sometimes signal gang territories. This introduced interesting questions in the classroom, including: who owns the *perception* of the blues of the sky and ocean? Who owns the meaning of one's own blue jeans? Can a color even be "owned"?

Students provided their own answers. On top of saying color should not be owned beyond an individual's personal perception, students described what indigo is to them against the backdrop of their surrounding environment: "Indigo is the color of the ocean, which brings life to the beautiful creatures!" "Indigo is the color of the big blue sky that you can look up at and wish for a beautiful day!" "Indigo is a traveler!" "Indigo is beautiful, just like life." "Indigo brings life!"[12]

Paraded within blue jeans, scarfed around hair, swaying from the classroom ceiling or patiently dripping from one's blue-stained fingertips, indigo has winsomely tinted the adventures of Silk Road Connect students throughout their school year. Indigo evokes memories of earlier places and times, like the Big Apple itself, where criss-crossing cultures and traditions flourished creatively, stemming from pure and tangible interactions between human beings, their crafts, and their natural environments.

In the self-centric and super-urban New York City, indigo viewed through a lens such as that presented in the Silk Road Connect is a point, or rather, *hue* of reference that allows for a reappraisal of the way we see the world.

Images courtesy of the Silk Road Project
and Jenny Balfour-Paul.

TIRANA, BEYOND COLOR
GJERGJ BAKALLBASHI, ENIDA MITRO, EGEST GJINALI

Gjergj Bakallbashi is principal of VIZA Arkitekts in Tirana. Bakallbashi has a Master in Architecture from Harvard Graduate School of Design and a BA from St. John's College, Annapolis, Maryland.

Based in Vienna, Enida Mitro is an architect and a graduate in sustainable design of the Technische Universität Wien.

Egest Gjinali grew up in Tirana and is currently based in Geneva. Gjinali studied architecture at the University of Waterloo and the École Polytechnique Fédérale de Lausanne (EPFL).

1 See Burdett and Kaasa in this volume.

2 Commissioner: Ministry of Culture, Youth, Sports and Tourism of the Republic of Albania; Curator: Gjergj Bakallbashi; Deputy Curators: Egest Gjinali, Enida Mitro.

3 Participants included: Hashim Sarkis Studios, Svetlana Boym, Gareth Doherty, New Geographies, Helidon Gjergji, Eve Blau, Ivan Rupnik, Peter Voit, Transsolar, Egest Gjinali, Zeinab Aghamahdi, GAC General Architecture / Collaborative, Michael Beaman, Zaneta Hong, James Setzler, Yutaka Sho, Sunmin Whang, Jessica Yin, Alexander C. Häusler and Silvia Benedetto, OFICINAA, Edgar Sarli and Tamar Loeb, Nuno Jacinto, Architect 51N4E: Johan Anrys, Peter Swinnen, Virginia Studio: Spiro Bakallbashi, Ihsan Prushi, Renato Konomi, Enida Mitro, Dritan Mesareja, Armand Vokshi, AVATELIER, with FIN and POLIS University, Gjergj Bakallbashi with FIN Students and photographic work by Dritan Zajmi, Luciano Bojaxhiu, UNDP-UNESCO Joint Programme, Culture and Heritage for Social and Economic Development, Eled Fagu.

There was almost no color in Tirana before the project of painted façades, initiated by Mayor Edi Rama.[1] Now there is color almost everywhere in the capital. The time is ripe to ask ourselves how we can move beyond color, while maintaining the tremendous momentum that the project of coloring the facades has created. "Beyond Color" was the theme of the first Albanian pavilion at the Venice Biennale in 2010.[2] Prompted both by the theme that Kazuyo Sejima set for the Biennale—"People Meet in Architecture"—and by our curiosity to speculate about Albania's most potent urban phenomenon, Tirana, as curators we decided to open up the pavilion to contributors from other countries and fields other than architecture.[3]

Through site-specific proposals, film, photography, interviews, and discussions, we create a topography to serve as future territory for collaborations on architecture and design for Tirana and, we hope, other contexts. Projects were selected to show that "Beyond Color" is both a place and a conceptual possibility. But why "Beyond Color"? Why not beyond walls, concrete, mass, density, beyond the boulevard, the streets full of cars, beyond now? Is there such a place? We chose to look at Tirana to begin to answer these questions. We wanted to be methodical in answering our questions and structured the pavilion into sections.

1. Looking at Colors: Through the colors project, Tirana has placed itself among those cities in Europe and elsewhere that want to reinvent themselves. As the projects shown in this section demonstrate, the use of colors and motifs is not place-, time-, or city-specific. The concepts, styles, and devices used go beyond the use of just color.

2. Looking at the Boulevard: Tirana's boulevard is its main public space. At one point it was imposed as an opening in the middle of an existing urban fabric. Its unfinished end, Tirana's derelict train station, invites us to ask, "What will happen with the boulevard?" We look at Zagreb to see how its Green Horse Shoe (Zelena Potkova) was planned in parallel with Vienna's Ringstrasse, how it was used by the city's planners and architects and, most important, how it was extended beyond its original boundaries. We look at Stuttgart to see the relationship between the use of open space, temperature gradients, and natural cold air supply in order to cast the question about the future of the boulevard in the context of its relationship with Tirana's climate and topography.

3. Looking at Spaces: Once we step out of Tirana's main streets and out of its boulevard, we find spaces that at first look extremely chaotic. Different layers of history, different scales, activities and forms coexist without any particular claim to order. Analytical projects and a short movie are attempts to understand these spaces and their accidental character. The student proposals show the potential of such spaces and the power they have to inspire a variety of projects.

Photomontage of the Tirana sky
by Dritan Zajmi.

4. Two Projects: Projects by 51N4E and Virginia Studio are chosen to show the scale of contemporary architecture in Tirana. Each is located in landmark areas and addresses different zoning regulations, urban conditions, and programmatic requirements. They employ formal gestures and cladding strategies to create focal points for the fragmented urban conditions in which they are located.

5. Looking for the Station: The rise of capitalism brought to Albania dreams and paradoxes. Owning a Mercedes as opposed to using public transport, overinvesting in the private at the expense of the public, gray concrete as opposed to green trees are all phenomena that belong to Tirana. The train station is a place where the monumental, the infrastructural, the public, the informal, the natural, and the derelict all overlap. We think that this site presents a perfect opportunity for Tirana to begin to imagine the potential of complexity of this multilayered overlap and the interesting interactions it may generate. Through different levels of temporality and scale, the projects/ideas propose visions for Tirana´s citizens, in a climate of rapidly declining public space.

6. Looking at Heritage: Tirana's Mosaic, presented in the "Looking at Spaces" section of the pavilion, is a reminder of the architectural heritage of Albania and its presence in active urban conditions. Including images of domestic, and religious architecture and military structures, "Looking at Heritage" is a conscious effort to underline the value of architecture heritage.

7. Carte Blanche: Seen through the eyes of an architect and an artist, this an artistic interpretation of the phenomena we encountered while looking at Tirana. It is a sensitive journey, exploring the urban topography of the city, searching for what identity is made of.

8. Tirana's Streets: The photomontages of Dritan Zajmi draw our attention to the way buildings create cutouts of the sky and configure it. Each cutout is special and identifies a particular place. Unusual in the way they are framed, these photographs draw attention towards the colors of the sky and its limitation by current Tirana architecture.

A BIT OF NOTHING DAVID BATCHELOR

David Batchelor is an artist and writer based in London. Batchelor makes three-dimensional works, photographs and drawings that relate to a long-term interest in color and urbanism. *Chromophobia,* was published in 2000 and is now available in eight languages. *Colour,* an anthology of writings on color from 1850 to the present, edited by Batchelor, was published in 2008. Text © TATE ETC. magazine.

My original motives for making monochromes – back in the late 1980s – were vaguely malicious. The subject was interesting because it seemed to be pretty much the dumbest kind of painting that it is possible to make. A single uninterrupted plane of flat unmodulated color spread evenly across a given surface – a monochrome appears to involve no composition, no drawing, no subtlety; and it requires no skill, and certainly no craft skill, to make one. Anyone who can paint a door can paint a monochrome. Or, as El Lissitzky put it in 1925: "Now the production of art has been simplified to such an extent that one can do no better than order one's paintings by telephone from a house painter while one is lying in bed." This was painting as low comedy, the reductio ad absurdum of high abstraction. Having said that, a part of what attracted me to the monochrome was also the awareness that for many artists this form of painting had promised a great deal more – the freeing of color from the tyranny of line, the liberation of painting from the register of representation and the possibility of a brush with some sublime void or other metaphysical nothingness. It's just that I didn't believe that anyone could still seriously maintain its claims to transcendence, be they formal, spiritual or otherwise.

So there was the monochrome: born in revolution (around 1920, say, in the tussles between Malevich, Rodchenko, Lissitzky and others); grown through tricky adolescence to some kind of ambiguous respectability in the 1950s and 1960s (think Yves Klein, Piero Manzoni, Lucio Fontana in Europe; Ad Reinhardt, Robert Rauschenberg, Ellsworth Kelly in the US; Hélio Oiticica in Brazil, etc.); and now old, fat and bloated, come to die as corporate decoration in the boardrooms and marble foyers of every other steel and glass office block, hanging over the head of the CEO like a halo, only rectangular and usually grey. At least, that's what I thought, back then. In truth it was difficult to think of that many actual corporate monochromes, but I loved the image none the less and that, for a while, was good enough for me.

The monochromes I started making began life as paintings, gradually turned into reliefs and then, after a few years of flailing around, ended up on the floor as objects. The first ones were black. They turned white over time, became silver for a while and occasionally went red – out of embarrassment I suspect. And all the while there was this nagging question: if the monochrome was so simple, why was this all taking so long? In retrospect, I realize one of my many difficulties was I had an idea of what I wanted without any obvious sense of what these things might actually be made from – which is only a problem if you are working in a studio surrounded by materials of one kind or another, and with some space to fill in an as yet unspecified and perhaps entirely imaginary gallery. Which is another way of saying that in art ideas are often much tidier creatures than objects. And then, to cut a rather long and very dull story short, at some point in the early 1990s my monochromes tripped up on a couple of

ready-mades and stumbled into some color. And in the process they began, just possibly, to have a life of their own, rather than one I had dreamed up for them.

In 1997 I also began taking photographs of what I called "found monochromes" in the streets around where I lived in London. My initial thought was that I would somehow refute a thesis I had recently heard being made by Jeff Wall in a lecture on the work of On Kawara. Wall had presented a rather vivid account of the history of modernism as the history of two opposed forces unable fully to escape each other and equally unable to be reconciled with one another. These forces were embodied in the painting of modern life, on the one hand, and high abstraction on the other, and they had found form in photo-journalism and the monochrome, respectively. As I understood it, he appeared to be saying that, in its logic of exclusion and emptying out, the monochrome was in some structural way unable to engage with or embody the experience of modernity. That seemed a very plausible argument – except I just didn't buy it. So I went out into the street, literally, with the aim of finding evidence that the city is actually full of monochromes, that modernity is a precondition of the monochrome and that, in all its artificiality, the city is the monochrome's natural habitat, an un- acknowledged museum of the inadvertent monochrome. None of which, I now realize, necessarily refuted Wall's thesis, but never mind.

On 17 November 1997 I photographed a monochrome I found on a street in King's Cross, near where I lived at the time. It was off-white and cracked, but I thought it would do the job if I could find another four or five to go with it. But then, slowly, or maybe not so slowly, some- thing happened. I

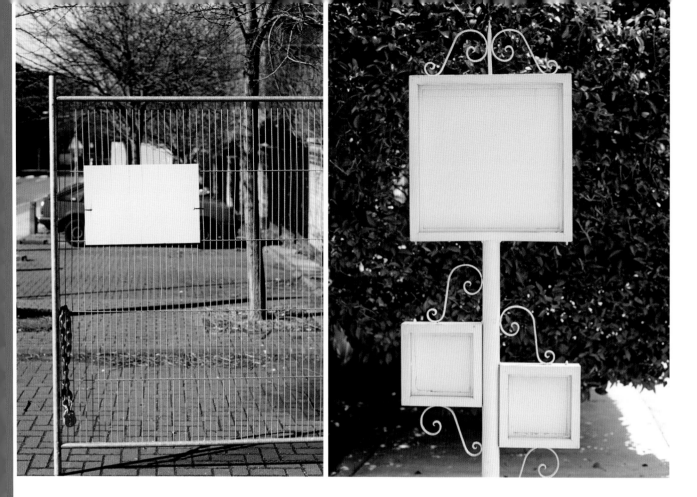

found there was something strange and rather compelling about these ready-made blanks. And from time to time I found new ones. So I photographed them too. And in the process I learned a few things: a found monochrome has to be a blank surface in the street, but not just any blank surface. It has to be rectangular or square, vertical, white and in some sense inadvertent, un- planned, or temporary. For it to work, the monochrome has somehow to detach itself from its surroundings. That's why white is better than black or other colors (I photographed some reds and blues and yellows too, early on). And in detaching itself from the surroundings, by being white and parallel to the picture plane, the monochrome plane can begin to form a small empty centre in an other- wise saturated visual field. A bit of nothing – but more nothing-much than nothing-ness; a presence that is more like an absence, at least for a moment or two. Or, to put it another way, the monochrome became more interesting – more am- biguous, more uncertain – than I had been pre- pared for it to be. Rather than just a dumb blank or just a bit of exotic emptiness, it appeared that it might occasionally be both, or it might somehow flicker between the two mutually exclusive alternatives. A plane and a void. But not a mysterious void-in-general, rather a contingent void, a void in a place, here, today, on this particular railing in this particular street; here today, and probably gone tomorrow. A void in a place, but not in every place: these incidents are not, I noticed, distributed evenly throughout the city; they have a tendency to cluster in more overlooked and transitional environments, and are scarce in more refined and elegant districts. For me, and perhaps only for me, these bits of peripheral vision are little heroic

moments, small monuments to modernity – if modernity can still, in part, be defined in that great phrase of Baudelaire's as "the ephemeral, the fugitive and the contingent".

Since 1997 I have found versions of these occasional void-planes in areas of London and in just about every other city I have traveled to. There were around 400 at the last count. I have come to think of the series as an open- ended project that changes shape as it grows and can be exhibited in a number of forms – as a slide show, as individual prints, as an installation of images pasted on a wall in a grid. Together the series forms a map of sorts: a city map; an autobiographical map; a mildly psycho-geographical map; and a map that principally indicates the location of something that is no longer there.

THE RED TENDA OF BOLOGNA
JOHN BERGER

John Berger is an art critic, novelist, painter and author. Berger won the Booker Prize in 1972 for his novel *G*. Author of *Ways of Seeing*, his most recent novel, *From A to X: A Story In Letters*, was published in 2008.

I should begin with how I loved him, in what manner, to what degree, with what kind of incomprehension.

Edgar was my father's eldest brother, born in the 80s of the nineteenth century at the time when Queen Victoria became Empress of India. When first he came to live with us, I was about ten years old and he was in his mid-fifties. Yet I thought of him as ageless. Not unchanging, certainly not immortal, but ageless because unanchored in any period, past or future. And so, as a kid, I could love him as an equal. Which I did.

According to the standards by which I was being brought up, he was a failure. He was hard-up for money, unmarried, unprepossessing, apparently without ambition. He ran a very modest employment agency in South Croydon. His principal passion was writing (and receiving) letters. He wrote to pen-pals, distant members of the family, strangers, and people he had once encountered on his travels. On his dressing table there was always a book of stamps. What he knew or surmised about the world fascinated me. And as an adolescent I loved his alternative vision, his shabby and royal intransigence.

He and I seldom embraced or touched one another; our most intimate contact was made through gifts. During three decades our gifts conformed to the same tacit, unwritten law: any gift had to be small, unusual, and addressed to a particular appetite known to exist in the other.

Here is a random list of some of the gifts we exchanged.

A knife for opening envelopes

A packet of Breton galette

A map of Iceland

A pair of motorbike goggles

A paperback edition of Spinoza's *Ethics*

One and a half dozen Whitstable oysters

A biography of Dickens

A matchbox full of Egyptian sand

A bottle of tequila, the eau de vie of the desert from Mexico

And (when he was in hospital dying) a flamboyant wide silk necktie, which I tied around the collar of his striped flannel pajama jacket, laughing so as not to howl. He too knew why I was laughing.

I also loved him for his imperturbability. He believed in general and in principle that the best was to come. A belief hard to sustain during the twentieth century, if one didn't close one's eyes. And he carried with him everywhere three pairs of spectacles—each pair with different lenses. He examined everything. He died in 1972.

Was he the most compliant man I've ever met, or the most persistent and independent? Perhaps he was both. He was never where you expected him to be.

He practised Pelmanism and Esperanto and was a pacifist. He got around on a staid, upright bicycle with a luggage rack behind, onto which he strapped books that he was exchanging or bringing home from the Public Library in East Croydon. He had three cards from this library so that at any given moment he could take out at least a dozen books.

Before mounting his bike, he attached a pair of bicycle clips to his legs and they gathered in his trousers just above his ankles. Like this he had a slightly Indian look, although the skin of his body was pale, and for a man, particularly soft—reminiscent of what the French call *le pain au lait*. He didn't possess a driver's license, although for two years when he was thirty he had driven ambulances on the Western Front during the First World War.

Whenever I stood beside him—in the figurative or physical sense—I felt reassured. Time will tell, he used to say, and he said this in such a way that I assumed time would tell what we'd both be finally glad to hear.

Beside letter-writing, his other passion was traveling. At that time many people traveled, but tourism as such did not yet exist. Travelers, rich or modest, planned their own journeys. He was a modest and persistent traveler. He believed that travel broadened the mind. One of the many biographies I remember him reading was one of Thomas Cook, who founded the first travel agency. Another was of Berlioz whose music, according to my uncle, was, *par excellence*, the music of travel. *Bien sûr*. He smiled with a kind of pride when he used French phrases and—less frequently—Italian ones.

After an early supper in our dining room, he used to go upstairs and read in his very small bedroom, often until the small hours of the morning. The room was less than double the size of a wagon-lit cabin. In it was a radio and a typewriter, on which he typed out with two fingers his letters and thoughts. Most evenings as a boy and young adolescent I went to say goodnight to him, and I often had the impression there were at least three of us in the room with the single upright chair (I always sat on the bed when we were discussing together). The third person was either the writer of the book he was reading or one of his favorite characters in the book. It was in this cramped room that I learned how printed words when read can summon up a physical presence.

Much of what my uncle read was related to the next journey he was planning or the one he had just made. The years passed and he traveled to Iceland, Norway, Russia, Denmark, India. (Maybe I'm exaggerating. Maybe one or two of these journeys were only planned in low-voiced conversations between us when we met in his South Croydon office.) He certainly did go to Egypt, Greenland, and Italy.

He went south to study history and north (which he preferred) to be at home with nature.

In Italy he discovered two cousins of ours who were music teachers in Rome. Before visiting Florence he read Burckhardt's *Renaissance* and spent weeks planning exactly what he wanted to see each day and in what order. Plan your work and work your plan. Later he became fascinated by the city of Bologna.

By this time I was at art school and so I mentioned to him that Bologna was the city of Morandi. And no sooner had I said this than I saw in a flash that he and Morandi could well put on and wear each other's shoes without either of them noticing the difference! Neither of them was married: both had lived at various times with a spinster sister. Their noses and mouths had the same expression of seeking an intimacy that is not carnal. The two of them liked solitary walks and both were continually curious about what they saw as they walked. The difference between them was that Morandi was an obsessional, great artist and my uncle, who was no artist, was a passionate letter writer.

To have said any of this would have been an impertinence, and so I simply repeated several times that he should look at Morandi's paintings when he went to Bologna.

He's a very quiet man Morandi, my uncle told me on his return.

What do you mean? He's dead. He died last year.

I know. I only saw his pictures of pots and shells and flowers. Very careful and very quiet. He could have been an architect too, wouldn't you say?

Yes, an architect.

Or a tailor!

Yes, a tailor. Did you like the city?

It's red, I've never seen a red like Bologna's. Ah! If we knew the secret of that red.... It's a city to return to *la prossima volta*.

In the Piazza Maggiore some steps lead up to the east face of the Basilica of St. Petronius, which like many of Bologna's historic buildings is constructed in brick. For centuries people have sat on these steps to watch what's happening in the square and to notice the minute differences between yesterday and today. I'm sitting on these steps.

No traffic except bicycles. I notice that some people crossing the square, when they are more or less at its center, pause and lean their backs against an invisible wall of an invisible tower of air, which reaches toward the sky, and there they glance upward to check the clouds or the sky's emptiness. In conversations about tomorrow's weather, opinions here continually differ.

Five teenagers are demonstrating their talents with a football, imagining a stadium. An elderly woman, to her evident surprise, meets a five-year-old girl whom she recognizes and who appears to be here alone.

Probably they live in the same district, a bus ride from the center, a district of worker's flats like San Donato. The woman buys the girl a helium balloon from a street vendor. The balloon has the body of a tiger, with black and yellow stripes. It slinks along, wafting on high above the girl's head.

A man in his fifties carrying two plastic bags—he has been shopping for his groceries—puts them down, stoops towards me and asks me whether I have a cigarette. I take out a packet and offer him several. He has the eyes of a man more used to reading print, than looking at buildings. Only one! he insists. His canvas shoes are frayed and dusty. He uses his own lighter to light the cigarette.

At the university, ten minutes' walk away to the right of where I'm facing, 60,000 students study today. In medieval times, the first secular university in Europe was established here.

The girl, with her tiger, walks toward the shop windows of the Pavaglione. Her steps are as feline as the animal above her. Even life-size tigers look weightless when walking. Way behind the tiger stand two towers; the taller of the two, built in the twelfth century, is almost 100 meters high. During the Renaissance there were many such towers in the city, each one built by a rivaling mercantile family to demonstrate its wealth and power. One by one they collapsed, and within a century you could count on one hand those that remained. After the city was annexed by Rome in the sixteenth century, the population suffered from poverty and pestilence. No wages, no work, no outlets. In the last decades of the nineteenth century, thanks to Marconi, the radio, and to light precision engineering, it began to prosper again, and then became a capital of skilled labor.

The girl with her floating tiger is so enchanted that, as she looks up smiling, I imagine her listening to some bars of music. It's an improbable city, Bologna—like one you might walk through after you have died.

I leave the piazza and wander east toward the university. There are continuous arcades on both sides of the street. People here argue not only about tomorrow's weather but about how many kilometers of arcades there are crossing the city.

The tradition of the "porticoes," as the arcades were called, began in the early Middle Ages. Each mansion had before its door a small plot of land that gave on to the street. A number of householders had the idea of roofing over their plots. Like this they could accommodate unforeseen travelers, allow extra servants to sleep overnight, or rent accommodation to poor students from the university. At the same time the public walked from portico to portico, benefiting from the shelter, and leaving the street proper open for wagons, horses, and animals. With the passing of time the city persuaded its rich house owners to take a pride in what they were offering the street, while imposing a certain standardization. Thus finally the porticoes became arcades.

For those living here, the arcades are a kind of personal agenda, made of stone, brick, and cobbles. You can visit your creditors, your secret love, your sworn enemy, your favorite coffee shop, your mother, your dentist, your local office of unemployment, your oldest friend, or a bench where you regularly sit down utterly alone, adjusting the small bandage you've put over a sore wart on your index finger—you can keep all these rendezvous without ever being exposed to the sky. And what difference does this make to the facts of your life? None. Yet under the arcades the echoes of those facts sound different. And in the evening Pleasure and Desolation take their evening stroll along the arcades and walk hand in hand.

All the windows I pass have awnings and all of them are of the same color. Red. Many are faded, a few are new, but they are old and young versions of the same color. Each fits its window exactly on the inside, and its angle is adjustable according to the amount of light desired indoors. They are called *tende*. The red is not a clay red, it's not terracotta, it's a dye red. On the other side of it are bodies and their secrets, which on the other side are not secrets.

I want to buy a length of this red *tende* linen. I'm not sure what I'll do with it. Maybe I need it only to make this portrait. Anyway I'll be able to feel it, scrumble it up, smooth it out, hold it against the sunlight, hang it, fold it, dream of what's on the other side.

I inquire about a possible shop.

Try Pasquinis, a woman tells me, near the Neptune fountain.

On my way there, in a corner of what was once long ago a pottery market, I pass a long high wall with several thousand black-and-white photographs, behind glass, displayed on it. Portraits of men and some women, with their names and their dates of birth and death printed across the bottom of their chests, where one might listen to their hearts if one had a stethoscope. They are arranged in alphabetical order. Mid-twentieth century. How many foresaw their portraits being placed along with thousands of other martyrs, side by side, row above row, on a public wall in the city center? More than we might guess. In alphabetical order they knew what was at stake: in this area of Italy one out of every four antifascist Partisans was to lose her or his life.

I read some of their names, hearing them spoken out loud. Their faces look confident, most of them, and with the confidence there is pain. Looking at them I vaguely remember something written by Pasolini. And now, while writing, I have found the lines I wanted to remember:

> ... The light
> of the future doesn't cease for even an instant
> to wound us: it is here to
> brand us in all our daily deeds
> with anxiety even in the confidence
> that gives us life...

After 1945 and free elections, Bologna became a Communist city. And the City Council remained Communist, election following election, for fifty years. It was here that management was obliged to accept workers' control committees in the running of their factories. Another consequence (so easy to forget how political practice often operates like a loom, weaving in two directions, the expected and the unexpected) was that Bologna became the best conserved city in Italy, famous for its small luxuries, refinements, and calm—and Europe's favorite host-city for trade fairs (sports installations, fashion knitwear, agricultural machinery, children's books, etc.).

The Pasquinis shop is on a corner. From the street you see nothing except the announcement: *Tessuti lino, cotone e lana, tendaggi.* Inside it looks as though nothing has changed for fifty years. Maybe some of the textiles on sale are 75 per cent acrylic, but you wouldn't guess it.

There are three high counters, and between and behind them are hundreds of bolts of colored fabrics, stacked up horizontally from the floor so that they make a wall. You think of a log stockade. A corral for colors.

Behind each counter a man stands in his shirt sleeves, wearing a wide leather belt with a pair of large scissors, a meter rod and a ruler stuck into it. The counters are high so that when one of these men unrolls a bolt of cloth, and, if the customer approves, cuts it with his scissors, he can work standing up, without bending.

There are two women before me. One is touching the velvet, over which she's hesitating, as if it were her daughter's just-washed hair. The other is counting out loud her steps as she strides across the floorboards, calculating how many meters of a floral calico she will need.

At the end of the shop, near the entrance door, there's a high podium with a stool, table, and cash-till placed on it. Seated on the stool, the shop owner oversees every operation taking place. At the moment he's reading his newspaper.

The light, like the quiet, is diffused, muted, as if all the rolls of cloth had given off, over the years, a very fine, unidentifiable white cotton dust—the same dust that settled on the objects painted by Morandi, who surely knew this shop.

When my turn comes, I explain to the young assistant what I want. Like his two companions, he has the air of a rancher rather than a draper. To extract the 2-meter bolt of red linen, he shifts with great dexterity several others. Then he places the bolt on the counter and with a flourish unrolls about a meter. I finger the cloth.

It's a heavy linen, he says.

How much a meter? I ask.

19 euros.

Okay. Give me, please, 3 meters.

He takes scissors and rod from his belt, looks at me again to check (mistakes can't be corrected), I nod, and he cuts. Folding the length I've bought four times, he slips it into a bag, writes out the bill with a pencil, also attached by a string to his belt, and nods in the direction of the podium.

I pick up the purchase, take out three 20 euro notes from my wallet and go to pay, holding the notes up high, above my head. The owner leans forward and down to take them from me, and our eyes meet. I recognize him. He pretends not to recognize me. His conspiratorial expression is familiar. The last time he put it on was when I had given him his tie and was saying good-bye to him in the hospital. Behind his bifocal glasses the swiftest flicker of one eye (his left) says: I'll see you round the corner—when the time comes.

I leave the shop without a word, return to the steps in the Piazza Maggiore, and there I look at what I've acquired and compare it to the awnings I can see in the top-floor windows, surrounding the square.

Time will tell.

I turn things over in my mind. Then I fold the cloth another time, place it on the step beside me, and stretch myself out to lie along the step with my head on it, as if it were a pillow, eyes shut.

We made three voyages together, before I was fourteen years old. One to Normandy, another to Brittany, and the third to Belgium and Luxembourg. When we arrived in a town—be it Ghent or Rouen or Carnac—after we found the hotel, booked by him in advance, we had a special procedure. I might say ritual—except that it was so discreet.

We had something light to eat—perhaps a small glass of white wine—and then we followed, street-name by street-name, a trail he had already prepared. Along it were surprises, for me total surprises, for him anticipated ones. Canals like streets. A gallows. A shop window with a display of white lace as fine as the stars in the furthest galaxy.

Sometimes the trail called for a taxi to take us cross country. To cheer the Tour de France as the riders came in at the finish of the day's stint. To watch a fisherman's boat leaving at night at a quayside, an oil lamp on its mast, flame flickering and never going out. To search for a megalith one could lie on—like I'm now lying on this step in the Piazza Maggiore.

All these finds that we came upon together were as secret as wrapped presents. In fact more secret, for, once unwrapped they still remained secrets. He would put his finger with the wart on it to his lips, as a sign to remind me not to tell, to keep it to myself.

Even at that early age, I sensed this was something more than a childish game. He had learned how persistently many people need to look away from, to neutralize, what surrounds them. And one of the frequent devices they use to achieve this is to insist that everything is bound to be ordinary. The advantage of the untold is that it cannot be dismissed as ordinary. God is the unsaid, he murmured to me one evening in St. Malo, drinking, before bed, a glass of Benedictine.

In the Via Caprarie we are going to find a kilo of *passatelli* in a paper bag that looks as if it were made to hold truffles. After Easter, during the summer heat, the Bolognese stop eating lasagne and tagliatelle, which are too heavy, and move on to *passatelli*, a pasta *in brodo*. You want the list of ingredients. 400 gr. white bread crumbs, 240 gr. Parmesan cheese, 1 teaspoon of flour, 6 eggs, 1 small nutmeg, 50 gr. butter?

Teaspoons fascinated him, and on his travels he collected them. He had half a dozen teaspoons from Dublin that he kept in a flat box, like a box for war medals. Inside it the spoons lay on a dark blue velvet.

In the Via Marsala we'll eat the best mortadella in the world. Mortadella was invented here at the beginning of the seventeenth century. Its name comes from the fact that it is seasoned with myrtle berries. When it's good, it's eaten in chunks, not thin slices. With it, drink a white wine from Alto Adige. He raises his glass to touch mine.

Now some coffee? A merchant in the Via Porta Nuova. Here, as you see, the coffees are listed with the year of their harvesting, like wines. There are good years and poor ones. Time will tell. Coffees from all over the world, Brasil sul de Minas. Java Wib. India Parchment. Let's go straight to the best. Blue Mountain from Jamaica. When they receive a new delivery of this coffee, they put it, each night, in the safe along with the bank notes! After drinking it, the taste stays in the mouth for fifty minutes. It keeps the whole brain company.

Lying on the step, I keep my eyes shut.

When you can taste it no more in your mouth, go to the church of Santa Maria della Vita.

I open my eyes to look up into the empty sky above the Piazza. I already know the church; there's a *compianto* there.

A group of life-size figures made in terracotta. Fifteenth century. Christ lies dead on the ground and standing around him are Joseph of Arimathea, the rich man who bought the tomb so Jesus could be buried, Mary the mother of the apostles John and James, Mary the mother of Jesus, John the storyteller and evangelist, the Mary who was Jesus' aunt and Mary Magdalene. The sculptor is Nicolo dell'Arca who worked most of his life for the city of Bologna.

The two men in the group are calm, the four Marys are caught in a hurricane of grief. The vortex of the hurricane is Mary Magdalene. What the wind does to her clothes, the way it tears at them as she rushes forward, is the same as what her grief has done to her mouth and throat.

Yet is grief the right word? Her grief has become her own determination. Nothing will stop her.

The night after next she will be alone in the same place. The tomb will be open. Christ's body will have disappeared. Only the shroud and head cloth will remain. And she will ask the gardener where he has placed the crucified body so she may find it and tend it. And the gardener will look at her and she will instantly recognize him, and he will say: Do not touch me. And for the first time she'll believe he means it. Tell my disciples I have gone to my Father...

There are a few figures in art who have ended up in the wrong setting. In a painting by Velasquez there's a Madrid stone mason, exemplary for his care and patience, who has ended up as Mars the god of war! In this *compianto* over the dead Christ, Mary Magdalene ends up representing every martyr—Lucy, Teresa, Cecilia, Catherine, Ursula.

She is intrepid, and in face of her nothing is mitigated.

When I arrive at the church, there is nobody else. I'm alone and I hang the *tenda*, folded as it was four times over itself on the counter, on the wrought iron railing that surrounds the *compianto* group at the level of my knees.

There I wait. It crosses my mind that a *tenda*, as well as being a blind for keeping sunlight out, may also be one for keeping grief in, and for cultivating determination.

After some time, I leave the church of Santa Maria della Vita. The hurricane it contains never blows itself out. Outside the evening is peaceful. People are discussing tomorrow's weather. I enter the Pavaglione shopping center, for I have a premonition. There is a certain place where two arcades cross under a dome. In the corners of this space are tall pilasters. Pigeons often fly through there. The sparrows don't come because there are no tables with people eating. It's a place of passage. Perhaps when the Pavaglione was used, as an indoor food market, it was the quietest place. Anyway there's an acoustic phenomenon. Which might be called "the whispering shout."

If you stand against a particular pilaster and look diagonally across the octagon to the corresponding one on the other side, and if somebody happens to be standing there, you can talk to them, and they can talk to you, and your voices will be very distinct and loud, however many people are passing between you, and nobody else will hear your words. The idea of a secret is stood on its head. To share a secret here you move far apart, the words resound in public, and only the two of you hear them.

My premonition is that if I wait by one of the pilasters in question, he may come.

I wait for what seems a long while. It's not that with age I have become more patient. I'm as impatient as I was when I was eleven; it's simply that I believe in time less. A dog comes up to me wagging its tail. Dogs in Bologna are rare. The dog's mistress scolds it, frowns at me, and walks on, remembering, and at the same time fatally forgetting, her youth.

Suddenly he's there. He's perspiring. He has no jacket. His hands are gently clasped behind his back. He knows about the invisible acoustic telephone. He speaks with the quiet confidence of somebody who, apparently talking to himself, knows he will be heard.

Don't forget, martyrs are ordinary people, they are never the powerful. Afterward, a little power may accrue because of the example they've set. An example sustaining thousands of little hopes. Little hopes like the pursuit of little pleasures.

He mops his brow.

It's only under this dome in the Pavaglione that we can talk of such paradoxes. Who would ever dream of putting martyrs and Blue Mountain coffee side by side? Yet they are closer than the moralists pretend, very close.

He peers through his glasses at me.

Martyrs are enviable. They're to be pitied for the pain they suffer, for at one moment it is pain, very harsh pain. Yet they are also enviable.

I nod.

They have learned how to be touched—that is the special gift of martyrs, warriors never learn it.

One of the buttons of his white shirt is undone and he does it up with his right hand without glancing at it, while continuing his whispering.

They know before they die that their life has served for something. Many would envy that.

Even if the cause they believe in was lost? I ask.

I believe so, yes. Anyway, I'm not sure history has winners and losers any more than justice does. Martyrs die to have a home everywhere. That's why they are honored by the poor. When they are honored in palaces, the martyrs, they revolt and disappear—leaving behind only their relics.

He takes off his spectacles and wipes them on a handkerchief he takes from the breast pocket of his shirt.

Surely the little pleasures, I reply, belong not to death but to life.

So does martyrdom. He says this as if he wants me to hear every letter of the words. It's the coincidence of opposites. Among martyrs, and in the pursuit of little refined pleasures, there is something of the same defiance, and of the same modesty. At a different level naturally. But the coincidence remains. Both defy the cruelties of life.

You make me think of a painting by Caravaggio.

What of?

The martyrdom of St. Ursula.

His laughter fills the dome, and nobody apart from me hears it. People are walking faster before the shops shut.

Ursula is rumor from beginning to end. He opens both palms in a gesture of humility and resignation. Street gossip. The woman lived in the third century and her story was told only in the ninth. Some respect for the facts. At the end of the fourth century, a basilisk near Cologne was being repaired and the masons discovered a mass grave, all of women, said to be virgins. They carved an inscription without citing a name or date. Four centuries pass, and along comes a storyteller. This storyteller finds the name of Ursula on a grave somewhere else. The grave of a child, who had died aged eight. Misreading the Roman numerals, he further proposes that Ursula, who has become overnight the daughter of the King of England, was accompanied on a pilgrimage by 11,000 other virgins! There were understandably not enough ships for them to cross the Channel. So the ships had to be built. While waiting, the women themselves learned to sail and to become intrepid sailors. They crossed the Channel together, they sailed up the Rhine as far as Basel, and from there they walked over the Alps to Rome.

He shakes his head and waits, and we both watch the people passing through the arcade.

It was on their return journey that disaster befell them. Not far from Cologne they fell into the hands of Attila and his thugs and all of them who resisted were massacred.

He passes his thumb slowly along his lower lip.

There have always been rumors. They're inevitable. They help us to come to terms with what is forcefully denied and may be true.

He dabs at his mouth with his handkerchief. When he takes it away, his mouth is smiling.

So be it. Bologna! Bologna! Near the Porta S. Vitale there's a bar called the Bocca d'Oro, where they serve, if you insist on the one made by the capo's mother, the best limoncello you've ever tasted. It promises everything.

Only the pilaster now. He's gone. In my ears only the sounds of the city.

INTERVIEW WITH PETRA BLAISSE
NICOLE BEATTIE

Petra Blaisse works in a multitude of creative areas, including textile, landscape and exhibition design. In 1991 she founded Inside Outside. Blaisse invites specialists of various disciplines to work with her and currently the team consists of about ten people of different nationalities.

Nicole Beattie is a doctoral candidate at Harvard Graduate School of Design. Nicole's objective is to contribute to architectural design and urban planning strategies that promote a healthy built environment.

NB: Your work addresses the importance of establishing context, the "process of knowing." You write about discovering "what do water, trees, flowers, colors symbolize" in each site. How does color significance vary culturally? How do you use transparency and light to effect color and perceptions of space?

PB: These are very different questions. Of course if you work somewhere, if you write about a certain culture or if you design within a certain context, you have to know your host and where you are. The getting-to-know is not only about the place and the people who work on it but also about the environment that we want to create as a team; and about the wishes of the future users. The first process is always to go through all these layers of information: culture, site, climate, use, inhabitants and, of course, the local flora and fauna. Then you ask about color: if we take the color green for instance, this to us is a good but simple and day-to-day color. Yet if you are in a desert climate, each tiny bit of green grayish or bluish green or maybe even brownish green because of the perpetual sand dust has a huge impact. If you drive through the endless, monochrome desert and all of a sudden you see these isolated bluish, silverish shrubs, it becomes a sensation. Or if you are in barren mountains high up and all of a sudden you see a single flower of a deep ultramarine color, you get extremely excited, even moved to tears! It s all a matter of context. In China, for instance, we are working in Shenzhen and in Hong Kong where it s very moist and green, everything is growing, even under highways and in the deep shade of bridges. From every crack plants emerge, through the smallest gap roots push themselves upward, literally strangling the architecture. You want to find something else to balance this aggression, you want to stop it, to escape it! That is what I mean by working with objets trouvé: the influence of what is already there on your own instincts and design plans.

I think that the most exciting part of our work is this kind of anthropology, sociology, the spontaneous moments before you become a 'designer', before you have a plan. You are a human injected somewhere, expected to create something there and then. And then each person you start working with has a certain color palette, certain energies, preferences or wants.

In the Seattle Public Library, for example, we asked the future users: "Do you like being in a gray or white environment? Or do you prefer pink or blue, brown or orange?" Well, they all hated orange for some reason. But they liked brown, beige, dark green and burgundy. In Korea we included black and white and pure colors that in Holland don't mean very much outside a given context. In Europe we interpret white as a sign of purity in the context of a wedding or a religious occasion, but in Korea white symbolizes death, even when it is in the form of a white-blooming tree. Colors can be banned for political or religious reasons because they represent the wrong parties; they can be

forbidden because their pigment base is considered environmentally harmful, or simply because fashion predictors and production companies decide that it is time for a change. If you look around, the colors that one saw everywhere in the fifties and sixties—the colors of Technicolor ©—simply don't exist any longer;" they literally disappeared from our general color scope—even in the color charts of large paint firms they are no longer included.

We are now working in the Taipei Theater, and we are in conversation with the local client and architects. In one of our first conversations with them we said: "We have a proposal for the interior finishes of the three auditoriums. To compensate for all the different architectural materials applied such as concrete, metal, steel, aluminum, plastics etc., and in contrast to the lushness and hectic of the given site and the average climate of Taipei (including moisture level and smog) we would like to propose a single color blue for all the auditoriums." And they immediately said: "Please don't!". We asked why, and they explained "blue stands for military, blue represents the most disliked political party right now, blue has all kinds of negative meanings for Taiwan at the moment." Then we asked if there was anything else that they didn't want

The Netherlands Embassy, Berlin: large planes of green pull the garden into the interior space and create a literal connection to the vegetation outside. Designed by Inside Outside.

Chasse Terrein: red "artery" path connects all five entrances. The warm color is used to animate the colorless building site and the Dutch winter weather. (Image: Petra Stavast).

us to use, and after some thought they said: "Yes: also please no green and no red; and also: the color gold is not considered as 'chic' here in Taiwan." Wow.

We thought: how can we achieve the (Dutch) architect's preference for blue anyway? There are of course many hues to a color. Some might not trigger the same reactions. So we needed to find an alternative blue, for instance a more grayish-blue—without being too 'navy'; and not too light 'baby' blue, which would be too innocent; with a warm yellowish gray tint to it. That is now what we will be using for each auditorium: one single color from top to bottom, as if the spaces are dipped in a can of monochrome paint—chairs and lamps included!

One and the same color will become a totally different thing if printed onto velvet, concrete, paper or leather, on plastic or wood; in daylight or when used in a (synthetically) lit or dark auditorium; even in combination with the acoustic quality of a room. Also the size of the field of color matters: small or large, a thin straight slither, a meandering line or a rectangular plane of substantial size? Far away or close up? Shiny or mat? Opaque or transparent? With or without colors or a black or white layer—hidden or visible—underneath? So you have to do endless tests and learn to predict the effect of color according to all these givens, and you will discover that you will hardly ever use the actual color that you initially wanted to achieve the effect you envision, in the end.

The first curtain I made was for the dance theater in The Hague, in 1987. I wanted to make it out of metal particles, but it was too heavy to make it of real metal. Also, a stage curtain has to close off light and sound. To achieve the effect of the initial idea we attached lines of 6cm dots of golden foil to a heavy wool velvet of matte gray color. This was done by pressing the foil onto equal circles of heated glue, applied with a silkscreen roll that we made. The effect of these 'floating' metallic dots on that soft, undulating surface of velvet is that of a waterfall, rain, fire, sunrise, a silver moon or a plane full of holes.

Because we control the lighting in theatres very carefully, it is exciting to introduce chance, to let the outside enter the interior. Natural things such as the changing light from morning to night, spring through winter and the shadows of passing clouds; but also the bleaching effect of UV light, staining and the wear-and-tear through use, all play an important role in the changing character, structure and overall effect through time.

NB: Color elicits emotions. Sanford Kwinter writes: "Blaisse's architecture both generates and suspends desire." Your spatial construction, the use of color and light, are instruments for emotional (desire, sensory) experiences. How do color, light, transparency, and acoustics help build and define these spatial responses?

PB: It depends on whether we are working with curtains or carpets or gardens; with horizontal or vertical planes and in what scale. Curtains, with their flow and movement and tactile presence produce a strong sensory response; but they also create space, open up views, mute sound, filter light, darken a room, cool or heat up a space. Carpets mute the sound of steps, inviting people to settle, to take a rest; they define areas, lead visitors in a specific direction and can communicate the intention of a room, institution or inhabitant. Gardens are a prolongation of; or the introduction to the house, it is a private space—however public they may be—that offers protection, that invites for meditation and thought, stimulates social interaction, cultural events and festivities. Gardens are the connection between man and nature, the reminder of 'true' values. All three subjects address the issue of trajectory, sequence, and time. All three subjects trigger ones inherited memory, wherever one comes from and of whatever age, religion, or culture one is. For all three subjects color is the most essential ingredient.

Acoustics make an enormous difference for your perception of a space. For example, in an OMA exhibit I designed at the IFA (Institut Francais d'Architecture) in Paris in 1989, we wanted to present the biggest models of large city plans that OMA, at that time, had made for Parc de la Villette and Melun Senart in the smallest room. The IFA inhabits a very old building, each room with its rustic seventeenth- or eighteenth century unpredictable details: crooked walls, rounded ceilings, a toilet in the corner—really funny! We painted the tiny room completely matt black and covered the windows with black felt, so you saw no form, no shape, no boundaries. Then we added a sound system that made this space seem enormous. It was the sound of a train passing by, coming from really far away, and moving closer and closer—then passing and moving away. We also had sounds of a tennis game, the hits and the grunts and the balls going from left to right … so of course we laughed a lot, but the effect was actually quite fantastic because while the sound was very soft in the background, it created enormous space—re-enforcing the spaciousness of the projects shown.

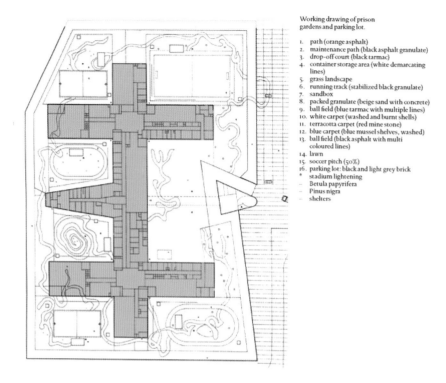

Working drawing of prison
gardens and parking lot.

1. path (orange asphalt)
2. maintenance path (black asphalt granulate)
3. drop-off court (black tarmac)
4. container storage area (white demarcating
    lines)
5. grass landscape
6. running track (stabilized black granulate)
7. sandbox
8. packed granulate (beige sand with concrete)
9. ball field (blue tarmac with multiple lines)
10. white carpet (washed and burnt shells)
11. terracotta carpet (red mine stone)
12. blue carpet (blue mussel shelves, washed)
13. ball field (black asphalt with multi
    coloured lines)
14. lawn
15. soccer pitch (50%)
16. parking lot: black and light grey brick
*   stadium lightening
–   Betula papyrifera
–   Pinus nigra
–   shelters

Landscape plan for the State Detention Center by Inside Outside.

NB: Can you talk a little bit about your work with prisons, in particular the three gardens you designed for the prison in Holland in 1997? Prisons are usually severely devoid of color. In this prison project you had to work under highly restricted guidelines as well as in your material choices, vegetation, and color palette. In the context of the prison project: how important was color in your design? How dramatically did light, movement, and color condition the perceptions of space you were creating? Especially in the context of the prison population, which might need color and light just as much or even more?

PB: Just as much or even more. Well, because it is Holland we were allowed to use color and planting and even trees with trimmed stems (to prevent suicide by hanging), which was nice. The rhythm of all the prison cells and the floor plans was very repetitive. I imagined that if you were in that building you would not know where you are, as there was nothing to orient yourself. For that reason color became very important, so we saw to it that each garden not only offered a different composition, but also a different color. In this way you experience immediate recognition looking through the cell windows; and you undergo different atmospheres when entering a garden: you might jog in the orange (terracotta) garden one day, play a ball game in the blue (mussel shell) garden the next day, walk in the black-and-white (asphalt and white shell) garden the third day and play a game of soccer in the green garden (fake lawn and mixed flower field) after that. In each of these activities you have completely different experiences, even though the size of the gardens are the same and the building in the background and the gates and all the terrible things you don't want to see always look the same. Here color, form and seasonal changes have a critical value. We visited the jail again in 2007, ten years after its completion, because we were working on the *Inside Outside* book and wanted to be critical about our own work over time; we didn't only want to show the work when it is just finished and everything is beautiful. When we came back we were worried that the gardens would be completely dilapidated. But because our design was so simple and strong, because the paths and forms we created were so graphic and bold and the gardens can be easily maintained, our design survived. The trees were growing and looking great, the paths still meandered endlessly and uninterrupted and when the prisoners started to appear, it was clear that they used every inch of the spaces. Also the gardens matched their tattoos pretty well!

We are now working on two Belgian prisons, thirteen years later. The safety and maintenance regulations for exterior spaces are much more strict and possibilities have drastically reduced. Yet we managed to make two very different gardens for one and the same building, that is to be placed in two different contexts: one sub-urban and one country side environment. The form language and the color use for both exterior areas—that, like in the Dutch project, include gardens, sports fields, drop off areas and large parking lots—is totally different: for one project we applied an agricultural organization of irregular angular plots, each planted with different mixes of plants, herbs, grasses (fields of different greens) and pink and white flowering trees; for the other we applied a very regular linear organization of fields that were either covered with lawn or with black asphalt (zigzagging green-black stripes); then covered with a confetti of one type of red-leafed tree. In both projects the gardens enter the buildings to become patios or interior gardens, adding daylight and a lively glow of (green or red) color to the prisons' interiors. **NB: Speaking about the maintenance and validity of a project over time: Color is not for the shy. Perhaps because color is subject to the capricious and transient forces of style, so provocative and emotionally charged, it tends to either be overused or not used at all. How do you solve color's problem of time, so that the spaces you create can stay valid, not becoming obsolete and dated? And what would you say to those who are afraid to use color?**

PB: I would say: "Keep it this way" that way they can hire experts to do this work for them (Petra laughs). I'm sure that people are not afraid of color in their private lives, so it has something to do with professionalism and a need for concentration and respect. Maybe it is about democracy or diplomacy; or about humorless awe for modernist architecture! In any case, the idea of decoration is something that the architect of today really has to chew on—Venturi and Scott Brown notwithstanding! It is so strange that we live in such inhibited times, because throughout history people were not afraid of color at all! Roman architecture and architecture up to the seventeenth century and again in the first half of the twentieth century was, as far as I can tell, very much involved with the importance of decoration, with added layers and visual narratives as integral part of it. Paintings were drawn directly on walls, ceilings and columns, colorful mosaics were inserted in surfaces, adding color, three dimensionality, light and (illusionary) spatial effects both to the interior and exterior spaces. And without exception, color would fade or change into a different color, depending on pigments, adhesives, climate, use and the amount of daylight. So this fear of color (and the wear of color through time) is a sign of our times. Everything needs to be predicted, prevented and controlled in the 21st century, it's just ridiculous and insulting. So actually I don't know what to say, I could say: "Don't hesitate, go for it!" but then again: if it's bad architecture that you want to patch up with cheap painted stucco, it might add some joy on opening day, but it won't work for long. Color and decoration really need to be part of the whole intent from the first conceptual thought.

NB: The interdisciplinary nature of your work creates new geographies and explores spatial connectivity. How important to your choice of color and projects, then, are health and well–being?

PB: Biology is essential when one speaks about color. I always liked to read books about animal behavior when I was young. When I started on our *Inside Outside* book, with Kayoko Ota and Irma Boom in 2005, I had a few conversations with Dutch biologist Tijs Goldschmidt, to introduce this aspect of my interest to the book through him. As he visited our full-of-colored-samples-studio, the first thing we talked about was color, specifically addressing the color RED of the smocked stage curtain for the Hackney Empire Theatre and its conceptual counter-part: a boldly striped, black and white 'fringe' curtain. We told Tijs that the latter was harshly rejected and that the red curtain was welcomed with enthusiasm by the Theatre staff and the Arts Council. This was no surprise to him, for as he explained, the color red is a sign of health and potency, meaning that it is a guarantee for reproduction and survival. If we look at scaring off an enemy, on the other hand, stripes or large dots in contrasting colors (as indeed in black and white) are most effective, as this form of mimicry represents a larger, more poisonous and much more dangerous species than the one addressed. So our first design basically communicates the message "back off!" and who the … would want such a curtain?

We also discussed the techniques for defining territories and boundaries, the function of repetitive trajectories and the methods of leaving traces, the meaning of color and patterns, and the logic of evolutionary mutations as necessary adaptation to a changing environment. They were conversations that brought about interesting moments of insight and recognition, as for example the phenomenon of weaving. Not literally like the intricacy and inventiveness of woven bird or fish nests, but more as in food chains. In the ocean, for example, animals inhabit a particular horizontal space where they find their food. But when the light or temperature changes, they start to move up or down through these horizontal "food bands", vertically weaving their way through an invisible, horizontal organization.

In our work we talk a lot about weaving, knotting, folding, pleating, filtering, screening and veiling. The curtain or planting as a veil, disclosing, hiding, revealing or muting, opening up, wrapping or unwrapping architecture. Unwrapping and de-stabilizing is what our curtain intervention does in our project for the Haus der Kunst in Munich, where we made a huge curtain for the central hall, the biggest and most public space. In this fascist building of the 1930's, we shifted the curtain off center, undermining the rectangular logic of the space and the linear and regular placement of the columns; disturbing the mathematic organization of the room, putting it off balance. That effect is so evident and strong, yet the act is so simple. But one more move undoes the effect: storing the curtain in two corners of the space (forming column-like bundles), the mathematical organization of the room re-appears and is as pertinent and powerful as ever.

Yet the most fervent discussions during this two-year process were not about this "revolutionary" design decision or the technical aspects of the undertaking, but about the color of the curtain: according to the curators of the institution, its color needed to be neutral to not disturb the exhibited ART around it. And what is neutral to art curators? GRAY. Gray, they seem to think, is just 'not there'. It took us a whole year of creative argumentation and sample production to convince the staff that a slightly bluer gray would really introduce more life and air to the place and that the ART could handle a blue hue too!

NB: What is your favorite color?

PB: Oh my God, I don't think I have one! Well, I used to have lime green as my favorite accompaniment, and I still like it a lot because of its absolute positive energy, its sunny glow, its imagined smell. I used it a lot, among others for the curtains for the embassy in Berlin, the curtain running along the south façade, where it connects to a group of acacia trees (the curtain hanging opposite to it is the same Angel Root design in black and white). This lime-green makes me so happy, the more of it there is, the better, and even the fruit itself, every aspect of it: whole or cut open, pressed or peeled or mixed in or dried to a hard brown ball—it provides me with an enormous optimism, an energetic urge for life and a need to create! I just can't help it. It must be scientifically proven somewhere by someone that lime green creates this kind of reaction, don't you think? So as I said, I used to like that color and I still do; I just think I owe it to myself to grow up and to find another, "more deep" favorite color … soon.

COLOR, POWER, VELOCITY
WILLIAM W. BRAHAM

William W. Braham PhD FAIA is Interim Chair of the Department of Architecture at the University of Pennsylvania and Director of the Master of Environmental Building Design. Braham's book, *Modern Color/Modern Architecture: Amédée Ozenfant and the genealogy of color in modern architecture*, was published in 2002.

1 Beginning in 1946, *House and Garden* began publishing an annual color report and forecast each September and coordinating it with manufacturers and retailers. The citations are from two of those annual issues. The color use surveys were conducted by the Rahr Color Count for the first two years, and subsequently by Faber Birren, the prolific color consultant.

2 www.pantone.com/pages/pantone/Pantone.aspx?pg=20705&ca=4

3 Gottfried Semper, "Style: The Textile Art," *The Four Elements of Architecture, and Other Writings* (Cambridge: Cambridge University Press, 1989), 240.

1948, House and Garden

This year our findings as to the current palette (taken from the Rahr Color Count) are far more significant than ever before because an infinitely larger number of votes were cast—in all, 400,000 by 115,000 women. We found people are growing tired of the tan and beige scale; maroon and wine tones are on the wane. In their place are a variety of cool water-greens, blue-greens, and clear high pitched yellow-green that has some of the freshness and excitement of the first leaves on the willow. With the exception of Sprout Green and Flame, the palette is shifting toward the cool side. Upholstery grows clearer and brighter, rugs lighter. Women today want their kitchens and bathrooms to look like the rest of the house, not like laboratories.[1]

2010, Pantone

Pantone is pleased to announce PANTONE 15-5519 Turquoise, an inviting, luminous hue, as the Color of the Year for 2010. Combining the serene qualities of blue and the invigorating aspects of green, Turquoise inspires thoughts of soothing, tropical waters and a comforting escape from the everyday troubles of the world, while at the same time restoring our sense of wellbeing.[2]

The colors of twenty-first–century cities are largely determined by the competition among consumer products and commercially produced coatings and finishes, which vie for recognition in ever more visually saturated environments. Not that cities haven't always been colorful. In a contribution to the architectural color disputes of the nineteenth century, Gottfried Semper cited a description of the clothing worn in the ancient city of Ephesus: "the Ionians have violet-blue, purple, and saffron-yellow pattern undergarments… Their sarapeis are apple-green, purple, and white, at times also as dark violet as the sea."[3] Ephesus was home to the colorful Temple of Artemis (one of the seven wonders of the ancient world), and Semper used the passage to demonstrate the deep connection between the color of buildings and of clothing. He also assumed a natural identity between the local, Ionian culture and the particular colors displayed in clothes and buildings, a connection overwhelmed by the power and velocity of global, commercial culture. Even the cities of the Victorian era, which coincided with the "great masculine renunciation" of fashion and the invention of the black business suit, still had their locally specific polychromies. What has changed in the last century is our ability to produce more kinds of color in more kinds of media than any previous generation could have imagined. This hasn't altered the range of colors that humans can see, but has inspired a parallel revolution in techniques for manipulating color tastes, or at least for controlling the range of colors available for public display. These techniques seek to harness the power of color and control of the particular dynamics of mass color preferences.

"The look," by Pierre Cardin and Mary Quant, *House and Garden*, 1966

Put directly, color is powerful, and power is always contested. Restated in the form of a syllogism: people are visual, color attracts the eye, therefore color has power over people. It could also be the reverse. People seek power, color vision evolved to help distinguish the threat or utility of things, therefore people are visual. Whichever direction we start with, color and power are intertwined, though it is worth getting something clear from the start. One color by itself, even the brightest, is visually boring and slips almost immediately from awareness; our eyes are tuned to detect contrasts among colors, to spot the red berry among the green leaves or the flush on the pale cheek of a potential partner. So in a visually cluttered and competitive world, people, products, and buildings seek memorable color combinations that can be distinguished from their environments. Using tactics as old as eyes themselves, flowering plants, tribal banners, military uniforms, and sports teams all exhibit distinctive color contrasts. And though the eye can distinguish millions of colors, the number of memorable combinations is a scarce resource, limited by perception—think of the puzzling and often weak color combinations of new sports expansion teams—which makes the competition over color even more fierce.

The increasing size of global urban centers has only intensified the pace and sophistication of the struggle for color attention. The population circulating through urban centers has grown dramatically, as has the number of entities competing for their attention, and the variety of channels through which colors are transmitted. It is frequently reported that the average American is exposed to anywhere from hundreds to thousands of commercial messages a day, and those are only the explicitly formulated ones.[4] Exposure is a weak term and the estimates include product labels passed in a store, pages of classified ads, and the many sidebar, pop-up, and banner ads that hover at the edge of focused attention, but it highlights the challenge faced by manufacturers seeking to brand their products or institutions trying establish a memorable visual identity. With the sheer number of colored experiences being developed and tested constantly, the eyes of the population become both more jaded and more sophisticated.

The recent proliferation of digital techniques in public settings has further increased the rate at which highly visible color combinations can be displayed, but despite the velocity and magnitude of this visual assault, many color combinations retain their associations for years, while other colors become suddenly and widely popular in all manners of products. McDonald's has held

4 Google Answers has a good compilation of these estimates: answers.google.com/answers/threadview?id=56750. Among the more cogent summaries was from the Media Guru. "This statistic is only used for 'hype' purposes, usually to portray advertsing as some kind of social evil. The Guru has recently heard numbers cited between 3,000 and 20,000. These numbers are ludicrous. When challenged, those citing them will hedge and say they meant 'informational messages' or some such and include product labels passed in a grocery store…. The Guru has

Pastel colors of Kelvinator refrigerators, advertisement in *House and Garden* mid-1950s

"Committee members build the palette for Fall, 2009," Color Association of the United States

5 Leatrice Eiseman, "40 Years of Color: Pantone Looks Back at Four Decades of Color and Culture," www.pantone.com/pages/pantone/Pantone.aspx?pg=19758&ca=4

6 A. L. Kroeber and J. Richardson, "Three Centuries of Women's Dress Fashions, a Quantitative Analysis" in Anthropological Records 5, 2 (1940): 111–153.

onto its yellow and red since 1953, while Clinique has used its subtle green since 1968. Stable color identities are not limited to commercial products; the color of the Tuscan soil used to make the walls of Sienna is still known by the city name, as are a family of earth-based paint pigments, and of course Crayola has two well-known crayons of the color "burnt sienna and raw sienna." Conversely, the bright colors of the iMac introduced in the late 1990s were taken up by manufacturers and designers in many different fields and products (as was their translucency), extending and diluting the success of that color identify. Despite the persuasive stories of color commentators, it is nearly impossible to say what causes a particular color trend. Is it the association with an innovative product, the appeal of particular colors, the contrast of those colors to the current offerings, or the affiliation with the "spirit-of-the-times"?[5] Achieving a recognizable identify is a primary goal of marketing and of design, and color always forms some aspect of an overall image or appeal, but in the contemporary commercial city, marketing and design are rarely sufficient to secure a durable brand, and manufacturers have long sought to predict and control which colors will succeed.

FORECASTS AND PREDICTIONS

Apparel has followed seasonal cycles of variation for centuries, driven initially by seasonal variations in climates, but ultimately becoming a vital component of the retail cycle, used to inspire consumers to buy new items. Seasonal styles were propagated from fashion centers like Paris, which circulated their annual offerings in brochures, runway shows, or as prototypes displayed on modeling dummies and sent around the world. In an elegant study prepared in 1940, Kroeber and Richardson charted the length and width of the women's skirts shown in the annual Parisian reports from 1787 to 1936, illustrating their behavior as a kind of dynamic system, smoothly oscillating between the extremes of short and long, full and narrow.[6] The constrained and tidy oscillation of women's dress shapes began to break down a decade or so after Kroeber and Richardson published their article, with maxis and minis being available in the same season,

PANTONE®

fashion color report fall 2010

myPANTONE™ puts the power of the entire PANTONE Color Library in your pocket, enabling designers and design-savvy consumers to capture, create and share PANTONE Color Palettes wherever and whenever they find inspiration. Providing a portable, digital design studio and essential color tools at their fingertips, myPANTONE gives creatives the freedom to access PANTONE Colors anywhere, without the need to be in their office or carry multiple guides.

PANTONE FASHION+HOME SMART Color System Pantone is the only globally available, off-the-shelf color system that fashion designers and their vendors can trust for unsurpassed color accuracy. Using the new PANTONE FASHION+HOME SMART Color System, designers can reduce color development cycles by 50 percent or more.

The PANTONE Goe™ System The PANTONE Goe System is a color inspiration and specification system for the graphic arts industry, including 2,058 new PANTONE Colors, plus modern tools and interactive software for multimedia color reproduction.

For more information on these and other PANTONE Products, visit www.pantone.com.

Endive PANTONE 13-0632 C/M/Y/K **11 / 4 / 51 / 0** GOE **1-3-2**

Golden Glow PANTONE 15-1050 C/M/Y/K **7 / 31 / 95 / 0** GOE **9-1-3**

Living Coral PANTONE 16-1546 C/M/Y/K **0 / 61 / 50 / 0** GOE **21-1-2**

Lipstick Red PANTONE 19-1764 C/M/Y/K **13 / 100 / 65 / 5** GOE **26-2-7**

Purple Orchid PANTONE 18-3027 C/M/Y/K **34 / 79 / 0 / 0** GOE **37-2-6**

Chocolate Truffle PANTONE 19-1626 C/M/Y/K **53 / 86 / 61 / 34** GOE **26-3-7**

Lagoon PANTONE 16-6418 C/M/Y/K **73 / 7 / 39 / 0** GOE **104-3-3**

Woodbine PANTONE 18-0538 C/M/Y/K **49 / 26 / 90 / 10** GOE **135-4-3**

Oyster Gray PANTONE 14-1107 C/M/Y/K **16 / 14 / 24 / 0** GOE **141-2-1**

Rose Dust PANTONE 14-1307 C/M/Y/K **17 / 25 / 27 / 0** GOE **16-4-1**

for example, but even as fashion became more decentralized, or multi-centered, the attention to patterns of behavior became more focused.

At some point in the nineteenth century, the apparel industry began to focus more specifically on seasonal colors and to try to predict and regulate the colors used in the coming season. This began as a commercial precaution by various manufacturers whose products had to be produced in quantity and offered in a hierarchical and mass market. Specialized products, buttons, for example, had to be sold to apparel manufacturers who in turn sold them to retailers who then sold them to consumers. In today's terminology, they were all trying to minimize their risk, and the more coordination there was among manufacturers and between different industries, the greater likelihood that the colors of products manufactured would be accepted and purchased by consumers. Color forecasting is now a fully developed activity, with many competitors and specialists, but the first generally coordinated effort in the United States was by the Textile Color Card Association in 1915. As reported in the corporate history of their successor, now called the Color Association, the formation was instigated by an interruption in the flow of color information from German dyemakers.

Before 1915, it was the milliners, the US hat makers, who were responsible for setting color trends for the US textiles industry. Their judgments were based on the dyestuffs they got from Germany and fashion information received from Paris. After World War I cut off the means for continuing the milliners' seasonal fashion color forecasts, the wool and silk companies, who were particularly dependent on this data to market their clothing, decided to act on their own. As a result, a committee representing the textile and allied industries, including silk, wool, thread, button, and garment manufacturers, was selected to choose colors for the following season, have them dyed and issued in the form of an American color card. The proposition to prepare a color card resulted in

Fashion Color Report for Fall, 2010, Pantone®

Cover of the annual color issue, House & Garden, 1949-50

7 "About Us," *The Color Association of the United States*, March, 2010. www.colorassociation.com/site/aboutus

8 S. Lichtenstein, *Editing Architecture: Architectural Record and the Growth of Modern Architecture* 1928-1938, PhD Dissertation, Cornell University, 1990. Sweet's Indexed Catalogue of Building Construction, New York: The Architectural Record Co., 1906.

9 *House and Garden* was first published in 1901 by a group of Philadelphia architects as an architectural journal. After Condé Nast acquired it in 1915, it was refocused on interiors by editor Richardson L. Wright (1914–1946). The color surveys were begun under editor Albert Kornfeld (1946–1955).

the formation in early 1915 of the Textile Color Card Association of the United States (TCCA), the Color Association's predecessor:

The Color Association is the only forecasting service that selects its colors through a committee panel of eight to twelve industry professionals. The combined expertise of our committee members assures a thoughtful and innovative forecast, season after season.[7]

The development of a building products industry lagged somewhat behind that of apparel, but not by much. Sweet's Catalog was developed in the 1890s as a service of F. W. Dodge Construction, and first issued as a catalog in 1906 by the *Architectural Record* publishing company, of which it was a parallel effort.[8] Not unlike the history of the manufacture of apparel, building products moved rapidly in this period from items that were individually designed and custom fabricated on-site to engineered and mass-produced products. With that transition, building product manufacturers faced a similar challenge for items whose color was integral or fixed, and especially for colored coatings such as paints, stains, and dyes. The rapid growth of Sweet's Catalog through the 1920s and 1930s, both in its reach and the number of manufacturers it included, describes the change in the industry, but as with the apparel industry, color forecasting and selection was initially managed by individual manufacturers and industries. The critical moment of transition for building products seemed to be the economic activity that followed World War II, and the ever closer relationship between architectural magazines and manufacturers formed by advertising revenue.

It should have been the familial connection between *Architectural Record* and Sweet's that instigated coordinated color forecasting in the building industry, but instead it was the particular focus that *House and Garden (H&G)* magazine had developed on interior design, where products are typically more colorful and are changed more rapidly (though still not as rapidly as clothing).[9] *H&G* began its annual color reports in 1946, basing the description of "current colors" on nationwide preference surveys and coordinating the color forecasts directly with about 400 of the manufacturers who provided the materials from which next year's current colors would be chosen. In other words, the color choices they reported involved not only the determination of general preferences but the complex influences of mass media, and the interaction between polling data and coordinated consumer production. In this sense, post–war color palettes result from the complex systems phenomena of feedback and dynamic reinforcement, exemplifying, as well, their complexity—just because colors are coordinated doesn't mean they will all be popular. As one reads through the decades of annual color discussion provided by *H&G*, it is clear that *H&G* are no more in control of the outcome than the individual consumer. The retrospective comments offered in the reports, added to help interpret and position the annual forecast, seem to offer more historical perspective, but equally important insights can be discerned in the missed forecasts and the repeated struggle of the commentators to discover a logic that might explain changing color preferences.

How do we explain changes like that from the "light bright look of clear pastels" in the 1950s to the "deep, rich, bold" colors of the 1960s? Or the enduring use of earth tones, from the driftwood and sandalwood of '51 to the "tortoise-shell hues" of '63? What does the annual *H&G* color report actually describe, and what does it leave unsaid? Its breathless descriptions capture some familiar features of the post-war period: the lightening and brightening of popular colors and the sense of release from the Depression and the war. Such descriptions also convey the assumption that the one simply reflects the other, that there is a spirit-of-the-times adequately expressed by designer's color schemes and endorsed by the purchases of consumers. Color is certainly expressive; the categorical difference between hues—red, green, blue—and the exceptionally fine distinctions between different tints, tones, and shades, are all highly evocative. But as Russell Lynes observed in *H&G*'s 1957 report: "Freud has taught us that it is not as simple as that. We are now aware that our emotions, like our automobiles, are scarcely ever primary; they are at least two-toned."[10] And if color doesn't represent a simple expression of emotion, what kinds of cultural interactions are made evident by the constant change in colors of the moment, by the popular preference for one palette over another?

10 Russell Lynes, "You take the rainbow; I'll take the pot of gold," *House and Garden* (September, 1957). Lynes was the author of *The Tastemakers* (1949), which charted the interaction between high-, middle-, and low-brow taste in America.

From the beginning, the *H&G* report distinguished between color forecasts and the documentation of "current" colors. In that distinction they were following the practice established by the Color Association. When a color becomes a color-of-the-moment, there often remains "a popular and continuing demand" for it after the fashion has passed; it may even become a "staple" or "classic" color. And for all the influence exerted by an organization like *H&G* or the Color Association, there is little firm connection between a forecast and the collective decisions by which a color like Schiaparelli Pink crosses over to become a recurring favorite. Forecasting and coordinating alone are not sufficient. In historiographical terms, shelter magazines are documentary chronicles, situated somewhere between the raw data of historical facts and fully narrative histories. Chronicles endeavor to discern the patterns and motives later visible to retrospective histories. Such attempts are always fragmentary, often grasping at elements that appear minor in hindsight, and so convey the climate of uncertainty in which such decisions are actually made. Michel de Certeau illustrated this condition with a description of the difference between walking around in a city and planning or explaining it from above. Each imagines the perspective of other—the walker immersed in sights and smells imagines the coherent map, while the planner tries to remember something of the walk—and we need to grasp the interaction between the two to understand the collective activity that produces the city.[11] Like the city itself, color palettes appear more coherent when seen from a historical distance. They are an especially visible result of a quite unpredictable process driven by numerous forces and participants—designers, manufacturers, the media, and consumers—each of whom imagines the situation differently.

11 Michel de Certeau, *The Practice of Everyday Life* (Berkeley: University of California Press, 1984), 91–110.

Color palettes also involve critical decisions about how and where they are used. The color of flooring materials, for example, became a key advertising feature in the 1950s as the "new informality" made the floor an acceptable site for sitting. Through the 1960s, *H&G* reported the steady dissolution of other familiar color conventions—the abandonment of balanced color schemes or the discreet use of accents—so much so, that by 1967 the editors noted in despair that for color "everything is upside down as well as right-side up."[12] That condition of radical change had been the subject of canonical histories like Giedion's Space, Time and Architecture, which explained architectural modernism as the rational consequence of the massive transformations in science, art, and industry.[13] Revolution and progress were the order of the day, a condition resulting from the combined and destabilizing influence of new means of production, which constantly

12 *House and Garden* (September, 1967): 155.

13 Sigfried Giedion, *Space, Time and Architecture: The Growth of a New Tradition* (Cambridge: Harvard University Press, 1941).

14 This had already been noted by Marx a century earlier. *Karl Marx and Frederick Engels, The Communist Manifesto* (1948), chapter 1.

15 Susan Buck Morss, "Dream World of Mass Culture," *Dialectics of Seeing: Walter Benjamin and the Arcades Project* (The MIT Press, 1989), 253–286.

16 For example: www.trendhunter.com/; www.trendspotting.com/; www.bettynewmantrendspotting.com/; www.fashiontrendspotting.com/.

yielded new materials, colors, and finishes, and of new patterns of work, settlement, communication, and leisure leading to new demands and possibilities.[14]

The increasingly rapid generation of new products, new "wants," and new possibilities puts a premium on any indication of difference or novelty, and on any explanations which give such differences identity and authority. Colors are a most readily changeable and recognizable emblem of difference, which makes them the leading signifiers of any fashion, but such emblems must somehow be fit into the images and concepts that organize the dreamworld of consumption, that allow the new to make sense and to fit into existing concepts.[15] Any enduring color scheme must convey an equally compelling rationale, whether that explanation is historical (the Georgian house used this shade), scientific (these colors are complements), therapeutic (this green is calming), symbolic/psychological (purple means power), cultural (these are Chinese reds), or simply aesthetic, though the later requires a highly branded authority like that of Schiaparelli to be effectively enduring. Tracing the genesis of such authorizing discourses constitutes the most challenging task in analyzing color palettes, and allows us to understand the kinds of cultural, political, and architectural differences being negotiated.

Inquiring about the colors of cities means asking about the shorter cycles of fashion forecasts, in which the "big news" can be "earth tones," the longer cycles of brands and classic colors, and the enduring effects of local climate and geography. Much of twentieth-century architecture has involved an effort to resist the shorter cycles of change, at the same time that the architectural avant-garde has become identified with the activities that define the next fashion. This paradox reveals at least two different issues affecting our consideration of urban color. The first is the complex interaction between "high," "middle," and "low" culture, now thought to involve a host of competing and interpenetrating taste cultures or lifestyles, and the other is the intentionally experimental nature of avant-garde culture. In the classic model, high culture seeks to define and police good taste, which is undermined and overwhelmed by the low-culture appreciation of kitsch and the middle-class pursuit of status.

In current marketing practice, different lifestyles are viewed as nearly equivalent and can be chosen nearly independently of class or culture. As the marketing and brand consultants, Whitaker International, argue, the key is "understanding and defining consumers by STYLE, versus 'fashion, demographics or statistics.' " Their distinction is worth considering. The "style" of lifestyle is the result of a collective set of consumer choices that can be detected by careful observers and are only partly constrained by the offerings of the fashion industries or by social and economic factors. Manufacturers and designers who provide colors to the contemporary city succeed by paying attention to trends and tendencies as much as by orchestrating production.

Color is only occasionally the lead element in a trend, though it is usually one of the more memorable markers. A brief foray into any of the trend–hunting or trend–spotting sites, blogs, and feeds reinforces the point made at the beginning: the color of the contemporary city now arises from the seething mass of colorful activities, products, and events vying for public attention.[16] Any attempt at civic coordination of color must appear against the overwhelming commercial backdrop. Even the notion of a discrete trend seems to involve a tremendous act of visual focus, and yet durable color identities emerge, as they do in natural ecosystems. The surrealists were intrigued by the color displays of color-blind creatures like butterflies, which come not from design but from selective, evolutionary interaction with their environments. What is the color of the year but a survival strategy for manufacturers and designers faced with the twenty-first century city?

The terms of the restless color struggles in the contemporary city are only partly regulated by the color palettes prepared by color consulting groups and industry forecasting entities. The predictions for the paint colors of Fall 2011, for example, will succeed by limiting choices and organizing production, but they can still fail to persuade the populations that must purchase, use, and exhibit them. *House and Garden* predicted the demise of the pastel color palette for years before it finally gave way to the hotter, brighter palettes of the 1960s, and their frustration suggests the real complexity in the color of contemporary urban experience. Publically agreed upon palettes are shaped by many factors, from the memorable color distinctions determined by visual perception to material production, climate-geography, and culture, now commonly called "lifestyle." The fracturing and commercialization of public space is recorded in the proliferation of various lifestyle palettes, which employ, deploy, and redeploy arguments to give them authority, from "natural" colors to symbolic or psychological meanings and therapeutic promises.

COLOR AND THE CITY RICKY BURDETT AND ADAM KAASA

Ricky Burdett is Professor of Urban Studies at the London School of Economics and Political Science (LSE), director of LSE Cities and the Urban Age Programme, and Global Distinguished Professor at the Institute of Public Knowledge at New York University. He is Chief Adviser on Architecture and Urbanism for the London 2012 Olympics and the Olympic Park Legacy Company, and was architectural adviser to the Mayor of London from 2001–2006.

Adam Kaasa is a PhD candidate in the Cities Programme at the LSE with a focus on the circulations of ideas about architecture and urbanism. He is the Communications Manager for LSE Cities and the Urban Age programme, and coordinates the NYLON seminars and conferences, a transatlantic intellectual working group between universities in and around London and New York.

Santa Fe, Mexico City Informal Settlements and use of color (Image: Philipp Rode).

Shanghai Skyline from Jin Mao Tower (Images: Philipp Rode).

Graffiti in Goiânia, Brazil (by Santhiago Vieira Selon).

1 The Urban Age program is part of LSE Cities, an international center of excellence located at the London School of Economics and in partnership with the Alfred Herrhausen Society. From its beginnings in 2005, the Urban Age has hosted conferences in New York, Shanghai, London, Mexico City, Johannesburg, Berlin, Mumbai, São Paulo, and Istanbul.

Color is not expensive like moulded decorations and sculptures, but color means a joyful existence. … Let blue, red, yellow, green, black and white radiate in crisp, bright shades to replace the dirty grey of houses.
—Bruno Taut, *Call for Colored Architecture*, 1919

Now we have many problems to solve in the city, but we have a city. And this has been the beginning of it through just this very simple change of the mindset by putting some color in the middle of nowhere.
—Edi Rama, Mayor of Tirana, Albania, 2009

THE VISUAL AND THE SPATIAL: WHAT ROLE FOR COLOR IN THE URBAN DEBATE?

An internal debate within the London School of Economics and Political Science's urban fraternity revolves around the question of whether we should use the term "visual" rather than "physical" when it comes to determining how space and society are interlinked. Some of us argue that the concept of physicality is instrumental in conveying the impact of new housing or urban typologies on the people who live in them. Think of the gated communities of Johannesburg and Mexico City, with their fences and walls turning their backs on sprawling informal settlements, and you get the picture. Others argue that the eye is more sensitive to spatial measures that induce social exclusion and that research in this field should emphasize the sensory and the perceptual over the formal.

As the LSE Urban Age research program has investigated the social and spatial conditions of major world cities such as London, Istanbul, and São Paulo, we have become increasingly aware of the power of the "visual" to mobilize individual and collective action.[1] In this context, the visual encompasses all that the eye can see. A painted wall in a São Paulo drug-torn *favela* provides a narrative for children who wish to escape their entrapped condition. In Shanghai, a senior Party official orders that all rooftops visible from the top of the tallest hotel tower in Pudong be painted green, red, or blue—as in a Monopoly game set—so that foreign dignitaries will not be offended by the drabness of its Communist roofscape. Architects and politicians still attempt to mark difference or uniformity through the use of color in the built environment. Color, it seems, is not neutral. It remains an instrument of social control that has the potential to create a sense of solidarity and identity within the increasingly complex landscapes of the contemporary city.

Housing by Bruno Taut / Martin Wagner 1925–1930 (Images: Großsiedlung Britz, Hufeisensiedlung).

2 See Iain Boyd Whyte, *Bruno Taut and the Architecture of Activism* (Cambridge: Cambridge University Press, 1982).

3 Color was common in the Weißenhofsiedlung, though you would not know it from the descriptions or photographs—black-and-white photography was crucial in flattening International Modernism's diversity. Mark Wigley, in his book *White Walls, Designer Dresses: The Fashioning of Modern Architecture*, argues that because of the cheap reproduction of black-and-white photography, the Weißenhofsiedlung "facilitated the reduction of diverse tendencies and contradictions of the avant-garde into a recognizable 'look' that turns around the white wall" (Cambridge, MA: MIT Press, 1995, 302). Color is often related to fashion, and thus the colors white and black, as classic neutrals, come under fire by Wigley, who explains the very non-neutral elements in their meaning and use.

4 See Evan McKenzie, "The Dynamics of Privatopia: Private Residential Governance in the USA' in *Private Cities: Global and Local Perspectives*. eds. Georg Glasze, Chris Webster, and Klaus Frantz (London: Routledge, 2005), 9–30

5 Whyte, *Bruno Taut and the Architecture of Activism*.

BRUNO TAUT: CONSISTENCY AND ACTIVISM

But this is not an exclusively twentyfirst-century phenomenon. The Prussian-born architect Bruno Taut turned heads and angered contemporaries in refusing to toe the "colored" line at the Weißenhofsiedlung housing exhibition in Stuttgart in 1927. The event was organized by Mies van der Rohe and contained submissions by most of the leading architects of the time, including Le Corbusier, Walter Gropius and Peter Behrens; only eleven of the original twenty-one buildings remain. Still, this collection of International Style homes was one of the most important architectural spaces of the early twentieth century.[2] Taut's *Number 19* astonished critics by using vibrant primary colors on all external and internal walls. While other architects used some soft colors, Taut's striking red, blue, yellow and green exterior walls, paired with pitch-black flooring and yellow ceiling interiors, broke the architectural dialogue of consistency and began to push aesthetics into the realm of activism.[3]

The resulting backlash against *Number 19* is similar to the proliferation of consistency not only in urban zoning laws of the 1950s onward but more recently in the attack on diversity stemming from community regulations in suburbs the world over around housing style and, most important, color.[4] In an exponentially increasing number of suburban neighborhoods in the United States, for example, the growth of homeowners' associations and their CCRs (covenants, conditions and restrictions) amounts to an authority akin to a kind of "volunteer zoning." In an effort to raise land values through consistent rules of style and color (in effect lifestyle), these associations mean that painting your house a color beyond the tailored palette could bring legal action. In central business districts and entertainment zones in global cities, a consistent style of architecture exuding carefully tailored narratives of cosmopolitan lifestyles breeds a similar aversion to color. Although *Number 19* is one of many houses no longer standing in Stuttgart, Taut's intervention has lasting effects because of its apparent rupture from a consistent whole, and appearance to do not only with the style of architecture but through his use of color.

Equally avant-garde in terms of the relation of color to the city—an architectural site as much as a social one—was Taut's political roles in the cities of Magdeburg and Berlin. From 1921 to 1923, Taut was the director of municipal construction for the city of Magdeburg and implemented on a large scale his manifesto of 1919. He painted the primarily gray-colored housing (cheaply made after the Great War) with bright façades. He continued this work in a series of high-profile projects in Berlin in 1924, creating with the city's building planner, Martin Wagner, more than 10,000 new flats, using color to accentuate them against the Berlin palette. Speaking about his goals, Taut said that they were "not aesthetic, but ethical, since the aim was to give the inhabitants of the most sordid tenement and the most sinister rear court a spark of joie de vivre, however modest."[5] By just creating buildings, then, Taut was an early advocate of the sociopolitical importance of color to creating a sense of belonging to place in the social site of the urban.

ARCHITECTS ON COLOR

Much color theory since Taut has been functional or psychological, rather than political. The polemic 1976 edition of *Color for Architecture* brought together

Housing units, Santhiago and Iquique, Chile (by Elemental).

6 Tom Porter and Byron Mikellides, eds., *Colour for Architecture* (London: Studio Vista, 1976) 10.

7 Faber Birren, "The Need for Colour and Light in Future Man-Made Spaces" in eds. Porter and Mikellides, 8.

8 Dr Peter Smith, "The Dialectics of Colour," in eds. Porter and Mikellides, *Colour for Architecture*, 21.

9 Porter and Mikellides, eds., *Colour for Architecture*, 24.

10 Richard Rogers, "The Colour Approach of Piano and Rogers," in eds. Porter and Mikellides, *Colour for Architecture*, 60.

11 Ibid., 61.

leading architectural theorists, historians, and practicing architects, including Richard Rogers and Norman Foster, in an attempt, as the book's editors outlined in their introduction, to "avoid the possibility of future grey, monochromatic towns and cities" and to "reorientate [sic] our concept of space-form relationships towards a deeper awareness of colored space and colored form."[6]

Some contributors were decidedly optimistic about the direction of progress; "Men of future generations will not only travel in space but possibly live there".[7] Others were fascinated with the potentialities of a science of cerebral urbanism; "More than ever, there is a need for environmental presentations which enable the neocortex and limbic system to experience creative synthesis. ... Color in environment has a crucial role to play in keeping alive the cerebral interactive rhythms by nourishing the needs of the right side [of the brain], and by keeping active the dialectic routes between the centres of reason and emotion."[8] Still others were conscious of the historiography on which rests our understanding of the "color" of antiquity; "The idea that the Parthenon would come to be a source of study in monochromatic excellence would have puzzled Ictinus and Callicrates because they had originally designed it to be completely painted, gilded and detailed in rich colors."[9] Overall, there seemed to be an agreement that the function of color is to "humanize" cities in their relationship between people and buildings.

For architect Richard Rogers, an architecture of civil action and individuality is essential for a productive and equal urban sphere. Rogers wrote that color "has much to do with our interest in personal participation. In other words, we would like to come towards the idea that people could slip in their own red, pink or blue house-panel into a parent structure."[10] Color becomes the user's agent in a kind of flexible or democratic architecture. Rogers also argues that color is a way to accentuate values and morals. By "using color to underline what is important," Rogers insists on an inclusive urbanism.[11]

Norman Foster's practice, on the other hand, points to the role of visual distinction that color adds to a project. Rather than demarcating color's relationship to the psychological, Foster highlights the mediating space of color in relating a building to its environment. The use of color is not so much about the agency of creators or users in a building but rather how it speaks to its surroundings. In viewin the use of color as an aesthetic as much as a political act, the practice concludes that the primary motivation in choosing color is "the

visual excitement of the juxtaposition of vivid colors and their effect on an object in the landscape."[12] Without claims to a certain kind of politics, Foster and Partners recognize the effect of visual distinction in terms of legitimacy and representation in the urban realm.

From both of these architects, we can take away the importance of color not only in terms of creating a visual juxtaposition—a marker or urban event out of the relationship between color and built form, the landscape—but also in terms of its democratic potential.

TIRANA: COLOR AND POST-ARCHITECTURAL POLITICS

Nearly eighty years on, and in a city of equal transition to that of postwar Berlin, Edi Rama, the artist-turned-mayor of Tirana, capital of Albania, seems to be taking a cue from Taut. As mayor, Rama initiated a scheme to paint the dour surfaces of his post-Socialist city in bright, iconic colors. The move triggered interest from architects and artists around the world who came and were commissioned to paint buildings in the capital. But rather than turn Tirana into a living art museum (and coming close to it with the *Tirana International Contemporary Art Biannual* just concluding its fourth edition) Rama, speaking at the Tate Modern during the Architecture Foundation's *Architecture + Art : Crossover and Collaboration series*, noted:[13]

But in the beginning, this is very important, it was not an artistic operation. It was just a way to get through this terrible and very, very thick wall between people and authority, and individual life and social life.[14]

The color choices were not, as for Le Corbusier, meant to reveal or enhance the architectonic elements of the building but rather to create a social condition of newness, a break, a discontinuity from the historical weight and candor of Soviet Socialism. This, according to Rama, was the most important outcome of the project, not just a beautification scheme, nor simply an attempt to enter the international glitz of the biennale circuit, but rather to recreate, or indeed, create again for the first time, the "city."

12 Foster Associates, "On the Use of Colour in Buildings," in eds. Porter and Mikellides, *Colour for Architecture*, 62.

13 See http://www.tica-albania.org/TICAB/

14 Edi Rama, Mayor of Tirana, Albania, speaking at the Tate Modern as part of the Architecture Foundation's *Architecture + Art: Crossover and Collaboration* series, 19 October 2009.

Edi Rama's color project in Tirana, Albania (Images: David Dufresne).

Speaking to the importance of creating community, Rama recalled that:

It's important to give the people a sense of belonging to space. A sense that they [had] lost. Communism used so inflationarily [sic] all the key words of a common life: belonging to the country, belonging to your land, solidarity, volunteering—all these words lost sense in Albania. Using these words at this time sounded totally Communist. So the colors helped to build a common ground for discussion. And then we started to talk to people to build small communities.[15]

Where Rama departs from Taut is in his political position. Taut was commissioned by leading mayors at the time, or at least given the freedom to move on his own. Rama is mayor and artist in one. Without formal training but recognizing the distinct connections between place and politics, Rama is elected to a position of authority and then uses this position to make tough choices, to bring about new-ness through a system of shocking colored architectural moves.

While Edi Rama's work in Tirana is nothing if not inspirational, the political construction of a communal good, a communal city, a social body, weighted in place by urban planners past, but invigorated with a colorful modern future, has taken it's toll, and reminds us of the limits of top-down political action. In a telling moment, having been asked by a member of an international audience about the need for destruction to "create" the new Tirana, Rama spoke frankly about the demolition of illegal housing, and the poignant attempt by these urban poor to use the symbol of this new urban commune—color—as a sign of both political legitimacy, solidarity, and political activism:

Another collateral effect was that this process was accompanied with a very very heavy process of demolition, because all these spaces were cleaned up from build-

15 Ibid.

ings. For example, in the river side we had to demolish buildings of 1 to 8 floors. We removed 123,000 tons of concrete. And the people trying to protect their illegal building, they painted it with very strong colors. Because they had the hope that this would impress me so much that I would say, "Please protect this jewel because it's so beautiful." But in fact, you know, it was a vain additional expense because they would be demolished anyway.[16]

Do Cortiço da Rua Solón ao Edifício União, São Paulo, regenerated with color façade (Alfred Herrhausen Society).

16 Ibid.

The categorical use of the term "illegal" to legitimate and rationalize the destruction of homes and the relocation (or not) of inhabitants is a sign both of Rama's comfort speaking to an international audience and the limitations of color as political agency.

The conditions of use of color in the city of Tirana were directed by the (democratically) elected mayor. And yet the political recognition of color-as-social stopped where the need for development and "cleaning up the city" began: "they would be demolished anyway." As much as Tirana would have brightly colored building façades, it needed a riverside free from settlement to showcase the new city to strolling foreigners and locals alike. The right to the city stopped where the need for the photographic and international gaze ended. While the city of Tirana is changing the way the social and the visual worlds engage, the destruction of housing and the consolidation of control over the visual and political representation of the city remains.

COLOR FROM THE GROUND UP: A LATIN AMERICAN PERSPECTIVE

Where Taut and Rama provide an inspirational, if official, sense of the relationship of color to cities, a host of local initiatives in Latin America remind us that the complexity of color extends to the micropolitics of neighborhoods, and of the need for social belonging in a diversity of individual spaces. We encountered two initiatives as part of the LSE and Alfred Herrhausen Society's Urban Age program, an ongoing series of international conferences hosted in cities around the world, that illustrate this relationship.

The first of these initiatives is the Rua Solón in São Paulo, Brazil. Like many other buildings of its period, 934 Rua Solón is a raw, partially completed concrete-frame multistory structure located in the Bom Retiro neighborhood close to São Paulo's central district and its range of economic activities. Constructed in the 1970s, the building remained unfinished due to the death of the developer and was subsequently taken over by squatter families in the 1980s. As with many other "invaded buildings," the early residents established a precarious system of electrical and water supply with exposed wires and unreliable water provision, and a very basic form of waste and garbage disposal. Overcrowding became severe with seventy-three families crammed into the building, using all available spaces including the incomplete elevator shafts. Following a project with students from São Paulo's Faculty of Architecture (FAU) efforts to improve the site began.

The building needed improvement if this vulnerable population of the urban poor was going to keep a safe and habitable roof over their heads. Through varied partnerships, including local government, the university, public institutions, human rights groups, and private enterprise, part of the task became one of raising resources and "de-densifying" the building. More than thirty families were rehoused, and the remaining residents focused on raising living standards for the entire community. With resources secured, the architecture students decided to live in the building with the residents for one week.

The action resulted in three immediately visible results. First, *mutirões* or collective initiatives between students and residents were organized to clean the site, beginning with the common areas and with the often blocked access to the building. Second, the installation of a collective power grid enabled each family to have a reliable measure of their electricity bills, thus providing improved economic stability beyond removing fire risks. Third, and important for this discussion, they improved the façade of the building by painting it a bright orange, adding security gates, and finishing it with letters giving the name of the building, *Edifício União*.

Inspired by the bright new color of the building and their own agency in making it happen, the physical improvements to the "look" of the building and its common areas triggered a newfound motivation that led many residents to make improvements inside their own apartments. Internal walls have been rendered and painted, and new kitchens and bathrooms have been installed, with a determined interest in the collective improvement and maintenance of the site. Openings have been introduced into dark corridors and stairwells to improve the environment and reduce electricity consumption.

While these infrastructural improvements made possible through the partnership between the university, future practicing architects, and the residents of the Cortiço Rua Solón are essential, the importance of making place, of building a sense of belonging and a sense of pride, are even more so. Consolidating a diverse vertical community around the hope offered in a few cans of paint delivers a promise to Henri Lefebvre's right to the city. As David Harvey so concisely noted, "The right to the city is far more than the individual liberty to access urban resources: it is a right to change ourselves by changing the city."[17]

The second initiative comes through the Chilean architect Alejandro Aravena and his work on providing flexible, unfinished housing, in recognition of the place-making capabilities of populations in Latin America. Aravena's "do-tank" *Elemental* is leading a small revolution in the way in which social housing is imagined. Rather than building finished houses, *Elemental* recognizes the Latin American auto-construction movement's capacity to complete the less

17 David Harvey, "The Right to the City," *New Left Review*, vol. 53, September–October, 2008, 1.

complicated parts of the home.[18] *Elemental* constructs the structure, plumbing and lighting, completing half the house, leaving enough space open for the family to expand their home in the long or short term. Part of the ethos relates to an economic rationale, but equally important is the social investment required in building or expanding the home.

When *Elemental* leaves the building site, the social housing is neutral in color, and half finished. In a lecture Aravena gave as part of the Urban Age public lecture programme *Understanding Cities*, he mentioned this imperative:

There's been an historical criticism to social housing which is in order to achieve efficiency, and to lower costs, it tends to be monotonous and repetitive creating very bad urban environments. Well, when you have money for just half of the house, you can prefabricate without bad conscience. I mean, the more monotonous the first half is, the better that half is going to be able to control the second half of which we cannot know the quality. The more neutral, dry and repetitive that first half, well the more it works as a frame, as a support for self intervention.[19]

Even though, or perhaps because, the house object begins as a monotonous one, within months—afternoons sometimes—the agency of the inhabitants creates a visual statement of ownership, feeding off the collective relationship with others in the area and inspiring a sense of belonging. More often than not, the first addition is one of color. Color gives the immediate sense of pride that extends not only within the housing block but throughout the relationship of the inhabitants to the political realm of their city. While the monotony of social housing may not be realistically avoided, the method of demanding personal and collective intervention in the built environment by providing livable homes with room for expansion, *Elemental* creates place-makers. Because citizens were offered the right to "change themselves through changing the city," they become citizens with presence and are more able to access a political agency. In an ironic moment, their right to the city is enabled by monotony and consistency, but enacted through color.

COLORING THE CITY

While costs and economic rationales, and increasingly (and equally reductive) methods of carbon calculation focus on the typology of the built environment, still color matters. Color is what angered Mies in Stuttgart when his apartment glowed red off the reflection of Bruno Taut's Number 19, challenging the homogeneity of the avant-garde. Color is how Mayor Edi Rama reinvented the social collective of a city, laying the groundwork for the difficult discussions that face post-Socialist Tirana. Color is the method through which people accessed their right to the city in two initiatives in Latin America by making place, and therefore, inspiring political presence. Urban interventions the world over enact in the dialectic of continuity and change, of monotony and diversity, of consistency and the unique. Debates over coloring the city is one way of navigating this dialectic and is at once a political necessity and an ethical imperative.

18 See Illiana Ortega, *Brick by Brick: Building Families and Houses in Mexico City*, PhD dissertation, London School of Economics and Political Science, 2008.

19 Alejandro Aravena, "Architecture as Investment: New Forms of Social Equity," *Understanding Cities* public lecture series, Urban Age, London School of Economics, 27 April 2009.

URBAN LIGHT AND COLOR
ALEX BYRNE AND DAVID R. HILBERT

Alex Byrne teaches philosophy at MIT. His main interests are philosophy of mind (especially perception and consciousness), metaphysics (especially color), and epistemology. He has written a number of papers on color with David Hilbert; they also edited a two volume anthology on the philosophy and science of color, *Readings on Color* (1997).

David Hilbert teaches philosophy at the University of Illinois at Chicago and works primarily on issues concerning color and vision. He is the author of *Color and Color Perception* (1987) and he edited a two volume anthology on the philosophy and science of color, *Readings on Color* (1997), with Alex Byrne.

MIT's Stata Center, Cambridge. Attached shadow on right-facing brick wall; cast shadow on metal cladding opposite (Alex Byrne and David Hilbert).

1 Tom Porter and Byron Mikellides, *Colour for Architecture* (London: Studio Vista, 1976), 10.
2 Tom Porter and Byron Mikellides, *Colour for Architecture Today* (Abingdon, Oxon: Taylor & Francis, 2009), vii.
3 Jean-Philippe Lenclos and Dominique Lenclos, *Colors of the World: the Geography of Color*, translated by Gregory P. Bruhn (New York: Norton, 2004), 86.

In *Colour for Architecture*, published in 1976, the editors, Tom Porter and Byron Mikellides, explain that their book was "produced out of an awareness that colour, as a basic and vital force, is lacking from the built environment and that our knowledge of it is isolated and limited."[1] Lack of urban color was then especially salient in Britain—where the book was published—which had just begun to recoil at the Brutalist legacy of angular stained gray concrete strewn across the post-war landscape. Perhaps because the most urgent need was to inject some hue into this architectural dystopia, one of the main innovations illustrated in the book involves nothing more than cans of paint. Dull unfinished concrete façades, the interior of a subway station, a cement works, and so on, are shown enlivened by fields of bright color.

The mood is more optimistic in *Colour for Architecture*'s successor, *Colour for Architecture Today*, published in 2009. The later book is itself more colorful as befits "these much more open, enlighted and adventurous times" (from Sir Terry Farrell's foreword).[2] Indeed, even the cans of paint are assigned to the ash heap of history, along with all that gray concrete—"the concept of the painted surface is passé," at least according to Jean-Philippe Lenclos.[3] Screen-printed glass, enamel, dichroic film, and other materials are used to achieve exterior effects that paint never could.

The two books contain a diverse selection of interesting essays, but what largely goes missing is an examination of how our perception of color is affected by a distinctively urban setting. At night the main factor is artificial exterior lighting from street lamps, storefronts, and cars, but what about daytime city life? The question raises large and complicated issues. In this short space, we will briefly discuss how a number of features of the daytime urban environment influence color perception.

COLOR VISION: SOME BASIC FACTS

The perception of color begins, of course, with light. Take a simple case of seeing an opaque object, say a brick, in sunlight. The brick will absorb some of the sunlight, and reflect the rest back. More specifically, the brick will reflect a fixed percentage of the energy at each wavelength in the visible spectrum—this is the brick's *(surface spectral) reflectance*. The reflected light can be characterized in terms of its *spectral power distribution* or SPD, which specifies how its energy is distributed among the wavelengths of the visible spectrum. The light then enters the eye of the observer, where it is selectively absorbed by pigments in the cones (photoreceptors used for color vision) at the back of the eye. The response of the three cone types is then subject to further processing in both the retina and various cortical areas, and the upshot is that the brick looks yellowish-red.

Reflectance is important because it is a major determinant of perceived color and, arguably, is the property we see as surface color. And, in fact, contemporary models of color vision usually assume that the primary computational task of the color vision system is to estimate the reflectance of objects from the *color signal*, the light reaching the eye.

But how is such estimation possible? The color signal from our brick, for instance, is the joint product of the SPD of the illuminant and the spectral reflectance of the brick. In principle, innumerably many combinations of illuminants and reflectance can produce the same color signal, so how can the visual system work out which of these combinations is the right one? It is as if the visual system were given an equation like "24 = X x Y", and told "Solve for X". Despite the fact that the visual system's problem is in this way "underconstrained," something close to the correct solution is often found—objects by and large look to have the colors they actually have, through a wide range of lighting conditions. The visual system accomplishes this remarkable feat—to cut a very complicated story short—by making realistic assumptions about the range of illuminants and reflectances in the real world and by treating each object in the context of the whole scene in which it is found. To re turn to our algebraic analogy, we can make an accurate estimate of *X* if we can discover from other sources that *Y* is either 6 or 8.

The stability of perceived color through variation in illumination is known as *color constancy*. This will be important in what follows.

ILLUMINATION

The ultimate source of outdoor light during the day is the sun. Typically, an object in the direct sun will also receive a significant amount of light from the sky. This combination of direct sunlight and skylight is known as "daylight" (a technical term in the literature) and is a common reference point in discussions of natural illumination. The SPD of daylight varies with latitude, time of day, cloud cover, and other atmospheric conditions, with the standard daylight SPD rising quickly from the short wavelength (blue) end of the spectrum to a peak and then declining slowly toward the long wavelength (red) end.

In the urban core the usual properties of daylight can be modified to a significant degree. Direct sunlight is often not present, decreasing the intensity (often dramatically), and shifting the SPD toward short wavelengths. Sometimes there is direct sunlight but comparatively less illumination from the sky, decreasing the short wavelength component. Less precisely but more plainly, this makes city daylight dimmer and bluer, or slightly yellower, than daylight in a setting lacking parallel rows of very large opaque objects.

Various atmospheric components can also significantly alter the SPD of daylight. Aerosols (small airborne particles, such as water vapor, smoke, and dust) produce variation in the SPD of daylight everywhere, while in the urban core a number of common pollutants are optically significant, including smoke, and the nitrous oxides from vehicle exhaust. Some of these effects are most visible late in the day or early in the morning, typically making daylight dimmer and yellower.

However, because of color constancy, the result of this all this variation is not to produce a dramatic shift in the perceived color of the cityscape.

When one turns a corner, going from direct sun into a street lit only by skylight, the significant change in the illuminant does not lead to a correspondingly large shift in the perceived color of one's clothing, automobiles, and the surrounding buildings. On the other hand, it is not as if there is no perceptible change—the dimmer, bluer character of the illuminant is also clearly visible.

One natural way of describing this complicated experience of stability and change is that we see both the unchanging colors of surfaces and the changing illumination. An alternative—and less natural—description is that moving from direct sun into skylight does change color appearances, and hence there is actually no color constancy, at least as we have characterized it. What is constant, on this view, is our judgment or belief that the colors have remained the same, not color appearances. We judge that the colors have remained the same, and that the illumination has changed, because we know that buildings and the like normally have stable colors, and that illumination often changes. The second view can seem plausible if the process of vision is analogized to painting on an internal or mental canvas, an analogy that many philosophers have found tempting. A painter only has differently colored paint to achieve the effects of different illumination. A naive observer might take a canvas to be uniformly colored and differently illuminated, although in reality it is differently colored. Similarly, moving from direct sun into skylight changes the mental paint on the mental canvas, thus changing color appearances.

There is a practical difference between these two descriptions. If the second is correct then, at least in principle, it should always be possible to adjust the reflectance of an object so that viewed under skylight, it looks the same as it did when viewed under direct sun. If the first description is correct, then there is no guarantee that such an adjustment will have the desired effect, since the illumination will sometimes be visibly different.

Interestingly, there is some evidence from the laboratory in favor of the first description. Subjects are sometimes unable to make two objects in different lighting conditions look exactly the same, despite being allowed to, in effect, adjust the reflectance of one of the objects at will[4].

SHADOWS

As just discussed, the SPD of city light differs from that of other sorts of outdoor illumination. One way in which it differs, worth noting separately, is in the prevalence of large shadows. These are less frequent in suburban settings with lower, more widely spaced buildings, or in rural environments. In forests, for example, light is dappled and filtered by the leaf cover, with fewer sharp-edged large shadows.

Shadows are sometimes classifed as "cast" or "attached." A cast shadow is formed when one object blocks light from striking another; an attached shadow is formed when one object blocks light from falling on itself, as when the front of a building faces the sun, preventing the light from illuminating the back. Both sorts of shadows are shown in the image on page 65. In the city, large cast-shadow boundaries are common; the illumination in a shadow is not just less intense than the illumination outside, but often differs in its spectral characteristics, being more similar to skylight than to direct sunlight.

4 D. H. Brainard, W. A. Brunt, and J. M. Speigle. Color constancy in the nearly natural image. I. Asymmetric matches. *Journal of the Optical Society of America A. Optics and Image Science* 14 (1997): 2091-2110; A. Logvinenko, and L. Maloney, The proximity structure of achromatic surface colors and the impossibility of asymmetric lightness matching. Perception and Psychophysics 68 (2006), 76.

Return to the painting analogy. Since shadows are depicted using differently colored paints, darker and often of a different hue than the paint in a neighboring unshadowed region, a proponent of the "internal canvas" would claim that urban shadow boundaries make buildings appear variably colored. But, again, this sort of description is not faithful to the phenomenology. The most natural way to describe how the metal-clad tower in the figure looks is uniform in color, with the leftmost part in shadow. Shadows thus provide another illustration of color constancy, of unchanging color appearance under changing illumination. They also vividly illustrate how the idea that we simply see the color of an object is mistaken—we also see its illumination-dependent features.

All this makes perfect sense against the background assumption that the visual system is in the business of estimating useful properties of the perceiver's environment, of which colors are merely a single example. Separating out shadows from darkly colored regions is worth doing, because shadows can provide information about depth, among other things. That is why the shadowing effect on the open windows of an Apple computer make the windows appear to float above the desktop surface. Color changes, on the other hand, can signal a change in surface composition, for instance from brick to glass.

DISTANCE

Inhabitants do not just see their cities at street level: Boston can be seen from the opposite bank of the Charles River, or from a plane approaching Logan Airport. And distance affects color perception. Again, the effect is reduced in suburbia, because towns and villages do not typically loom on the horizon like cities.

This is relevant to color perception because the human eye has a fixed ability to resolve spatial detail. Unlike a camera with a zoom lens, the only effective means of changing the resolution of the eye is to change the viewing distance. This implies that the color seen at a point on an object is the result of averaging over a portion of the object's surface that increases in size as viewing distance increases. For an object whose reflectance is not constant over its surface, viewing it at different distances changes its color appearance—from having a distinct pattern of color to having a more homogeneous color, or a different pattern. Older television sets viewed close up are dramatic illustrations, but these days the individual red, blue, and green components of a pixel are hard to see with the naked eye. Less ephemeral examples are pointillist paintings, such as Seurat's *A Sunday Afternoon on the Island of La Grande Jatte - 1884*.

The phenomenon can also be encountered by stepping outside the Art Institute of Chicago. For example, the Willis (née Sears) Tower is visible at a range of distances from a few feet to several miles. Increasing the viewing distance, the color appearance changes from the somewhat variegated range of dark grays seen standing close to the base of the building to a pattern of dark rectangular windows separated by black bands at approximately 1/2 mile, to large areas of contrasting shades of gray at 2–3 miles. For other buildings of modest size, there is the change from, say, the contrasting colors of the bricks and mortar seen from across the street to the more uniform reddish appearance seen from down the block.

This variability raises the issue of what viewing distance is the one from which we correctly perceive a building's color, but this question is

Willis Tower, Chicago. Appearance changes with increase in viewing distance. Left: approximately 1/2 mile. Right: approximately 3 miles (Alex Byrne & David Hilbert).

misguided. The average reflectance really does change depending on the size of the area over which the average is taken, and so there is no reason to deny that buildings have different patterns of color at different spatial scales. The effect of changing viewing distance is to change which of these patterns we can see, not to create an illusion.

SPECULARITY

In the example of the brick, we tacitly ignored any effects of viewing angle: the seen object was treated as if it reflected *diffusely*—that is, indiscriminately reflected light in every direction. Since many objects, including bricks, have a reflectance dominated by their diffuse component, this is often a useful simplification. However, for other objects, some made with common architectural materials, the color signal does depend on the angle between the light source, the seen object, and the eye. This is most obvious in the case of objects that have a mirror-like (or specular) component to their reflection, like modern office buildings with large exterior areas of glass. Although glass is an important element in older buildings, the glass used until the late twentieth century reflected relatively little of the illumination, and so the contribution to the perceived color of a structure made by its windows was determined by the light transmitted through the window from the interior. Since building interiors are typically much more dimly illuminated than building exteriors during daytime, windows in these buildings mostly appear as areas of darkness when viewed from outside, unless shades or window treatments are present. With the introduction of highly reflective glass, the appearance of large-scale specularity was introduced to the city.

Highly reflective glass has two principal effects. First, because the glass reflects a substantial proportion of the incident light, tinting can make it appear strongly colored. Second, because the reflection is primarily specular and not diffuse, other objects are seen reflected in the glass, as we can see ourselves reflected in a mirror. When these two effects are combined, the color of the glass can influence the perceived color of the reflected objects. Thus the blue appearance of Boston's John Hancock building blends the blue of the sky or the white of the clouds with the blue tint of the glass. If the glass is not tinted, then we primarily see the color of the reflected object, not the color of the building. Highly reflective untinted surfaces in the built environment therefore have a certain kind of invisibility, displaying the color of the objects seen in them rather than their own color. Since the reflection that is seen depends on a complex set of factors, modern buildings can acquire some of the variability in color appearance that is characteristic of large bodies of water, whose color appearance is also primarily due to specular reflection.

CONCLUDING PHILOSOPHICAL POSTSCRIPT

The discussion above assumed that colors are properties of objects in the environment—Chicago taxicabs and the John Hancock building, for instance. More specifically, the discussion assumed that the color of an object is intimately connected to its reflectance, that is, with the way in which the object changes the incident light. Indeed, we have argued elsewhere that colors are the same as reflectances[5], but there are other positions that also fit congenially with these assumptions[6].

5 See: David R. Hilbert, *Color and Color Perception: A Study in Anthropocentric Realism*

70

However, *Colour for Architecture* tells us that "Colour is a subjective sensation caused by light and is not properly a quality which is inherent in the object itself,"[7] a statement that appears unchanged in the successor volume.[8] This view has a long and distinguished history. Galileo, for instance, wrote in The *Assayer* that colors "reside only in the consciousness," and it must be admitted that some notable contemporary philosophers and scientists agree. But this is a controversial philosophical position, and certainly not, as *Colour for Architecture Today* goes on to say, one of the "basic facts...which are the result of decades of scientific investigation."[9]

The idea that color is a "subjective sensation" is closely connected with the painting analogy. If there is something like a painted canvas in one's mind when one looks at the golden dome of the Massachusetts State House, then if anything is colored, surely it is the canvas, not the State House. Why suppose that the dome is golden in color if the corresponding patch on the mental canvas is? To suppose that both are golden seems like gratuitous speculation. That is why colors, on this view, "reside only in the consciousness." More ecumenically, the dome may be said to be golden but only in a derivative way—it is golden in the sense that it produces splotches of golden mental paint in the minds of suitably situated observers. This is a view sometimes called the "secondary quality" theory of color.[10]

As we hope the preceding discussion suggests, taking color to be a subjective sensation is not theoretically fruitful. For one thing, it tends to force unnatural descriptions of our experience, making it easy to overlook the possibility that we see both the colors of objects and the ways in which they are illuminated. The fascinating topic of urban light and color is better understood by other means.

(Stanford: CSLI, 1987). Also, Alex Byrne and David R. Hilbert. Colors and reflectances. *Readings on Color*, Volume 1: The Philosophy of Color. ed. A. Byrne and D. R. Hilbert (Cambridge, MA: MIT Press, 1997); Alex Byrne and David R. Hilbert, Color Realism and Color Science. *Behavioral and Brain Sciences 26* (2003), 3–21.

6 For a discussion of one of them see Alex Byrne, and David R. Hilbert, Color primitivism. *Erkenntnis* 66 (2007): 73–105.

7 Porter and Mikellides, *Colour for Architecture*, 78.

8 Porter and Mikellides, *Colour for Architecture Today*, 13.

9 Ibid.

10 Alex Byrne and David R. Hilbert, Are Colors Secondary Qualities? *Primary and Secondary Qualities*. ed. L. Nolan (Oxford: Oxford University Press, 2010).

THE (CHANGING) COLORS OF THE AMERICAN CITY MARCO CENZATTI

Marco Cenzatti lectures at the University of California Berkeley. His research is based in critical theory and focuses on urban studies, economic restructuring, and planning theory. Recent publications deal with village development in China ("The City in Between the Villages," *Places*, forthcoming); the production of social space ("Heterotopias of Difference", Dehaene and Vervloesem eds, *Heterotopia and the City*, 2008); and urban industry ("The Permanence and Change of Urban Industry," *Harvard College Economics Review*, 2007.)

THE MAKEUP OF THE CITY

Today abstraction is no longer that of the map, the double, the mirror, or the concept. Simulation is the generation by models of a real without origin or reality: a hyperreal.
—Jean Baudrillard, *The Order of Simulacra*

When I started writing, Christmas had just passed and Berkeley was still bright with lights of all colors. Lights and colors succeed in defamiliarizing us from what we see in several ways. They change the built environment and urban typologies by highlighting forms and elements that are usually neglected. A bright blue bush in the front lawn of a single-family house at night is out of the ordinary, as are the green icicles dangling from the house's eaves. The color makes us see the bush or the eaves for the first time. But the bush and the eaves also make us see the color for the first time, making us realize how much color is missing, or unseen, in the built environment.

The decorations trigger an even more powerful defamiliarization at a larger scale, as they create new mental maps of the town, with new (if ephemeral) monuments and centers. Often clustered around competing households, the decorations transform quiet, usually ignored, residential areas into alternative short-range tourist destinations, suddenly more colorful, bright, and entertaining than downtown. (I have changed my office-to-home route to include, in the evening, a particularly festive street).

It is also part of this sense of defamiliarization that lights and colors do not have a connection with the real. They are signs suggesting a generic cheerfulness, but they are not signs that help us to understand what the city is, how it works, or even where we are. Christmas decorations and colors belong to a language, a code, different from the one that we usually use to read the city. They are what Baudrillard would call "signs of the third order," simulacra that do not relate (any longer) to reality, but construct a reality from and for their very existence.

After Christmas, returning to the normal city of the everyday, colors seem to be strangely absent, even when they are not. Buildings of different colors are present almost everywhere. With exceptions to which I'll return, however, those colors do not stand out like those of Christmas or Chinese New Year. In Western cities the colors tend to form a palette around a gray-whitish theme. In other places with other cultures and/or with different local materials, such as the "Red City" of Marrakech (red for the local sand used in the plaster of its buildings), or the "Pink City" of Jaipur or the "Blue City" of Jodhpur (both painted in those colors), the color is much stronger. What remains constant, though, is the sense of homogeneity that the dominance of one color and its variations gives to the entire city.

This is peculiar, because once they are no longer tied to construction materials (the red bricks, the gray concrete), a building's color can be easily changed, without the costs associated with modifying or rebuilding entire structures. In Las Vegas, as Robert Venturi and Denise Scott Brown pointed out, colors and other embellishments are used in this fashion, giving character to anonymous buildings by turning them into "decorated sheds." They are indeed decorations that hide the uniformity of the "sheds" and create a hyperreal urban experience.

THE STUCCO CITY

It is in the Renaissance that the false is born along with the natural…. In churches and palaces stucco is wed to all forms, imitates everything—velvet curtains, wooden cornices… The first order simulacrum never abolished difference. It supposes an always detectable alteration between semblance and reality.
—Jean Baudrillard, ibid.

But colors in the city are not only decorations and Baudrillardian signs of the hyperreal. In most cities—and in the residential parts of Las Vegas that are not tourist destinations—colors, or better their homogeneity, have an effect opposite to the decorated shed: they underscore and reinforce an urban sameness already present in most residential and commercial typologies. This effect is also contrary to the one of Christmas lights: uniform colors familiarize us with the city; they suggest a collective urban identity and make us feel part of it. Michel Foucault would perhaps call this a process of urban normalization. The limited color range is part, although a minor one, of the various mechanisms (legal, political, economic, ideological, etc.) aimed at establishing a social norm for urban living, and, by the same token, marginalizing as abnormal what and who lives the city differently.

In the United States, the narrative of the "melting pot" is a good example of normalization. Immigrant groups are supposed to proceed over time in a straight-line process of acculturation and assimilation. The spatial expression of this process is the passage from the different enclaves and ghettoes that serve as ports of entry, to middle- and working-class neighborhoods and suburbs where, progressively abandoning their language, cultural habits, and social and spatial relations, immigrants become fully acculturated and fit the overarching urban norm. They enter the city with different (abnormal) languages, social relations, and color codes and messages, which vanish in the melting pot, leaving only traces.

Many new suburbs corroborate this path to homogeneity-normalization with an added touch of tamed difference. Suburban developments, gated communities, and Common Interest Developments may claim their individuality by attracting specific social groups and by reinforcing their identity with names drawn from exotic locals such as Mediterranean villages or hilltop towns. More important, though, they also call, often in covenants, for building colors to be limited to a palette of "tasteful" colors (so-called earth tones) that merge them into the rest of the city.

Baudrillard uses the stucco ornaments of the Renaissance to indicate the moment when the false begins. Stucco reproductions imitate originals from which, however, they remain always intrinsically different. Many suburban developments show that Baudrillard's simulacrum is still alive and well. In fact, the simulacrum has become more inclusive, expanding from ornament to whole buildings. The material of the buildings is often (appropriately) stucco rather than the stones or bricks of the villages they imitate. Their urban residents are certainly different from the fishermen or peasants that their subdivision's name suggests. These developments simulate an isolation and independence of the originals from the city that they don't have; they are integral part of the broader city and feign a difference from other real estate developments that does not exist. Their tamed colors are but one indication of their structural sameness.

CASTE-LESS CITIES

In caste societies, feudal or archaic, cruel societies, the signs are limited in number, and are not widely diffused, each one functions with its full value as interdiction, each is a reciprocal obligation between castes, clans, or persons. The signs are therefore anything but arbitrary.
—Jean Baudrillard, ibid.

Baudrillard seems to present a sequence (a *precession*, in his words) of increasing separation of signs from reality. At our end of the series there are signs of the hyperreal. At the other end, far into the past, there were the "pre-simulacrum" signs, tightly linked to their object, limited to highly hierarchical, unchanging, premodern societies. Today, however, the relation between signs and their referent, however, has become more variable and multilayered. Different contexts give different and coexisting meanings to urban signs, and to the colors of the city among them. Various dynamics triggered by globalization (such as new waves of immigration and rapid and easy communication) and by post-Fordism (such as the rapid pace of change and fragmentation of consumer markets) have reshuffled the deck of Baudrillard's signs and simulacra.

Thus the billboards, canopies, insignias, logos, and brightly colored buildings of immigrant commercial enclaves—like the old Chinatowns and Little Italies, but also the new Little Saigons and Koreatowns—become two-sided markers of *both* tourist and shopping destinations and immigrant communities. From the former perspective, the billboards and colored shops function like the Christmas decorations. As in most shopping districts, the individual meaning of the colored signs is lost in the general sense of cheerfulness that characterizes shopping districts—"where the lights are much brighter" and "you can forget all your troubles," as the '60s song goes. Ethnic shopping areas have lost much of the perceived impenetrability and mysteriousness of the past and are more accessible to outsiders. Still, the difficulty that visitors have in "reading" signs of a different cultural code increases their hyperreal status, separating the experience from everyday activities and turning the individual colors and lights into a collective sign that refers to a real that the signs themselves produce.

Yet the signs and colors of commercial enclaves are also similar to Baudrillard's "non-arbitrary signs" that mark a precise social and spatial relationship. They are the more permeable part of spaces produced and maintained by a specific social group, with mechanisms of opening and closing that regulate relationships with other groups. Beyond the tourist areas, the "colors" worn by ethnic gangs that establish their right to a specific place and their graffiti that mark its territorial boundaries are signs that leave little doubt about the relationship with the real.

Also the suburbs are changing. If the narrative of the melting pot told the story of difference melting away, ethnic suburbs and neighborhoods indicate an opposite dynamic: of ethnic groups claiming their right to difference and eroding the homogeneity of the suburban development. Mexican neighborhoods, from Southern California to Texas, make their identity known, with front yards surrounded by fences, religious shrines, and vivid house colors. Similarly, green tiled roofs and "monster-houses" (often in pastel colors) identify the Asian ethnic suburbs of California's Fremont or Alhambra. Here colors and ornaments, far from referring to hyperreality, indicate a social place and a community.

These signs are strong and clear, but what they don't denote (and in the case of the old commercial enclaves, I should say, "what they have lost") is a hierarchy, an indication of submission or caste. Instead, it is the melting pot that shows a hierarchical and "caste" social structure and, with it, urban colors split between "normal" and "abnormal." But the norm is not as strong as it used to be. Increasingly the right to difference is replacing what was seen as abnormal, deviant, or needing to remain invisible. If this is a sign of a cosmopolis in the making, I am looking forward to being defamiliarized by different colors every day.

THE STREET AS VENUE FOR CHROMATIC EVENTS CARLOS CRUZ-DIEZ

Born in Caracas in 1923, Carlos Cruz-Diez began his research on color alongside the Kinetic Movement of the 60s. He describes himself as an artist with the discipline of a researcher: "In my work nothing is left to chance; everything is planned, programmed and codified. Freedom and emotion only come into play when the time comes to choose and combine the colors."

Crosswalk, Caracas, 1975.

For thousands of years, humans lived in fields and villages. Their collective behavior and notions of freedom were very different from ours and we are still learning to live in a constrained environment. Large urban masses are relatively new, continuously reducing living space; we must control our gestures and movements to avoid disturbing our neighbors.

The only solution we have found, as a way to coexist in this new way of living, is the repression of human beings, forcing us to be more obedient, more "standard," without many opportunities to be different.

In this situation, the dweller of the large city has adopted the attitude of an automaton, of an indifferent creature; he does not think, he just acts. In his daily meander, he crosses a pedestrian walkway or stops at a red light, obeying learned codes, without being conscious of the act. He moves through the multitudes without recollection of his actions.

In this difficult environment, which in the future is apt to be even worse, artists can have an important role—not only to express their creativity but to participate in structuring the spiritual well-being of humans in the megalopolis. In the coming leisure society, both art and cultural activities in general will be of utmost importance for social peace.

I believe that a work of art conceived as urban spectacle could achieve greater importance in the city of today. Through it, we could awaken dormant perceptions and transform the neutral, codified, or automated into motivating "situations," adding to the spiritual legacy of the robotic passer-by.

But a city should not be crowded with works of art. They would become banal objects and lose their fundamental purpose. Their installation on the street should be the outcome of a team integrated by the artist, the town planner, the architect, the engineer, the landscape architect, artisans, technicians, and promoters. Together, taking into account the concepts outlined above, they must orchestrate the best solution for the particular location, scale, and atmosphere of a given work.

Art on the street could promote further understanding, leading toward different levels of information and knowledge, and the ability to "see," not just to "look." Furthermore, the streets are also the ideal venue for ephemeral works. The artist can generate in passers-by a sense of surprise, of amusement and rapture, awakening their imagination.

In the past, a single person, "the artist," conceived and produced everything—the building, the artwork, both inside and out. The subdivision of knowledge caused the artist's actions to be divided among diverse professions and specialties. In a project, the artist should be part of the creative team from the beginning and not be called upon when everything has been decided, to decorate or mend a deficient space.

Currently the artist is seldom included in a team assigned to conceive environmental and urban projects. The artist's irreverent attitude toward dogmas could be the source of unforeseen solutions. He or she could awaken the imagination of a team wrapped up in professional routines.

In my search, I try to find nontraditional solutions to the perception of the chromatic world and plastic space. I am a researcher who from an early age believed that art is communication, and that the artist should not only provide works to museums and collections but also be present on the streets, in factories, and everywhere that is part of the collective.

I think that a work of art integrated into the community or the broader habitat should engender unprecedented events in constant mutation. The works I make for the urban environment are conceived as dialogues generated in time and space, while creating "situations" and "chromatic events," and modifying the dialectic between the spectator and the work. They are not referential discourses, as in the Gothic, the Renaissance, or the work of Mexican muralists. They profess a different starting point by which real time and real space replace time that is inferred or transposed. They are supports for an event that changes and evolves.

They are realities and autonomous situations: realities because events evolve in time and space; autonomous because they do not depend on the anecdotal that the spectator is accustomed to seeing in art. A different learning relationship is established. The spectator discovers the ability to create or to break down color by his own means of perception. He discovers the "making of color," emerging and disappearing before his eyes.

Crosswalk, Marseille, 1989.
Chromostructure Radial Barquisimeto, Venezuela 1983; Ambientación Aeropuerto Maiquetía, Caracas, 1974; Crosswalks, Chromatic Inductions, Houston, 2009, Marseille, 1989, Caracas, 1975, Fortaleza, 1986, (Carlos Cruz-Diez).

ACCUMULATIONS JULIA CZERNIAK

Julia Czerniak is an Associate Professor of Architecture at Syracuse University and the inaugural Director of UPSTATE. She is also a registered landscape architect and founder of CLEAR, an interdisciplinary design practice. Czerniak's design work, complemented by a body of writing, focuses on urban landscapes.

1 Simon Henley, *The Architecture of Parking* (New York: Thames and Hudson, 2007), 240–243.

2 In conversations with Roger Sherman, Spring 2008.

Little things grew by continual accumulation
—Samuel Johnson

The Dutch are known for their bicycles. Whether as index to bodily health, green living or personal freedom, they zip along roadways, cluster at parking units, and hang in rental shops. But the contribution of bike culture to the country's identity is both captured and extended through good design—a notable example at VMX Architects' Fietsenstalling, a parking station for 2,500 bikes built over a canal opposite Lover's Quay near Amsterdam's Centraal Station.[1] The impact of this facility is enabled by both the efficiency of the bicycle's size, allowing an enormous clustering in a small space, and the novelty of storing bikes in the car's convention of the multilevel parking structure, a formation whose impact has long since lost its effect. Perhaps even more memorable is the brightly colored ground plane that lends coherence to the accumulation. This project is a potent example of what urban theorist Roger Sherman calls "radical incrementalism," a design strategy "that utilizes accumulation as a means of producing character and identity" across an urban field in lieu of master planning. This strategy "promotes the invention and use of norms as a way of instigating, creating and using imageability as a loose means of building strong identity and coherence."[2] The Fietsenstalling prompts a question: What about the coherence of accumulated color?

In a city such as Syracuse, New York, where growth is not an option, accumulation is a viable, potent strategy for positive change. This brief reflection explores how cumulated color can lend identity and coherence to a large urban landscape, enabling projects to accrue over time while remaining legible. That the identifying color—red—of the Syracuse Connective Corridor has persevered through a series of project iterations, shifting design teams, stakeholder inputs, and review agencies is a testament to its promise of making a visible streetscape within a city of otherwise muted colors. Yet, for a project that will take years to evolve—dependent as it is on the vicissitudes of funding streams, stakeholder confidence, and approval processes—visibility is not enough. To perform in this way, the corridor must be *legible*, understood as an emerging urban design project replete with elements and systems—a condition here linked to the way it appears.

Like many Rust Belt cities that once constituted our nation's industrial heartland, Syracuse, New York, has been shrinking in population for decades—as evidenced by the loss of city fabric, the diminishment of social-welfare networks, the erosion of public schools, the loss of industry, increasing amounts of tax delinquent and vacant land, and crumbling infrastructure. The environment produced through these processes is disparate: partially occupied remnant fabric and parking surfaces join a still active downtown and an emerging visual and performing arts infrastructure in a mixture not all that promising for vibrant urban life. In this context, the Connective Corridor's ambition is to

Bike clusters at Fietsenstalling, Amsterdam (Photo by the author).

link Syracuse's arts and cultural venues and downtown businesses with the Syracuse University community and other neighborhoods in the city through a comprehensive landscape-architectural strategy that would hinge on a 2-mile multimodal transit system accompanied by vegetation, lighting, public art, and new technologies, creating a system with greater force than its individual assets.

    Now into its fourth year of development, the projects' winning competition entry by Field Operations in partnership with CLEAR advanced a concept still vital to the ongoing work—that the transit system of bus, car, bike, and pedestrian lanes inscribed into the old city fabric will leverage zones of investment. In addition to connecting disparate places and institutions, it will create an economic incentive framework to catalyze infill of the urban fabric, and address the profusion of vacant lots, abandoned buildings, and parking surfaces. We understood that the project's success would be contingent on its conception as a legible and resilient framework, able over time to absorb design and development initiatives by others while retaining its identity.[3] The initial competition images pictured vividly colored streetscapes made with inexpensive yet highly graphic materials including paint, resin, porous pavers, and textured concrete to both announce the corridor's presence and brighten up perennially gray skies. Illumination from street fixtures at multiple scales lighten up long winter nights and provide a clear route.[4]

    Three related frameworks offered robust guidance to the development of the design: a streetscape matrix, a color spectrum, and the concept of bundling. The use of color is not reduced to a singular application with immediate effect but accumulates as streetscape elements, environmental graphics, and lighting emerge along a color spectrum according to their own logics of formation, fabrication, and context of application. The first framework is a streetscape matrix of paving, furnishing, lighting, and vegetation that ensures both consistency along the 2-mile network and choice by various designers and stakeholders who wish to respond to diverse city contexts along the way. Inexpensive materials such as thermoplastic paint, new ones like resin, embedded

3 For more on this concept, see my essay "Legibility and Resilience," in *Large Parks*, (New York: Princeton Architectural Press, 2007), 214–251.

4 See "Doing More with Less" in *Lab Report: Phoenix Urban Research Lab* (Phoenix: ASU College of Design, 2008) 40–47.

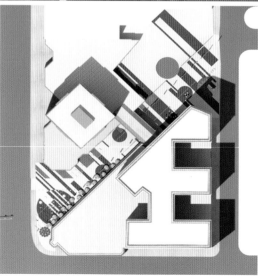

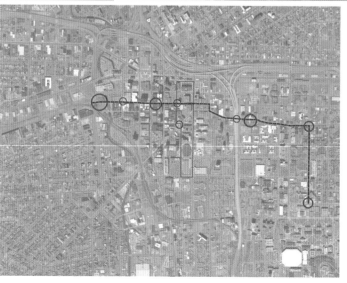

Top: Redosier Dogwood along the Syracuse Connective Corridor (Image courtesy of Olin Studio); Middle row, left and center: Paving materials and lighting effects, The Syracuse L (Images courtesy of Field Operations);

Middle right: Methacrylite bike lanes along University Avenue, Syracuse (Image courtesy of CLEAR); Bottom left: Banding along pavement surfaces of Symphony Place, Syracuse, and the route of the Connective Corridor

through the city (Images courtesy of UPSTATE: A Center for Design, Research, and Real Estate at Syracuse Architecture); Bottom right: Collateral materials for the Connective Corridor (Images courtesy of Pentagram).

5 The project team includes Pentagram, Tillett Lighting Design Inc., and Barton & Loguidice Engineers.

amenities such as lights and event tie-downs, join moveable furnishings, LED markings, and luminous paint to activate the route. The second framework, a color spectrum, further accommodates color use through the varying contexts through which the corridor passes. In certain places, such as tracts of empty parking lots, the boldness of primary red announces the route. In others, such as historic neighborhoods, color application of brick-red appeals to preservationists. Later in the design process, two distinctive contrasting color values were developed that both respect historic values yet energize the context.[5] Color variation is extended by the material to which it is applied—metal, wood, pavement. Both frameworks are being tested in the design of a small urban plaza at Hotel Syracuse, a historically significant but vacant hotel built in the 1920s. Although the color of the hotel is commonly perceived as brick-red, its seemingly homogeneous surface nonetheless displays tonal variation that opens audiences to other uses of color in historic context. Vibrant red bands that run perpendicular to the street that once passed through the site direct flows to connect ground floor retail. Trees that normally line and reinforce curb lines are collected in mounds. Minor in scope, these actions nonetheless begin the accumulations of color use and convention shift that will over time identify the corridor. The final framework, bundling, intends to build efficiencies into the way transit lines along streetscape systems work. When various transit lines (such as sidewalks and bike and bus lanes) run in parallel, their streetscape assets—benches, racks, and shelters—collectively appear. Their unbundling for separate uses—for example when a bike lane runs along a different street than a bus—enables an independent identity for the place. A perhaps less conceptual notion of bundling is to closely group streetscape elements for efficiency (construction ease), economy (cost of trenching), and effect (more for your money).

These preliminary frameworks have been expanded through an interdisciplinary team led by landscape architects Olin Studio, where color and its effects emerge in provocative ways as formations and temporalities, strengthening both the corridors' image and its identity. Environmental graphic designers Pentagram developed a unique typeface that, according to principal Michael Beirut, "reinforces the idea of the project—circulation, access, connections, and energy."[6] This typographic formation—what could be thought of as bundled transit lines or more specifically the continual red strip of methacrylite that marks the corridors' bike lane—informs a graphic language that will be uniquely associated with Syracuse, inviting people to "use" the city and its cultural assets. This linear formation informs the design of bike racks and benches, thickening and transforming to accommodate their use and value, as well as subtly echoing the vertical corrugations of the repurposed shipping container cum bike bodega. Tillet's lighting fixtures, limited to conventional pole-mounted luminaries and illuminating bollards, are nonetheless custom colored and grouped into formations that produce powerful effects. These vertical clusters mark entrances to institutions and other significant spots along the route, visible even during the winter of America's snowiest city.

6 Michael Beirut, project materials in client presentation, February 2010.

These enduring elements play a large role in the corridors' legibility. Yet they are supplemented by the temporal—even ephemeral—use of vegetation whose color bursts are seasonally dependent; promotional products and bus lines that index weather and schedule; and luminous surfaces that are fleetingly activated by shifting angles of light. These each suggest in varying ways how lived experience adds to the identity of this emergent place. Trees, shrubs, and annual selections lend a cyclical quality to the route's visibility. In the spring and summer, red poppies blanket open spaces, and planters outside storefronts boast deep shades of tulips and zinnias. These give way to vibrant red maples that line streets, whose leaves fade and fall. Most striking is the blood-red bark of red osier dogwood stems against the winter snow in parks and other public spaces. A perhaps unlikely but equally important component of color's appearance and performance along the corridor relates to Pentagram's design of promotional items that stand in for a project that still does not exist. Picture a streetscape of umbrella-carrying urbanites as they scurry from museum to gallery in the rain, or a flood of pedestrians toting coffee mugs signifying the workday's beginning. Or droves of shopping bags filled with goods, suggesting reinvigorated commercial activity. In a different way, budget constraints and light-fixture-filled streets is sponsoring one of the most evanescent of color effects. Tillet Lighting's use of luminous paint, a paint that gives off visible light, is planned for newly exposed parti-walls, along beam surfaces in parking garages, and as a component of public murals. Activated by headlights and the sun's lower rays, these measures bring color into the city in fleeting ways. The Connective Corridor bus, shrink wrapped with spectrum colors, is one early example of temporal color along its route. Its vibrant surfaces appear reassuringly and rhythmically, as scheduled, its presence an early sign of the streetscape to come. In these ways, color comes alive—through schedules (as in bus and work), cycles (such as light and season), lifestyles (shopping and coffee habits), and weather (rain and snow). Here in the North Country, we typically think of snow as covering up the city, homogenizing its surfaces into first white, then gray, then brown. Pentagram's brilliant advancement of red snow shovels bearing in large letters "use" suggests colors' bold appearance in an unexpected way.

To accumulate is to gather or collect, often in gradual degrees, to form a steadily increasing quantity. As such, accumulations connote the processes by which an entity comes into being. Accumulation promises coherence across vast urban fields in ways that are different than master-planning efforts, contingent as it is on celebrating the unknowns of taste, value, use, and support. As suggested here, the Syracuse Connective Corridor is a bold urban design project that will appear over time. In the ways described, color is a strategy to lend identity and distinction to a new landscape that must be visibly inscribed onto the old city fabric. Yet more important than the elements and materials themselves, the process by which this project is coming into being speaks of painstaking work to build investment and commitment. Syracuse is giving meaning to this color. It is an index of public/private collaboration between the university and the city, and the sometimes uneasy politics of which that speaks. It is the sponsor of economic development as new businesses open along it, willing to subscribe to its branding package. Color's appearance is intimately related to its performance in a Rust Belt city looking for a second chance. After growth comes cumulation.

GREEN BLACKTOP PETER DEL TREDICI

Peter Del Tredici is a Lecturer in the Department of Landscape Architecture at Harvard Graduate School of Design. He teaches courses on urban ecology, soils, and sustainable landscapes. He is a botanist and senior research scientist at the Arnold Arboretum of Harvard University.

Purslane (*Portulaca oleracea*) growing in a "trifecta" of granite, blacktop and concrete.

Bibliography

Arnold, C. L., and C. J. Gibbons. 1996. Impervious surface coverage: the emergence of a key environmental indicator. *Journal of the American Planning Association* 62(2): 243–258.

Baker, H. G. 1974. The evolution of weeds. *Annual Review of Ecology and Systematics* 5: 1–24.

Chocholoušková, Z., and P. Pyšek. 2003. Changes in composition and structure of urban flora over 120 years: a case study of the city of Plze . *Flora* 198: 366–376.

Del Tredici, P. 2010. *Wild Urban Plants of the Northeast: A Field Guide.* Ithaca, NY: Cornell University Press.

George, K., L.H. Ziska, J.A. Bunce, and B. Quebedeaux. 2007. Elevated atmospheric CO2 concentration and temperature across an urban-rural transect. *Atmospheric Environment* 41: 7654–7665.

George, K., L.H. Ziska, J.A. Bunce, B. Quebedeaux, J.L. Hom, J. Wolf, and J.R. Teasdale. 2009. Macroclimate associated with urbanization increases the rate of secondary succession from fallow soil. *Oecologia* 159: 637–647.

The plants that flourish on derelict urban wasteland are famous (or infamous) for their ability to grow under extremely harsh conditions. Through a quirk of evolutionary fate, many of them have evolved life-history traits in their native habitats that have "preadapted" them to flourish in cities. Indeed, several studies have shown that many common urban plants are native either to limestone cliff habitats and rocky outcrops or dry, open grasslands with neutral or alkaline soils (Gilbert 1989; Wittig 2004; Larson et al. 2004; Lundholm and Marlin 2006). The authors argue—by analogy—that cities with their tall, granite-faced buildings and concrete foundations are biologically equivalent to the natural limestone cliffs where these species originated. Similarly, they suggest that the increased use of de-icing salts along walkways and highways has resulted in the development of high pH microhabitats that are often colonized by either grassland species adapted to limestone soils or salt-loving plants from coastal habitats.

The concept of preadaptation is defined as "an anatomical or physiological trait which evolved under one set of ecological conditions and, by chance, proves advantageous under a completely different set of circumstances" (Del Tredici 2010). It is a powerful idea for understanding the emergent ecology of cities because it helps answer questions about why some species are common in urban habitats and others not. In general, plants that can survive and reproduce under urban conditions without human assistance need to be *flexible* (i.e. non-specialized) in all aspects of their life-history, from germination through seed production and dispersal. They also need to be *opportunistic* in their ability to take advantage of locally abundant resources (mainly water and nutrients) that may be available for only a brief period of time. And finally, they need to be tolerant of the stressful growing conditions caused by an abundance of pavement and a paucity of soil (Baker 1974; Del Tredici 2010).

In nature, these types of plants tend to come from habitats that naturally experience high levels of disturbance and/or environmental stress, such as seasonal flooding (river and stream banks), burning or grazing (natural grasslands and prairies), sun and wind exposure (cliffs and rock outcrops), soil disturbance (eroded slopes), and high soil salt concentrations (coastal and desert areas) (Salisbury 1961; Wittig 2004). Interestingly, a number of species that are commonly found in cities, mainly annuals of European origin, seem to have no known natural habitats. Many of these so-called anecophytes have arisen through the process of hybridization and show specialized adaptations to habitats associated with agriculture, urbanization, and/or industrialization (Salisbury 1961; Meerts et al. 1998; Wittig 2004).

THE NATURE OF URBANIZATION

One of the primary distinguishing features of the urban environment is the ubiquitous presence of physical disturbance associated with the construction

and/or maintenance of its infrastructure. At any given point in time, a significant portion of the urban fabric of economically vibrant cities is in the process of being torn up and rebuilt. This situation leads to the development of a constantly shifting mosaic of opportunistic plant associations dominated by disturbance-adapted, early successional plants, technically known as *ruderals* (Gilbert 1989; Kowarik 1995; Chocholoušková and Pyšek 2003; Kowarik 2005). In economically depressed cities of the United States—such as Detroit, Michigan, or Gary, Indiana—that are experiencing shrinkage rather than growth, a large percentage of the urban core has been abandoned for significant periods of time, upwards of forty years. In such cases succession is allowed to proceed without interference from people, and the vegetation comes much closer to reaching "maturity" than it does in more prosperous cities where ongoing maintenance and economic development promote a more rapid turnover in spontaneous plant associations (Muratet et al. 2007; Rink 2009).

A second distinguishing characteristic of urban areas is the abundance of concrete buildings and asphalt paving. Because such structures absorb and retain head—to say nothing of the cars, air conditioners, heating units, and electrical equipment that generate heat—the annual mean temperatures of large urban areas (i.e., with populations in excess of a million people) can be up to 3° C (5.4° F) warmer than the surrounding nonurban areas; on extreme occasions the temperature differences between the city and the countryside can be as high as 12° C (21.6° F) (Sieghardt et al. 2005). The abundance of buildings and impervious pavement in cities can also have a profound effect on hydrology by decreasing water infiltration, increasing runoff, and compacting the soil, all of which tend to reduce water availability and create stressful drought conditions for plants (Arnold and Gibbons 1996; Paul and Meyer 2001).

While increased temperature is probably the most ecologically significant factor that distinguishes the city from the surrounding countryside (Ziska et al. 2004; George et al. 2007), several other climatological features associated with urbanization can have profound impacts—often significantly positive—on the growth of plants, including elevated levels of carbon dioxide, altered solar radiation regimens, altered wind patterns, decreased humidity, increased or decreased ozone levels, increased soil temperatures, and extended growing season length (Gregg et al. 2003; Sukopp 2004; George et al. 2009).

A third distinguishing feature of the urban environment is its high concentration of non-native plants relative to the surrounding countryside (Kowarik 1995). Some of these plants have escaped from cultivation for agricultural or ornamental purposes; some are unintentionally introduced, disturbance-adapted "weeds"; and some are native to the area. Together they form cosmopolitan vegetation associations that dominate abandoned, degraded, or neglected urban land and mimic the diversity of the human population of the cities in which they grow (Del Tredici 2010).

When one couples the ecosystem impacts of well-adapted, spontaneous vegetation with the ubiquitous disturbance and environmental stress that is characteristic of cities, one has all the components necessary to describe a cyclical succession pattern that is constantly being interrupted by human activity and dominated by so-called pioneer species. With apologies to J. P. Grime (1977), the simplistic model presented in Figure 1 is a reinterpretation of his three basic plant strategies—the ruderal, the competitive, and the stress-tolerant—as drivers of succession in urban environments.

Fall Panicum (*Panicum dichotomiflorum*)

Tree of Heaven (*Ailanthus altissima*)

Prostrate knotweed (*Polygonum aviculare*)

Spotted spurge (*Chamaesyce maculata*)

Gilbert, O. L. 1989. *The Ecology of Urban Habitats*. London, Chapman and Hall.

Gregg, J.W., C.G. Jones, and T.E. Dawson. 2003. Urbanization effects on tree growth in the vicinity of New York City. *Nature* 424: 183–187.

Grime, J. P. 1977. Evidence for the existence of three primary strategies in plants and its relevance to ecological and evolutionary theory. *The American Naturalist* 111: 1169–1194.

Kowarik, I. 1995. On the role of alien species in urban flora and vegetation. In Plant *Invasions—General Aspects and Special Problems,* eds. P. Pyšek, K. Prach, M. Rejmanek, and M. Wade, pp. 85–103. The Hague: SPB Academic Publishing.

Kowarik, I. 2005. Wild urban woodlands: towards a conceptual framework. In Wild *Urban Woodlands*, ed. I. Kowarik and S. Körner, pp. 1–32. Berlin: Springer.

Larson, D., U. Matthes, P. E. Kelly, J. Lundholm, and J. Garrath. 2004. *The Urban Cliff Revolution*. Markham, Ontario: Fitzhenry and Whiteside.

Fig. 1

Meerts, P., T. Baya, and C. Lefèbvre. 1998. Allozyme variation in the annual weed species complex, *Polygonum aviculare* (*Polygonaceae*) in relation to ploidy level and colonizing ability. *Plant Systematics and Evolution* 211: 239–256.

Lundholm, J. T., and A. Marlin. 2006. Habitat origins and microhabitat preferences of urban plant species. *Urban Ecosystems* 9: 139–159.

Muratet, A., N. Machon, F. Jiguet, J. Moret, and E. Porcher. 2007. The role of urban structures in the distribution of wasteland flora in the greater Paris area, France. *Ecosystems* 10: 661–671.

Paul, M. J., and J. L. Meyer. 2001. Streams in the urban landscape. *Annual Review of Ecology and Systematics* 32: 333–365.

Rink, D. 2009. Wilderness: the nature of urban shrinkage? The debate on urban restructuring in eastern Germany. *Nature and Culture* 4(3): 275–292.

Salisbury, E. 1961. *Weeds and Aliens*. London: Collins.

Sieghardt, M., et al. 2005. The abiotic environment: impact of urban growing conditions on urban vegetation. In *Urban Forests and Trees*, eds. C. C. Konijnendijk et al., pp. 281–323. Berlin: Springer.

Sukopp, H. 2004. Human-caused impact on preserved vegetation. *Landscape and Urban Planning* 68: 347–355.

Wessolek, G. 2008. Sealing of soils. In Urban Ecology: *An International Perspective on the Interaction between Humans and Nature*, eds. J. M. Marzluff et al., pp. 161–179.

Wittig, R. 2004. The origin and development of the urban flora of central Europe. *Urban Ecosystems* 7: 323–339.

Ziska, L. H., J. A. Bunce, and E. W. Goins. 2004. Characterization of an urban-rural CO_2/temperature gradient and associated changes in initial plant productivity during secondary succession. *Oecologia* 139: 454–458.

THE URBANIZATION OF NATURE

One of the most ubiquitous and distinctive niches in the urban environment, and the focus of the remainder of this article, is the familiar sidewalk or roadway crack that develops when paving wears out the interface zone where one type of paving material is laid next to another, most often concrete and blacktop, but also including granite and brick. Because these paving materials have different densities and porosities, they respond differently to changes in temperature, pressure, and moisture (Wessolek 2008). This causes them to separate from one another when stressed by the weight of traffic or the formation of ice, thereby creating a relatively resource-rich microhabitat where soil and water (along with road salt and petroleum products) collect and plants can get established.

Observation has shown that many such interstitial "crack plants" share a number of life-history traits, including: 1) an annual life cycle; 2) seeds that germinate with warm temperatures in late spring or early summer; 3) a preference for or tolerance of neutral or alkaline soils; 4) a high level of drought tolerance; 5) a prostrate or mat-forming growth habit that is resistant to being stepped on by people or driven over by vehicles; and 6) a single dominant taproot (as opposed to producing adventitious roots along their stems) that allows it to fully exploit a minimal defect in an vast impervious surface (Salisbury 1961; Gilbert 1989; Del Tredici 2010).

In a striking example of what might be called *convergent preadaptation*, five of the most common crack species found in cities of northeastern North America—carpetweed (*Mollugo verticillata*) from Central America, purslane (*Portulaca oleracea*) of unknown origin (India, perhaps), spotted spurge (*Chamaesyce maculata*) from eastern North America, and prostrate knotweed (*Polygonum aviculare*) and smooth crabgrass (*Digitaria ischaemum*) from Europe—display remarkably similar morphologies despite their far-flung geographical origins and diverse botanical backgrounds. By exploiting the seams in the urban fabric, this quintet of prostrate, summer annuals demonstrates how natural selection, working through the mechanism of preadaptation, can adjust to the unnatural selection pressures of the city.

THE PINK AND RED DIAMOND
GARETH DOHERTY

Gareth Doherty is a founding editor of *New Geographies* and editor-in-chief of "Urbanisms of Color." He currently teaches Landscape Architecture and Urban Planning and Design at Harvard Graduate School of Design.

My hometown in Ireland used to be mainly grays, and whites, and beiges.

My grandfather lived in the square, called The Diamond, in a house called The Gem.

Grandfather liked a bargain, and got some paint on sale in the local paint store. It was pink. He decided to paint his house. We pleaded, "No! Please don't paint the house pink! Everyone will laugh at us!" Grandfather was undeterred, saying "It looks the same to me as every other color." Grandfather was colorblind.

The house was painted—pink—and surprisingly the pink house looked very good.

A year later, Pat, the local undertaker and publican wanted to paint his pub (which was mostly men-only) and asked for advice on a color saying, "I really like the color on your grandfather's house." "Why not paint your pub pink?" said I. "Okay," said he, "but if it goes wrong, I'll blame you." "Fine," said I.

The bar was painted—pink—and it looked very good.

A year later, the President of Ireland was visiting the village and I convinced my mother to paint her house. Called the Corner House, it is a prominent building in the Diamond. The yellow and blue was so bright at first that neighbors complained, and I did not get to paint the windows orange as planned.

The house was painted—yellow and blue—and it looked very good.

After a week, I noticed a strange thing happening. The Diamond was transforming into a bright and colorful space as other buildings were painted with much brighter colors than before.

"Why is this happening?" I asked myself. "There's no master plan. Nobody is coordinating this. It seems to be happening all by itself. And indeed if there was a master plan, no one would follow it, as they don't respond well to being told what to do." Looking around, I noticed that one thing that all the buildings had in common was that they had a business: businesses were using color to attract customers in the same way that flowers use color to attract insects. Businesses were competing with each other with color. If there was any rule it was that colors should clash: reds and greens, purples and yellows. Some said the village was starting to look like a bag of Dolly Mixtures.

A couple of years later, as I arrived home one morning to visit, the owner of the tallest building in the town, the other Corner House, was preparing the walls for painting. "What color are you painting it?" I inquired. "Beige, the same as always," he replied. "Would you consider something different," said I? "Like what?" said he. "Red," said I, "the same as the church ceiling." Okay, said he, why don't you go to the paint store and choose the shade you like. But if it goes wrong, I'll blame you." Fine!" said I.

And the house was painted—red—and it looked very good.

And after a week, an even stranger thing had happened than what had transpired before. The village was becoming red. Other buildings were being painted not just with bright colors but with the same shade of red as the tallest building. The red became dominant in a struggle between the colors. Red emerged as the strongest and fittest color. "It's known as the "Red Town" now," said one local. The Persian Bar, the hardware store, the jeweler, the souvenir shop, even a lawyer's, all were painted with the same shade of red.

Yet other colors continued to creep in. One businessman told me that he didn't have the courage to paint his property red, so he painted it yellow, which he felt was risky enough for an insurance broker's. Another told me he had painted his building purple for the same reason. Yet another used orange. The red was hybridizing into other colors as the color spread around the village.

Looking back, there were several factors at play, and Ireland was going through a moment of great economic, social, and political change in the late 1990s and early 2000s. It seems people realized the power of color, and saw that they liked it, and felt like they wanted to use it.

Today the village is still predominantly red, although the colors continue to adapt. It is no longer the gray and cream place it was before my grandfather painted his house pink. It looks especially good when it rains.

OLAFUR ELIASSON

Olafur Eliasson (IS/DK), born 1967, lives and works in Copenhagen and Berlin. A survey of his work, *Take your time*, was organized by SFMOMA in 2007 and traveled until 2010. His exhibition *Innen Stadt Außen* (Inner City Out) recently opened at the Martin-Gropius-Bau, Berlin, and includes various interventions in the city.

Green river, 1998
Realized in Tokyo, Japan, 2001
Photo/Film stills: Olafur Eliasson
Courtesy of the artist; neugerriemschneider, Berlin; and Tanya Bonakdar Gallery, New York

GREEN RIVER, 1998

To date, Eliasson has carried out this unannounced intervention in six different locations: Bremen, Germany, 1998; Moss, Norway, 1998; The Northern Fjallabak Route, Iceland, 1998; Los Angeles, USA, 1999; Stockholm, Sweden, 2000; and Tokyo, Japan, 2001. Uranin (fluorescein), a water-soluble dye used, among other things, to test ocean currents, was poured into rivers in both urban and rural settings, turning the rivers green. Carried along by the currents, the dye radically changed the appearance of the rivers and their surroundings. Response to the intervention varied greatly, depending on the location.

FEELINGS ARE FACTS, 2010

For *Feelings are facts* Olafur Eliasson teamed up with Chinese architect Ma Yansong to develop a site-specific installation at Ullens Center for Contemporary Art in Beijing. Eliasson introduced condensed banks of artificially produced fog into an expansive gallery, whose dimensions Ma had further altered by lowering the ceiling and constructing an inclined wooden floor. Hundreds of fluorescent lights were installed in the ceiling as a grid of red, green, and blue zones. The colored fog zones introduced a scale of measurement in the gallery, their varying size and organisation referencing urban-planning grids. At each color boundary, two hues blended to create transitional slivers of cyan, magenta, or yellow. Walking through the dense, illuminated atmosphere, visitors would navigate the space by using this intuitive color atlas. The premise of *Feeling are facts* was to challenge our everyday patterns of spatial orientation.

THE COLLECTIVITY PROJECT, 2005

Three tons of white Lego bricks were delivered to a public square in Tirana, Albania, where people were invited to build their vision of a future city. The project was also instigated in Oslo, Norway, in 2006.

COLOUR ACTIVITY HOUSE, 2010

Placed outside the SANAA 21st Century Museum of Contemporary Art, Kanazawa, *Colour activity house* functions as a zone of transition, mediating between the museum, the surrounding park, and the city. During the daytime, when visitors walk between the glass walls into the core of the pavilion, the colors are mixed according to their movement: cyan with magenta; magenta with yellow; and yellow with cyan. During the night time, white light shines from the sphere as a single light source. The pavilion thus becomes a lighthouse, primarily to be experienced from the outside. By adding a mediating color filter to people's experience, *Colour activity house* prompts visitors to critically reexamine their immediate environment.

Previous:

Olafur Eliasson and Ma Yansong
Feelings are facts, 2010
Installation at Ullens Center for Contemporary
Art (UCCA), Beijing, 2010

Olafur Eliasson
The collectivity project, 2005
All images © Olafur Eliasson

Olafur Eliasson
Colour activity house, 2010
Installation at 21st Century Museum of
Contemporary Art, Kanazawa
Photo: Hiromi Kurosawa; Studio Olafur Eliasson

COLORFUL LANDMARKS: HOW COLOR SHAPED PUBLIC SPACE IN 1950S SUBURBIA ALAN HESS

Alan Hess qualified the US's oldest McDonald's for the National Register of Historic Places in 1983. An architect, historian, and architecture critic for the *San Jose Mercury News*, he's written *Googie Redux*, *The Architecture of John Lautner*, *Viva Las Vegas*, and *Oscar Niemeyer Houses*. He is currently researching the architecture of Irvine, California.

1. The term "linear downtown" was used by Reyner Banham, *Los Angeles: The Architecture of Four Ecologies* (Baltimore: Penguin Press, 1971), 141.

2. Tom Wolfe, "The Hair Boys," *The Pump House Gang* (New York: Farrar, Straus and Giroux, 1968.) For more examples of Googie coffee shops, see Alan Hess, *Googie Redux: Ultramodern Roadside Architecture* (San Francisco: Chronicle Books, 2004).

3. William Bronson, *How to Kill a Golden State* (Garden City, NY: Doubleday, 1968).

The miraculous 2009 resurrection of Harvey's Broiler drive-in restaurant in Downey, California, restored a neglected historical fact to the streets: commercial architects consciously shaped the urban space of suburban metropolises blossoming in the 1950s, and color was one of their key tools. In this new landscape designed for the motoring public, coffee shops, signs, gas stations, movie theaters (both enclosed and drive-in), car dealerships, banks, and other commercial buildings blended light and color with the interior and exterior architecture to create the public space and urban place of the street.

Coffee shops, in particular, were exercises in bright splashes of organized color. Executed at a scale appreciable by drivers passing at 40 mph by day or night, they could also be appreciated by pedestrians walking in for coffee and pie. Dotted at regular intervals along the long linear downtowns of commercial strips, these coffee shops established a legible urban order and rhythm.[1] Open twenty-four hours a day, they served as a public commons for traveling salesmen, families, sales clerks, late-shift workers, and teenagers. A primary purpose of these designs was certainly commercial sales. But architects also used this function to create well-integrated Modern architecture that played a conscious urban role. As Hollywood's great cinematographers refined the novelty of colored movies into an art form conveying context and meaning, Southern California architects integrated color into the civic and architectural purpose of their coffee shops.

Harvey's Broiler (1958) by architect Paul B. Clayton was but one of these coffee shops, but a fabled one. There were "many streamlined modern shed buildings around Los Angeles, for drive-ins and car washes chiefly, also gasoline stations, with slanting roofs and a lot of upward hard-driving diagonal lines," wrote Tom Wolfe in his 1968 essay "The Hair Boys," but "Harvey's is the Dior, the Balenciaga, the Chanel of the new wave" of the teen fashion scene.[2] The social role of Harvey's and other establishments was to provide a place to see and be seen.

Though these designs responded to specific functions, to many critics these colorful spaces looked exaggerated and undisciplined. William Bronson decried the "quantity, vulgarity and chaos of visual huckstering" in California in 1968.[3] Author Raymond Chandler documented their visual impact on Ventura Boulevard in 1949: "There was nothing lonely about the trip. There never is on that road....I drove on past the gaudy neons and the false fronts behind them, the sleazy hamburger joints that look like palaces under the colours, the circular drive-ins as gay as circuses, with the chipper hard-eyed car-hops, the brilliant counters, and the sweaty greasy kitchens that would have poisoned

a toad," he wrote in *The Little Sister*.[4] The quirky term "Googie" (after the 1949 Sunset Strip coffee shop designed by John Lautner) was quickly attached to these ultramodern designs in a dismissive manner after *House and Home* editor Douglas Haskell wrote an essay with that title in 1952.

From the street view, they seemed wild conglomerations of roof angles, frequently clad in multicolor glass mosaic tiles or sparkle-stucco that glittered in the sunlight by day or the spotlight by night. Neon signs in radiant yellows, oranges, reds, blues, and greens formed jazzy names in jazzy fonts, or abstract animated patterns. It was even worse inside, to critics disposed to discount them. Ship's Westwood (1958), designed by Martin Stern, Jr., boasted orange and brown plaid leatherette upholstery on counter stools that clashed with tufted orange banquettes; salmon and tan Formica panels faced kitchen cabinets that contrasted with sparkling stainless steel, speckled terrazzo floors, red, yellow, brown, and white plastic lighting globes, turquoise faux-marble Formica counters, cultured stone walls, and inventive artwork screens of cast purple plastic embedded with gold-leaf versions of the abstract rocket ship neon logo of Ship's. Splashes of green philodendron leaves in planters (inside and outside) added another level of contrasting earth tones to the sleek high-tech of plastic and metal.

No wonder it took an inventive journalist like Tom Wolfe to label this phenomenon as "electrographic architecture" in a 1969 *Architectural Design*.[5] He accurately described these indescribable colors as "tangerine, broiling magenta, livid pink, incarnadine, fuchsia demure, Congo ruby, methyl green, viridine, aquamarine, phenosafrarine, incandescent orange, scarlet-fever purple, cyanic blue, tessellated bronze, hospital-fruit-basket orange" in his 1965 essay on Las

Interior, Ship's Westwood 1958

10877 Wilshire Blvd., Los Angeles, California

Martin Stern, Jr., architect (demolished)

4. Raymond Chandler, *The Little Sister* (Baltimore: Penguin Books, 1949).

5. Tom Wolfe, "Electrographic Architecture," *Architectural Design*, July 1969.

6. Tom Wolfe, "Las Vegas (What?) Las Vegas (Can't hear you. Too noisy) Las Vegas!!!!" *The Kandy-Kolored Tangerine-Flake Streamline Baby* (New York: Farrar Straus and Giroux, 1965), 9. See also Alan Hess, *Viva Las Vegas: After-Hours Architecture* (San Francisco: Chronicle Books, 1993).

Vegas, but their source was Southern California coffee shops; for example, Martin Stern, Jr., went on to design several seminal Las Vegas hotels.[6]

That historiographical link points toward a deeper fact about these colorful, popular commercial strip buildings: they were all part of a significant, ongoing expression of a well-studied, continually refined tactic both to create individual buildings and to assemble them into distinct, legible urban districts in the growing suburbs of America.

These design strategies, including the use of color, were shaped by location and function. To most people going about their daily lives in these suburban districts, they were anything but chaotic. The large, distinct signs provided unmistakable focal points to organize the jumble of businesses in the strip's vast spaces. Their brightly colored interiors, on full display behind plate-glass window walls, could not be overlooked. In fact, they projected a welcoming oasis of gathered humanity.

The coffee shops' use of color in signs and interiors also linked them to a culture-wide explosion of color technologies that heralded the new postwar era. From color television and pastel appliances at home to Technicolor movies and duotone and tri-tone auto paint jobs in the public realm, color clearly communicated something important about the times. Color distinguished the post-World War II era from the black-and-white austerity of the Great Depression's movies and diners. Color was opulence and prosperity incarnate.

Harvey's Broiler drive-in (restored as a Bob's Big Boy in 2009 after being partially demolished, illegally, in 2006) had been built at a strategic bend in Firestone Boulevard at the west end of downtown Downey, a southeast suburb of Los Angeles. Architect Paul Clayton utilized the urban design tactics that Southern California architects had evolved for such buildings and sites since the 1920s. Their modest size, scattered locations, mundane purposes, and

popular audiences would have been seen as shortcomings in traditional cities. Clayton, like others architects, flipped these qualities into actual advantages by placing Harvey's Broiler squarely in the line of vision of anyone driving east from the center of town, and then multiplying the power of that site with an enormous neon and incandescent sign.

Then he put the entire interior—green banquettes, colorful cartouches, Palos Verde stone walls, painted soffits, brass sconces—on display behind a long glass wall. The broad swaths of color, stainless steel, and stone were the backdrop for the customers themselves, dining at the counter or walking to their booths, and the colorfully costumed servers in uniforms were carefully coordinated with the architectural theme. The interiors of the Googie coffee shops became animated, three-dimensional, living-color billboards clearly visible from the cars driving by. At night, as the structural form receded, the light of sign and illuminated interior became the architecture and the landmark.

"Anyway, there are a lot of bright lights under the shed roof, and around it there are parking places for about a hundred cars," Wolfe reported, each of which contributed its own daub of yellow, turquoise, gun-metal blue, maroon, or pink to the architectural composition. Among the customers was Ed "Big Daddy" Roth, whose custom car shop was a few miles away. Roth could be counted on to drive a car with a boss paint job to Harvey's.

These strategies were by no means new at Harvey's Broiler. By 1958, two generations of architects had refined these as part of a compelling and spreading architecture of automotive urbanism and commerce in Los Angeles and elsewhere. Their challenge was to fluidly combine wideopen urban space with more intimately scaled interior spaces, all in one piece of architecture. The sign clearly announced the restaurant to the driver cruising past; the interior broadcast the image of a clean, popular, exciting space in which to eat. Unifying

left:
Harvey's Broiler (now Bob's Big Boy) 1958
7447 Firestone Blvd., Downey, California
Paul B. Clayton, architect
center and right:
Bob's Big Boy 1949
4211 W. Riverside Drive, Burbank, California
Wayne McAllister, architect

Googie's coffee shop 1955 S. Olive St. and W. Fifth St., Los Angeles, California Armét and Davis, architects (demolished)

auto/public and pedestrian/individual space in one design was an astonishing design achievement. This blending was not simple happenstance; architects who contributed to this strategy included the famous and not-so-famous: Armét and Davis, John Lautner, Martin Stern, Jr., Wayne McAllister, A. Quincy Jones, William Cody, Edward Killingsworth, Smith and Williams, and Harry Harrison.

Neon signs, first introduced commercially to the United States from France in the late 1920s for a Los Angeles Packard dealership, served an obvious advertising function, but architects soon noted how they also shaped the linear space of the strip. Neon's rainbow of glowing colors added a new medium to the architect's toolbox. The brilliant and impressive urban role of incandescent light bulbs (legendary on Broadway's Great White Way) gave way to an even more compelling medium. Neon tubing proved useful as thin sketch lines to write words, draw pictures, or create brilliant animated patterns against the night sky.

By 1935, Los Angeles architect Wayne McAllister discovered the power of neon's vivid indirect light reflected against architectural surfaces. In a series of Streamline Moderne drive-in restaurants that dominated the public boulevards, he exploited neon's impressive and inexpensive ability to create a tall, memorable tower of colored light. Louvered fins hid the tubing, but the stucco surfaces of the pylon reflected their glow. Another tactic was to place opaque, unilluminated lettering in front of neon-illuminated surfaces ringing the circular stands. These tactics gave a small building a large presence; the one-story Simon's drive-in on Wilshire at McArthur Park could rival the ten-story terracotta tower of Bullock's Wilshire nearby as a landmark. This design strategy solved the problem of giving the proper, readable scale to a small building in the sizeable spaces of the commercial strip at night.

McAllister developed this theme after World War II with a series of Bob's Big Boy restaurants. These were sizable buildings, with interior seated dining in addition to the car-hop service outside. The 1949 Bob's Big Boy on

Riverside Drive in Burbank (still standing) juxtaposed a tall vertical stucco pylon with the horizontal form of the restaurant and kitchen structure; a neon circle with the Bob's logo spills off the pylon's side to catch the eye of drivers blocks away; once they arrive at the corner, smaller neon signs in multiple colors point the way to the parking lot. The entire structure, signs and all, was an integrated, consistent design of shape and color, by day or night.

The widespread use of plate glass—a recent material advanced by Modernism—offered a second opportunity for the architects of coffee shops. A solid outer, enclosing wall was no longer needed. It vanished as the exterior wall became transparent glass, floor to ceiling. The interior itself was then revealed (especially at night) to the passing public. Southern California architects soon grasped the advantage of this in a restaurant building. The bustle inside the restaurant could be magnified by the careful design of colorful, boldly scaled seating, back walls, ornamental murals, and plastic chandeliers.

The public space of the boulevard was thus united with the interior public space of the restaurant. What is noteworthy is the degree of sophistication with which architects integrated the sign and the glass wall into the architecture. The sign was not simply a square placard on a pole; it echoed and amplified the aesthetic, lines, and colors of the entire building. And the colorful illuminated interiors were not alone for the enjoyment of the customer within, but also a projection into the public space.

The scale and spread of suburban commercial strips demanded a strategy for urban cohesion: bold, repeated visual anchors as focal points, the manipulation of scale, of bright colors or unmistakable forms. By creating real communal places along the long string of buildings reached by car or bus, Googie architecture created a new urbanism for the suburban metropolis.

It was virtually impossible for anyone not to notice the results. It was much easier, however, for critics to ignore them. Even when observers such as Wolfe, J. B. Jackson, Douglas Haskell, and Reyner Banham acknowledged, documented, and analyzed these phenomena, they did not take deep root in the evolving history of Modernist urbanism.[7] The minimalism of white International Style architecture, accented by splashes of primary color, became the mainstream high-art taste for interiors. Googie's opulent patterns, rich tones, and complex combinations of colors and textures exploiting the possibilities of plastic and radiant neon were rejected.

This was not without a fight, however. Frank Lloyd Wright, whose opinions were ever present in this era, used turquoises, Cherokee reds, golds, and other vivid colors in his architecture. His apprentice, John Lautner, explored mustards, rusts, salmons, and forest greens in his buildings. Such choices continued the approach to color in American Modernism stretching from Frank Furness's Pennsylvania Academy of Fine Arts to Louis Sullivan's Stock Exchange Room to Frank Lloyd Wright's Coonley house to Lautner's Googie's restaurant—the direct link from Organic architecture to Googie.

These boulevard coffee shops embodied the energy and excitement of the Modern era for the general public. But they represented more than a set of aesthetic choices on color. The popular American landscape of commerce and the auto contributed equally to the development of this architectural aesthetic, encouraging rather than inhibiting architects' creativity. The same commercial inspiration had been seen in the mesmerizing display windows of department

7. See J. B. Jackson, *Discovering the Vernacular Landscape* (New Haven: Yale University Press, 1984); Douglas Haskell, "Architecture and Popular Taste," *Architectural Forum*, August 1958; Reyner Banham. "Las Vegas," *Los Angeles Times West Magazine*, November 8, 1970.

8. One window dresser at the turn of the twentieth century was L. Frank Baum, who used color theory in his window displays before he created the Emerald City of Oz; see William Leach, Land of Desire: Merchants, Power, and the Rise of a New American Culture (New York: Vintage Books, 1993), 56.

stores fifty years before, which had established the role of color in selling product. Their lavishly designed displays also created a public space that drew people together for window shopping and strolling.[8]

These signs, exposed interiors, and spotlighted parking lots created strong visual and public anchors that helped to focus and organize the farflung space of the commercial strips of the suburban metropolises, pioneering a new kind of urban planning and design for the automobile public. All the more complex as designs because they worked equally well by day or night, the color and light was designed to reinforce structural, spatial, and urban roles. Especially at night, these living billboards created public oases, pools of organized light within the chaotic firmament of street lights, glinting chrome bumpers, flaring brake lights, and the welter of signs. The bold font within the graphic logo circle of McAllister's Bob's Big Boy, or the rocket-shaped neon logo of Stern's Ship's, or the neon pennants of Armét and Davis's Norm's chain, or the golden arches of Stanley Meston's original McDonald's stands, established visual focal points that gave order to the chaotic twentieth-century suburb in the same way that a county courthouse dome rose above the random skelter of businesses in the center of a nineteenth-century town.

The ultimate success of this strategy can be seen in the architecture and urbanism of the Las Vegas Strip in its great forward thrust in the 1950s and 1960s. Many of the architects who learned to use color, light, and form in Los Angeles roadside coffee shops and drive-ins from 1930 to 1960 also created the seminal architecture of the Strip: Wayne McAllister designed the first hotel casino on the Strip, El Rancho Vegas (1941), as well as the influential Desert Inn (1950) and Sands (1952). Martin Stern, Jr., designed the Sands (1967), the International (1969), and the MGM Grand (1972). The Strip was peppered with three Armét and Davis Googie-style Denny's.

This suburban electrographic metropolis was fully formed according to these urban design principles when Robert Venturi, Denise Scott Brown, and Steven Izenour arrived in 1968 with a group of students from Yale School of Architecture. They recorded, cataloged, and analyzed the new concepts that Las Vegas architects had already borrowed from the basics of Los Angeles commercial urbanism. The appropriately scaled signs, colorful neon imagery, bold animated façades, and the car-oriented district were conceptually the same, though in Las Vegas they were even bigger. The same strategy worked: colorful signs and colorful spaces brought a readable visual order to the enormous spaces of the car culture city

Las Vegas Strip, c. 1985

PURPLE IHRAM AND THE FEMININE BEATITUDES OF HAJJ MOHJA KAHF

Moja Kahf's book of poetry, *Emails from Scheherazad* (2003), was nominated for the Paterson Prize. She has a novel, *Girl in the Tangerine Scarf* (2006), and a scholarly monograph, *Western Representations of the Muslim Woman: from Termagant to Odalisque* (1999). Her short story *"The Girl from Mecca"* is forthcoming in Feminist Studies. Kahf teaches comparative literature at the University of Arkansas.

Images: Pilgrims, probably from South Asia, outside the Masjid-al-Nabawi in Medina (Transposition).

Pilgrims performing tawaf in Mecca, where the Ka'ba is circumnavigated seven times (Al-Muntada Al-Islami).

1 Muhammad ibn Ismail Bukhari (d. 870 C.E.), trans. Muhammad Muhsin Khan, *Sahih al-Bukhari*: Arabic-English (Beirut: Dar al-Arabia, 1983) Vol. II, 358.

O humankind! Indeed, We created you of a male and a female, and made you into peoples and tribes that ye may know one another. Indeed, the noblest of you in the sight of God is the most mindful.—Quran 49:13.

I was a girl of ten when I made my first hajj in the late 1970s. "In our hajj clothes, called *ihram*, all pilgrims look alike," my father said. My beatific mother chimed in: "Worldly differences erased, to remind us that we are all the same before God."

How groovy! So what do I wear? "Anything serves the purpose," my mother murmured.

My hajj would be valid in any color, any style. My mother chose one of her usual navy or tan caftans and one of her beige or blue scarves. I picked an elastic-waisted purple skirt and a chocolate brown blouse. Purpose would be served in purple (I used to mix up these two words as a child, anyhow).

My brother and father, meanwhile, had all sorts of rules for their hajj clothing. It had to be plain white. Untailored, unhemmed, undyed. They couldn't wear underwear, I giggled to learn, because that was stitched. Men have two specific pieces of cloth to wear. The bottom is a sarong (that better stay in place covering navel to knees, without benefit of buttons). The top is a shawl, often knotted over one shoulder. My brother and father could not wear headgear to protect them from the sun. No closed shoes, only sandals. Clothing outside the rules invalidates hajj for men, negating a journey they have gone to great lengths to undertake, and making atonement rites necessary, so they must be careful.

The only dress rule for women is that those who face-veil must go barefaced for hajj. A few dissenters manage loopholes around that, not imagining that God wants the indignity of bared faces for them.

Sahih al-Bukhari, a major Sunni collection of sayings of the Prophet Muhammad, peace and blessings be upon him, says that Aisha, blessed wife of the Prophet, wore a "mu'aSfar" dress on hajj.[1] *Mu'aSfar* means safflower. Safflower is an herb with large orange or red flowers; dyestuff from the flower heads gives a spectrum of colors including yellow, magenta–hot pink–fuchsia, and orange–vermillion–tangerine. Muhammad Muhsin Khan translates this as "yellow," not appreciating the range, perhaps unable to imagine that Aisha may have worn red, and on *hajj*. Aisha's hadith approves *"muwarrad"* clothes for *ihram*. Literally "floral," *"muwarrad"* is translated by Khan as "rosy." By extension, it describes printed fabrics.

Pilgrims on my hajj displayed a color variety against the scrubby brown hillocks around Mecca that fill with white tent cities during hajj season. Gowns of emerald green—color of brocade robes of paradise, the Quran

Samia Mubarak on hajj with her husband Osama Bianouni (Photos by Kashmira Contractor).

says— signaled Kuwaitis and Emiratis; other Gulf Arabs wore their usual black *abayas*. Yoruba folk sported geometric patterns on crisp *bubus* (tunics) with scooped necklines, topped with towering *dikus* (head wraps) in cobalt blues, Kelly greens. Kurdish farmers wore flowered britches under polka-dotted muslin dresses. Hip-length circular scarves with strings tied back from temples to nape of neck distinguished Malaysians and Indonesians. Sudanese pilgrims wore the *tobe*, their wraparound traditional dress, usually in muwarrad fabrics.

We do not all dress alike for hajj.

Ihram clothing does not white-out differences among tribes and nations. Women's *ihram* preserves sartorial symbols of difference. One trend in hajj clothing is that women sew flag patches onto headscarves or sleeves—literally wearing their national identities on their sleeves, flying their colors for their communities to rally around in the immense crowds. *Ihram* clothing, far from erasing difference, draws attention to the role of women as keepers of group identity of which color is a rich marker.

The notion that hajj clothing has the purpose of minimizing our awareness of national, ethnic, and racial differences is popular among Muslims. You see it in textbooks about Islam, teaching films about hajj, and hajj memoirs, a famous example being Malcolm X's hajj account in his *Autobiography*. The Muslim African-American singing group Native Deen repeats the fallacy. "Don the *ihram*, where we all put on white, putting on the sheets so that we all look alike," goes their energetic song "Labayk." It may be a noble myth, but erasure of difference is not mentioned anywhere in Quran or Sunnah as the purpose of *ihram*. Perhaps we've made it up because it sounds attractively like the "melting pot" model of modern democratic pluralistic states. For whatever reason, it has become a staple of modern Muslim discourse.

We've used male experience of uniformity in *ihram* clothing to set a universal expectation about *ihram* clothing that women's experience does not match. Even women mouth the cliché, ignoring their experience to squeeze their brains into another male-specific thing masquerading as a universal human thing. There is even a notion floating about that women should prefer white for *ihram*. Women's white-wearing for *ihram* has zero grounding in Islamic jurisprudence. Where does it come from?

From modern hajj supply companies, you can buy "*ihram* sets" for men and women—a completely unnecessary purchase, since you can tear any unseamed white fabric into two pieces for men's *ihram*, and there is no such thing as specific clothing for women's *ihram*. When hajj companies supply this unnecessary product, they invariably supply women's *ihram* dress *in white*. This is a thing concocted.

Where else could it come from, women's white-wearing trend? Eleventh-century Islamic scholar al-Ghazali suggests *ihram* clothing is a practice shroud (*"kafn"*) because of its similarity to the death shroud He develops an extended metaphor between hajj and death.[2] It is brilliant but, again, only works for men. Men's two-piece white unsewn shroud and two-piece white unsewn *ihram* are similar. There is no similarity between women's *ihram* clothing and women's *kafn*, which is seven pieces of undyed, unseamed fabric wrapped in a particular way around the corpse. Here again, we take male experience and act as if it is universal, when it doesn't fit women's actual, factual bodily experience. I wonder if Ghazali's metaphor influenced some pre modern women to seek white for hajj.

2 Abu Hamid Al-Ghazali (d. 1111 C.E.), *Ihya Ulum al-Din* (Beirut: Dar al-Ma'rifah, n.d.), Vol. 1, throughout his "Book" (chapter) of Hajj.

Many women seem to want their *ihram* dress to be white, as if craving rules tailored for men where there are none for women. Do they think God forgot to tell them what color to wear? This negative reading sees women's freedom in *ihram* clothing as a lack, similar to assuming that women's exemption from *salat* (ritual daily prayer) during menstruation is a lack. Why not celebrate and ponder that freedom instead of pining over white *ihram*?

"Hajj" is an Arabic word meaning "pilgrimage." In Islam it means pilgrimage to holy sites in and around Mecca on designated hajj days: the eighth through the thirteenth of the Islamic lunar month called "Dhul Hijjah" (which, conveniently, means "that Hajj month"). It is one of the religion's core rituals.

If you're smirking and saying: Yeah, but it's a logistical nightmare; what about pilgrims who die every year, crushed in tunnels and whatnot? You know what—they die ecstatic. They leave home knowing every step, like in any journey, may be their last. Say you live in the Midwest and it's your dream to go to New York City. Do you not know how many people die in Manhattan every week? But you feel the rush; you see the massive skyscrapers; it's your dream! Hajj is our rush, the long-awaited union with the Beloved. This is the sacred ground, the gleaming glass high-rises that now tower over the marble courtyards of the Ka'ba notwithstanding. You're chanting with a surge of voices, "Labbaik!" which means roughly, "Here I am!" or "Catch me, God! I'm falling toward you!" like the trust game, when your toddler jumps at you, "whooooooeeee!" Better than the running of the bulls at Pamplona, and people risk their booties for that. This is some people's Everest. And they train for it, with purpose, and know where they're going and why.

Hajj is marvelous, a life pinnacle. Like any ritual, it's got a ton of rules. It must be approached through these protocols. When you pass the Mecca city limits, the sacred precincts, intending hajj, you enter a state of personal sacredness called *ihram*, marked by donning a fresh set of clothes. *Ihram* has behavioral aspects such as no sex, no hunting, no cursing, no fighting: and bodily care aspects such as no using perfume, no cutting nails, no shaving, waxing, tweezing, haircutting. These are identical for men and women. The only gender difference in *ihram* is clothing.

Hajj is equally mandatory for men and women. Even if a man is not traveling with women, he's going to see many women. Hajj is a babe magnet. That's why there's a famous *hadith* criticizing men who go on hajj to meet women.[3] Rites are not segregated by gender. Camping at Mina, collecting pebbles from the ground at Muzdalifah, pelting with those pebbles three pillars representing Satan's threefold attempt to tempt Abraham, circumambulating the Ka'ba seven times, followed by the ritual march ("*saeey*") along the path between the boulders

3 Yahya ibn Sharif al-Nawaw (d. 1278 C.E.), *An-Nawawi's Forty Hadith*, trans. Ezzeddin Ibrahim and Denys Johnson-Davies (Damascus: Holy Quran Publishing House, 1977), Hadith #1.

Hajj pilgrims gather in Arafat © Ali Haider/ epa/Corbis.

that we traverse seven times, commemorating our foremother Hajar, who ran between those hills of Safa and Marwa seeking aid for her dying son, Ismaïl—male and female pilgrims move together, culminating in the climb up the Mountain of Mercy to the Plain of Arafat for a day of prayer outdoors.

I performed my second hajj when I was eighteen, in the 1980s. Padding along the *saeey*, I glimpsed a little family ahead. The man stood supplicating at Marwa's base, his toddler on his shoulder. I couldn't tell where he was from, just that he was tall, olive-skinned, bearded. The crowd parted and I saw his wife, and from the cut of her dress and scarf I knew exactly where she was from: Egypt, rural, working class.

Anyone who has been on hajj has hundreds of these mental pictures yet we seem to edit them out cognitively to fit the cliché that national differences are whited out by *ihram*. But it's simply not our real visual experience.

Where does this sense of awe-inspiring unity come from in Hajj? Perhaps from the joyous synchronicity of motion. If key hajj rites are not conducted on three core days, performing them does not equal the sacramental obligation. Because of this required synchronicity, if you look at aerial photographs of the hajj, you see a huge congregation of humanity moving like one elongated body through the same places at the same time.

Mecca's cityscape may morph from wood-latticed Ottoman-era homes to tall gray apartment buildings and villas with cream-colored stucco

Women pray at the Mosque of the Prophet in Medina during hajj © Kazuyoshi Nomachi/Corbis.

walls covered with hot-pink bougainvillea, from souqs with tattered ochre awnings to multi storied malls and black-tinted glass hotels glinting in the sun, but the seemingly more ephemeral humanscape is, over the centuries, constant on these Dhul Hijjah days. The fluid intentional kinesis of masses of people generates spiritual energy, evoked in blurred time-lapse photography of the ambulation around the Ka'ba. The contrast of white-clad men dotted with color-clad women making a kind of slow-spinning pinwheel around the Ka'ba, or a long Chinese ribbon dance spiraling up the road to Arafat, moving all together in one flow amid the breathtaking racial and national diversity is what we experience. Perhaps a secondary factor comes from our sense of hearing: the sound track of the pilgrims' overlapping choral and individual chanting of "Labbaik, here I am, Lord, here I am." Hajj enables us to see, not ignore, the diversity of the global Muslim *ummah* (community), then, while experiencing kinetically that our spiritual purpose is One. Maybe we mentally edit the kinetic unity into a false sartorial uniformity.

Ihram is a ritual. We cannot know the intent behind ritual. We can only examine its effects on bodies and selves. To explore that, we have to be open to our fresh, first-hand sensations of the ritual—even if those visceral reactions seem unpious at first. All religions that have high ritual—Judaism, Islam, Catholicism, even Paganism—are saying that the body counts. We are not airy spirits divorced from matter. Ponder the body. In Islamic terms, ponder the signs God has placed in our bodies and, in hajj terms, the array of bodily experiences that ritual makes possible.

God arranged for Aisha to get her period right before Arafat, the pinnacle moment of Hajj. He arranged for me to get my period on Arafat, too, right at sunset, when I made my second hajj at age eighteen. Luckily, neither Aisha nor I was wearing white.

Aisha, who at seventeen was near my age on my second hajj, cried thinking that her bleeding put her whole hajj in jeopardy. Her husband said comforting things to the effect of, "There's no need to see this as a sad thing, Aisha. All women get periods. They're from God." Periods are not a curse, in Islam, not God's punishment for Eve eating the apple. Menstruation is so rich in meaning that the enormous ritual of hajj must rearrange itself around the egg's ritual flow down its Fallopian paths. Aisha went back to the Ka'ba and did tawaf when she was done menstruating. And I hopped the bus back from Jeddah a week later.

Hajj waits for no one—except us. Because of our periods, Aisha and I both got to have a woman-specific experience of hajj ritual split over fragmented time. So even the kinetic unity of hajj is not really true. One-fourth of women pilgrims, or one-eighth of all pilgrims, will break rank with that fluttering Chinese ribbon.

Are there insights to be gained from this added layer of women's hajj experience? There will always be a minority's experience that is not going to adhere to the supposedly desired unity of the *ummah.* Maybe that minority's nonconformity is just as important to the flow of the community, and needs to be celebrated, against the potential tyranny of majoritarian expectations. One hundred percent unity, it turns out, is permanently elusive, in the grand blueprint of hajj. By the design of our bodies, we, the one-eighth, save hajj from utter uniformity.

Men's experiences are valid in themselves, but not the default for humans or the norm for women. There are two points I'd like to offer from specifically observing men's bodily experience of *ihram*. Both suggest that *ihram* may indeed serve as an equalizer, but not of ethnic difference—of gender.

First: What if the bodily effect of male-specific *ihram* gives men a period of feeling naked and vulnerable in their bodies? Maybe *ihram*, counterbalanced against the way pilgrims dress outside *ihram*, offers moments of border-crossing in gender. Muslim men are supposed to cover from the navel to the knees. To put Muslim men into garments that are in constant danger of slippage around this "*awrah*" (pudendal nakedness)—remember, there's nothing underneath!— perhaps helps them to know what women experience from the focus on their bodily coverage more typical of non-hajj time.

A second way the difference in *ihram* clothing may offer one gender a bit of the experience of another gender is this: Men in *ihram* suddenly have to be very careful about the most minute jurisprudential rules regarding clothing. Bukhari's and Muslim's hadith collections devote pages to these questions: may men wear turbans on hajj? What kind of footwear is permitted for men in *ihram*? All over the internet, you find Muslim men preparing for hajj engaged in anxious Q&A sessions asking religious scholars what is and isn't allowed for them to wear in *ihram*. The level of detail almost matches that lavished on women's dress outside *ihram*.

The Quranic verse that says God "created you of a male and a female, and made you into peoples and tribes that ye may know one another. Indeed, the noblest of you in the sight of God is the most mindful"[4] is often cited to encourage people to "know one another" across ethnic and national differences. That its exhortation to best conduct might apply, too, to the categories of male and female mentioned at the beginning of the verse is often overlooked. These differences are not insurmountable barriers to understanding our shared humanity as we move, sometimes like particles and sometimes like waves, some by circuitous flow and some by linear fits and starts, on the sacred path. Instead of erasing national and ethnic difference, perhaps *ihram* makes differences more visible while opening modes of understanding across both national-ethnic groups and genders.

Hajj: a stimulus to gender egalitarianism? A fruitful Islamic feminism is not based in agendas of cultural imperialism. Nor is it shaped around defensively reacting to those agendas, which is just another way of being defined by them. Constructive Islamic feminism might ignore those assumptions utterly, exploring new questions unexamined by those agendas, while thinking critically about assumptions in Muslim discourses.

My parents took me on my first hajj. My in-laws graciously hosted my second hajj. I'd like to go on a third hajj, self-sponsored. When I do, *inshallah*, my daughters and I will glory in all the colors of *ihram*, on purpose and in purple. We will wear vibrant safflower like Aisha, emerald green the color of paradise, rosy "*muwarrad*" prints. Like baby's breath among tulips, my husband and son in white *ihram* will complement our ebullient colors. Maybe that's the reason for the color difference in men's and women's ihram dress: maybe men have to wear white to make a plain canvas against which God highlights the glorious bouquet of *us*.

4 Quran 49:13.

A BIT OF COLOR DOESN'T HURT
ALEX KRIEGER

Alex Krieger FAIA is a Professor at Harvard Graduate School of Design and past Chair of the Department of Urban Planning and Design. His publications include editing *Urban Design* and co-editing two volumes of *Harvard Design Magazine*. He is founding principal of Chan Krieger NBBJ, an architecture and urban design firm in Cambridge, Massachusetts.

1 *Broadway Boogie Woogie* can be viewed online, for example see MoMA's website: http://goo.gl/OM5D5

One of my favorite twentieth century paintings is Piet Mondrian's *Broadway Boogie Woogie*. It is a remarkable interpretation of New York especially, but of great cities generally. The city as a grid-ordered cacophony of diversity, ethnicity, and propinquity—syncopation and improvisation as in boogie-woogie jazz, played out in perpetual street life, and in vivid colors[1]. Cities, as on a Mondrian canvas, are experienced in color. Paris is *La Ville-Lumière*, the City of Light, for being the first city in Europe to use extensive gas lamps for night lighting, but whose slogan evokes the light of culture, art, and colors, too. Venice is remembered as muted primaries as reflected in its canals. These are faded colors in Venice, but otherworldly beautiful nonetheless.

Sometimes a single color emblemizes a city. Boston is masonry red, at least pre-20th century Brahmin Boston, and the pressure to extend the tradition remains, or a logic required to explain why varying from tradition in new construction is acceptable. Jerusalem is gold; both for the unique golden hue of Jerusalem stone, the mandated local material for all buildings, and for the city's setting on a ridge overlooking the Judean desert. *The White City* is a moniker used variously, for places as different as Chicago's late nineteenth century Columbian Exposition, and Tel Aviv, for the predominance of its early twentieth century whitewashed Mediterranean Bauhaus structures. Miami in our imagination is pink, though the actual color is not so prevalent, except more abstractly at certain seasons and times of day, caused by a distinctive semitropical sunlight glow.

Although cities are experienced and even more so imagined in textures and colors, buildings in people's mind are more commonly monochromatic, especially on the outside, and especially those built across much of the last century. For the color-hungry among us, that is a pity.

While colors and color theory bloomed with the nineteenth and early twentieth century revolutions in art, modern architecture proceeded for a long while to become grayer. *The Machine Aesthetic* seemed to favor few bright colors. But a more fundamental reason for the general absence of color in everyday architecture is people's anxiety about color, and bold colors in particular. There is after all a difference between the sense of a color experienced at the scale of an urban panorama—reddish Boston—or on a canvas, and confronting, head on, a particular and strong color at the scale of a building.

My favorite color is yellow, I think. What is yours?

Such a typical exchange about color may explain why architecture often winds up "grayish" in tone. For many, of course, the subject of color itself is troublesome, with responses to a particular color a personal matter, often accompanied with a little insecurity. So, we think, if I am not so confident myself, how could I subject others who may be even more color challenged, or the public at large, to my sensibilities about color? It is safer to remain neutral, subdued, warm gray, maybe off-white.

And if the creative architect, we assume, comes to such timid conclusions less frequently (though recall that in apparel architects seem to prefer black) the client, the investor, the developer, the facilities manager, the homeowner all find it easy to acquiesce to safe choices in the use of color. Whether it is worry about taste, cost, upkeep, changing fashions, public reaction, or municipal approval, there are myriad reasons for staying conservative when it comes to color in architecture. Only the (crass?) commercial world seems uninhibited in its use of colors. Or is it that the permissive use of color indicates commerce's crassness and lack of sophistication?

Not least of the concerns among architects about the use of color is how color interacts with and affects the appreciation of architectural form. Consider, for example, two of Frank's Gehry's projects; the Bilbao Guggenheim and Seattle's Music Experience Project. The Bilbao Guggenheim, exterior coolly monochromatic, is universally acclaimed, as it deserves to be for many reasons. The Music Experience, with its audacious purple, red, blue, and gold interrupting the silvery continuity of the stainless-steel skin, has received far less attention. Yes, Bilbao was the jaw-dropping breakthrough project. But what if the Music Experience had come first? Somehow I suspect the response would have been different. No less astonishment, perhaps, but surely some skepticism expressed about the use and effect of the colors. Do the colors in Seattle add or detract, one would have asked, make the form more or less sublime? Just maybe multiple colors are better reserved, as they are in the entrance plaza of Bilbao's Guggenheim, to Jeff Koons's amazing flowering *Puppy*.

Accustomed to building exteriors as generally uncolorful, we are taken aback when encountering the opposite—seeing, for example, the subdued (in color) monumental remnants of Greece and Rome rendered as they originally appeared, painted somewhat garishly throughout in primary colors. A color photograph of Geritt Rietveld's De Stijl masterpiece, the Shroeder House of 1923, is at first surprising. The building's Piet Mondrian-like use of yellow, blue, and red stripes is unexpected in comparison to the more familiar black-and-white photographs of the house that appear in older books on the history of modern architecture. The exuberance in decorative motifs and use of color in a Gaudí, within the Art Nouveau movement, or among the Viennese Secessionists were also subsumed by grainy turn-of-the-century photographic reproductions, and by the modernist's more ascetic sensibilities. Color was a medium for eccentrics.

Then there is the story, perhaps apocryphal, of Richard Meier appearing before a design review commission with a color palette consisting of thirty-two shades of white—this in response to a local code forbidding white as a primary exterior residential color, and thus a request of Meier to show alternatives to his preferred use of white. For Meier, as for those who are skeptical about Gehry's Music Experience, color seems unnecessary, perhaps even detracting from the act of architectural form giving. Elegance for many twentieth-century architects, and architecture's admirers as well, resided in the subtly of a chosen color palette. Efficiency, restraint, abhorrence of decoration, and "truth" in the assembly and presentation of materials were the more valued goals throughout the modernist period—leaving color, unless integral to a material, as an appliqué,

Brigham and Women's Hospital, Boston; Nicolas Athletic Center, Cambridge; Beth Israel Medical Center, Boston, Massachusetts.

a technique not held in high regard among serious modernists, Le Corbusier's later experimentation in painting concrete in primary colors notwithstanding.

But as an accomplished painter as well, Le Corbusier saw fewer conflicts and more interactivity between color and form. And the sources for his artistic inspirations broadened with age: indigenous villages and primitive art, for example, often full of uninhibited color. Among those with the least means it seems it is possible, actually necessary, to become colorful, not just black-and-white minimalists.

Surprisingly, in the midst of our more permissive, un-minimalist present where limitation on shapemaking has virtually disappeared, color in buildings still arrives primarily in applied form, as for example in the older neon and newer giant LED screens attached to the façades of buildings from Times Square to Tokyo's Ginza, and throughout urbanizing China.

There are, of course, wonderful exceptions. Beijing's Olympic *Water Cube* is one. Its surreal blue exterior evokes program—aquatics—and is the result of the double layer of transparent fluorocarbon-based polymer material (ethylene tetraflouroethylene, ETFE) with which its exterior is clad. For the color-hungry among us, the outside of the *Water Cube* delivers a troika of pleasures. It offers vibrant color *sans paint,* construction innovations with striking color, and color associated with a place's function. The "Cube" promises a more color-filled world to come as newly engineered materials such as ETFE become more common, and can be impregnated in thousands of colors.

As an architect I've always looked to a more color-filled future, and so have snuck color in as often (and as much as clients would tolerate) into our own buildings.

For an inpatient cardiovascular center for Boston's Brigham and Women's Hospital, we designed bright yellow eyelids to provide some protection against solar gain in the patient rooms. Why yellow? Well, it is my favorite color, but here it provides a subtle, sunlike glow. Recovery time among hospitalized patients is clinically proven to hasten in rooms that provide ample natural light. That is why all of the patient rooms at this cardiovascular center have such expansive windows, but these do require solar protection. Why not, in offering that protection, also provide an illusion of sunlight even on a cloudy day?

At the Greater Boston Foodbank hundreds of foot-high reflective tabs, made of the same material as stop signs, help reveal the mission of the organization. As the headlights of the tens of thousands of vehicles that daily pass by this highway-hugging warehouse illuminate these tabs, the random pattern of the tabs momentarily transforms into an image of the Foodbank's wheat logo. Some will call it a Robert Venturi-inspired gimmick, billboard architecture rediscovered. But why not bestow a large, prominently located, and necessarily utilitarian structure, storing and awaiting additional donations of food for a region's poor, with a bit of an "in-your-view attitude"—in full color. The reflectivity of the tabs and thus the perception of the shaft of wheat vary in intensity during different times of day and under different light conditions, but few daily commuters fail to make a connection between the wheat figure and the building's purpose.

The directors of the Discovery Museum in Bridgeport, Connecticut hoped that additions and modifications to their original gray concrete home might become more poetically expressive of art and science for their young adult audience. They asked: can the museum itself, and just not the collections, heighten the natural curiosity and wonder that young people bring to learning? Finding in the museum a collection of the boards that Josef Albers used in his Yale color theory classes gave us the idea of using glazed brick in primary colors to create the new facades of the museum as "Albers-like" color boards. The green, blue, yellow, and red bricks are composed in a Broadway Boogie Woogie–inspired composition. The effect is playful and hopefully educational, or invites inquiry. The color compositions of the exterior along with the opaque and transparent geometric volumes, layered translucent surface inside, and articulated joints between columns, beams, and built-in furnishings are meant to evoke that sense of wonder about the place, and architecture itself as an exemplar of a union of art and science, or at least technology.

These are modest efforts in the deployment of color by comparison to Beijing's *Water Cube*. In tradition-minded, reddish-brick Boston, materials such as ETFE are not readily embraced (nor, by the way, do exterior LED screens yet flourish around the city). So the introduction of a common material such as masonry in uncommon ways and colors serves in our work as a halfway mechanism to less conservative color deployment. In several of our projects, such as at Beth Israel Hospital's Ambulatory Center and at the Nicolas Athletic Center, the threading of glazed brick courses through more conventional masonry surfaces leads our clients to haltingly advance to a more color-filled architectural future.

Greater Boston Foodbank.

Surely an entire neighborhood of Water Cubes would be exhausting. Nor do I advocate a Disney cartoon-rendered architectural future. I'm not sure many relish more orange roofs, golden arches, and the remainder of the colorful mishmash of the suburban commercial strip. All around us misuses of color are more prevalent then masterly color compositions. Indeed, the deployment of color requires a careful and discerning eye, and even then considerable restraint. As James Cameron's visual alchemy in the movie *Avatar* intentionally reminds us; when in *The Wizard of Oz*, that now ancient film but among Cameron's inspirations for *Avatar*, Dorothy's black and white world first becomes Technicolor, a smile was hard to suppress.

Discovery Museum, Bridgeport, Connecticut
all images Chan Krieger NBBJ.

URBAN IMPRESSIONS SYLVIA LAVIN

Sylvia Lavin, Professor and Director of Critical Studies and MA/PhD programs at UCLA, writes for an international spectrum of journals and is completing her next books, *The Flash in the Pan and Other Forms of Architectural Contemporaneity* and *Kissing Architecture*. Lavin is also a curator of experimental work in architecture and design.

Robert Venturi once explained his love of Rome as an expression of his affection for the dusty orange in which he was surprised to find the city empowdered during his first visit there in 1954. Gotham, in the renderings of Hugh Ferris, is black and white and every imaginable shade of gray in between. Who does not instantly recognize the pink stucco of a cheap LA apartment building? And Tunis without the brilliant aquamarine blue of endless window shutters might just as well be Houston. Such colors, like Proust's madeleines, are perfect evocations of particular places and our memories of them. But are these characteristic pigments, building materials, and renderings really what we mean to provoke when we conjoin color and the city today? Do we want our urbanity, already under extreme pressure from competing systems of signification, to collapse further under the weight of the semantics and vernaculars of color? And do we understand that this is what is at risk when our urban imaginary is taken over almost entirely by the rubric of current urbanisms and their exploded axonometric diagrams color-coded within an inch of their lives with the supposedly natural colors of landscape—colors which, with the aid of Pantone and Photoshop, become easily grafted onto program and then onto life itself? So colored and overdetermining has urban representation become that all other nuances of color are, hue by hue and at the very moment that color seems just in reach after a long period of exile, fading into nothingness as the field inadvertently starts to bleach the colorfulness right out of our capacity to think new forms of the urban.

Meaning is not what color does best. Instead, color is most productively understood as a means of describing—indeed provoking—a contemporary sensibility and of privileging intellected and social experience over sentimental and personal feelings and memories. Color is never absolutely perceptible alone: many forms of interference, from degrees of illumination to the adjacency of other colors, render color an always mutating and yet ever present element of perception. Colors are momentary locations on the spectrum of light that culture and science are always trying to pin down into a stable system and nomenclature. Yet it is precisely in their constant shifting and interdependency that colors can model an active and convivial urban sensibility. Because of all their codependencies, colors are corrosive to clear and stable boundaries between autonomous forms, tending instead to blur individual objects into hazy contact with nearby objects. And yet at the same time, in any single moment of perception, color and the experience it provokes (if left free of predetermination by name and meaning) is always new and singular.

The Paris of Impressionism and its increasingly global urban progeny, terrains filled with soft pastel colors and the baubley words of Baudelaire, are cities filled with the shifting, hazy hues of colorful urbanity. Filled at every turn with what Baudelaire called presentness, these urban impressions intoxicate the viewer with the enticements of a virtual city, an urban field crowded with the colors of prostitutes, *flaneurs*, and their quixotic allures, each in and of itself

vague and hazy but coalescing at any moment to produce the experience of the now. Such urban impressions unleash forms of experience—convivial, changeful, intense, and irreducible—for which the city emerges as the most potent model.

      A collaboration between John Baldessari and Rem Koolhaas for a competition to house the headquarters of Caltrans in Los Angeles, the state agency responsible for roads and transportation, suggests how this might work. The collaboration was wide-ranging and there are many intriguing aspects of this little-known project, yet I will mention only this simple fact: they proposed to paint each truck in the Caltrans fleet a different color. Every morning as the trucks left the parking structure they would have become animated points—part Seurat, part Space Invaders—moving across the city, covering Los Angeles with color by day and then retreating each evening to their color-coded parking spots. Each day, then, the city would leach the building of its hue, briefly expanding its effects across an entire region and transforming the single building into an urban atmosphere. These molecules of reddishness and pinkishness moving across the urban field used the necessarily diffuse and genial effects of color as a means of exploding architecture into urbanity. In this urban field, experience might be vivid and thoughtful, rather than sentimental and coded, susceptible to novel affects rather than adjudicating the proper proportion of various program, and could move perception beyond a concern with wayfinding and sign systems to open up alterative ways of being.

Georges Seurat, French, 1859-1891, *A Sunday on La Grande Jatte* - 1884, 1884-86, Oil on canvas, 81 3/4 x 121 1/4 in. (207.5 x 308.1 cm), Helen Birch Bartlett Memorial Collection, 1926.224, The Art Institute of Chicago. Photography © The Art Institute of Chicago.

Following spread: Caltrans, John Baldessari and Rem Koolhaas (OMA).

REDBRICK IN RIO MOISES LINO E SILVA

Moises Lino e Silva is currently a PhD candidate in Social Anthropology at the University
of St Andrews. He holds a BA in International
Relations from the University of Brasilia (UnB)
and an MSc in Social Anthropology from the
London School of Economics (LSE). His research
centers on the Anthropology of Freedom,
Postdevelopment and Urban Anthropology. His
research in Brazil was supported by the Foundation for Urban and Regional Studies.

1 My own translation.

2 Jorge Barbosa and Jailson de Souza Silva,
Alegria e Dor na Cidade (Rio de Janeiro: Senac,
2005), 24.

3 See Max Weber on the concept of status
groups. In editors H. Gerth and CW Mills,
From Max Weber: Essays in Sociology (London:
Routledge, 1991).

4 "Center for Urbanistic and Social Orientation."

Favela Amarela / Yellow *Favela*[1]

Favela amarela / Yellow *favela*
Ironia da vida / Irony of life
Pintem a favela / Paint the favela

Façam aquarela / Make watercolor
Da miséria colorida / Out of colorful misery
Favela amarela / Yellow *favela*
—Jota Júnior and Oldemar Magalhães

What is a *favela*? Jorge Barbosa and Jailson de Souza Silva open their book
Alegria e Dor na Cidade (Happiness and Pain in the City) with this very question.[2]
They maintain that many people think that a *favela* can be defined as a place
that "lacks"— order, sewage, asphalt, and so on. I am unable to give a definite
answer to the question; however, after having spent more than a year living and
conducting research in Rocinha—one of the biggest *favelas* in Rio de Janeiro—I
am certain that the apparent "lack" of things should be carefully considered. Here
I want to tackle the issue of the lack of paint in the landscape of some *favelas*.
Discussing deeper social dynamics within *favela* life however can be a more effective means for defining what a *favela* is than the mere "lack" of something.

Why do people living in *favelas* tend not to paint the exterior of
their houses, although the interior of these same houses are often very colorful?
I suggest that it has to do with the type of status one achieves—or doesn't—by
decorating the exterior of houses.[3] I have often been surprised when visiting
places in Rocinha that I judged from their exterior appearance to be very simple
and found highly elaborate colors inside. This issue seems to go beyond the mere
lack of resources.

A few weeks after Michael Jackson's death in June 2009, people
from the *favela* where I lived were excited to visit the place where the music
video for the song "They Don't Care About Us" was shot, in *Favela* Dona Marta,
in 1996. During our visit to the rooftop where Michael danced so intensely, one
of my friends found it odd to look out and notice that colors in that *favela* were
so diverse. She thought the mix of colors was ugly and preferred the more neutral
red-brick and cement-gray tones of Rocinha. At this point, another friend—a
student of architecture—told us more about a color project run by the municipality
through the local POUSO (Posto de Orientação Urbanística e Social).[4]

In this project, people were given a neutral color with which to
paint the exterior of their houses, and the choice of a second color for building
details. The latter would be chosen by the dwellers themselves: orange, purple,
red, or others. The result was an ongoing transformation of the *favela* landscape.

Coincidence or not, however, this is the same *favela* in which permanent policing units were placed in 2008 as a pilot project that attempts to obtain control over the *favela* territory and eliminate drug trafficking.

Would a *favela* without organized crime, and looking more colorful than ever, still be a *favela*? Given the historical government desire to eliminate *favelas* and, more recently, to "solve the *favela* problem," I would expect public authorities to hope the answer would be "no."[5] But during our visit to the colorful Dona Marta, people still spoke about the place where they lived in terms of a *favela*.

In Dona Marta, not just the colors were different; those in charge of the territory were different, and the inhabitants claim that even the popular *favela* "baile funk"—a kind of block dance party—had been forbidden by the police to keep "order."[6] However, "*favelas* are similar but different" is what I often heard during fieldwork. It therefore becomes easy to accept the idea that some *favelas* have the presence of organized crime and others do not. Some have a stronger presence of "militias," and others a greater presence of the police. Some *favelas* are becoming more colorful, while others remain red brick.

A recent article on Rocinha's "official" website discusses the possibility of a partnership between a multinational paint company and the governments of both the municipality and the state of Rio de Janeiro, with the objective of

Images by Moises Lino e Silva

5 The book *A Century of Favelas* contains a discussion on various initiatives for the elimination of favelas over the past 100 years; Marcos Alvito and Alba Zaluar, *Um Século de Favela* (Rio de Janeiro: FVG, 2006).
6 The movements and lyrics of funk music can sometimes be sexual, aggressive, or glorifying of organized crime, depending on the type of event.

painting more *favelas*.[7] The authors, Isabela Bastos and Luiz Ernesto Magalhães, argue that there seems to be a historical desire on the part of the government to minimize the "visual impact" of *favelas*.[8] The question I would like to put is: what "visual impact"?

In my home *favela*, I lived in a one-bedroom ground-floor flat. The wall outside my house was made of cement. The interior, however, had a combination of tile patterns on the walls and floor. The tiles in the kitchen and tiny bathroom were blue; they were beige in the living room and brown in the bedroom. Meanwhile, the top parts of the walls—the tiles went up only halfway—were yellow in the living room, light yellow in the bedroom, and deep blue on the ceiling of the kitchen and bathroom. The house was very colorful inside, but rather monotone on the external walls.

Upstairs lived a family of four: Raquel, Carlos, and their two children, Clara and Jefferson. Before living with Raquel, Carlos had lived with another woman and, with her, had an older son called "Mano" and a daughter called "Mana." Raquel told me that Mano's house was beautiful and that she wanted to take me there someday. The first time we started climbing stairs uphill to get there, I became tired. Mano lived a lot further up the hill than we did. The narrow ways leading to his house were sometimes challenging, steep and dirty at some points. Most houses on the way were red brick on the outside. We finally reached a hidden door in a gray-cement rendered building. Raquel knocked. Mano's partner opened the door and invited us up through a staircase covered with brown tiles. Inside the house, there were three floors and many colors on the walls. The living room was highly decorated with pictures, good-quality furniture, and small colorful objects everywhere. The upper floors were equally impressive. The contrast between the elaborate interior and the simple exterior struck me. The couple obviously had ample means to color the exterior of their house had they wanted.

On a different occasion, I was walking around Rocinha with a friend, Goianiro, who offered to teach me some shortcuts. We went all the way uphill through "becos"—narrow alleys—and then back down using a side way near the big rock just beside the area where I lived. At a certain point we stopped to rest, and from that spot had a great view of the *favela*. Looking at the red-brick tones that dominated the scene, I asked my friend: "Why is it that people don't paint the outside of their houses?" He didn't think long before saying: "Because they don't care about that." A few seconds later, though, after giving more thought to the question, he said that it was not worth spending money on the exterior if it is the interior that matters. The answer was important to me as an anthropologist, but I felt it sounded a bit too obvious. As we kept going down, he brought up the topic again and said that it was expensive to take building material all the way up to the *favela* just to decorate the exterior of a house, when that doesn't make any difference to your life.

Months after this conversation, I traveled with Raquel and Clara to Ceará state in northeast Brazil. Raquel had migrated from there to the *favela* in Rio where she had been living for more than twenty years. A few days after we arrived in Ceará, we went to visit the house of another friend I had made back in the *favela* in Rio. Her house was still under construction, with the walls bare red brick. She was a bit embarrassed about the house and told us that the building work was not finished; the inside and outside walls still had to be painted. I was surprised that she would be concerned about that. "Will you paint

7 Isabela Bastos e Luiz Ernesto Magalhães; *Parceria com fabricante de tintas permitirá pintar barracos,* http://www.rocinha.org/noticias/view.asp?id=1029 (accessed February 24, 2010).

8 Their argument is based on the work of Brazilian historian Milton Teixeira and presents other historical initiatives that led to some favelas in Rio being painted. The projects mainly reflected top-down approaches.

A wall in a school in Rocinha where color is used to teach French.
(Image: Luciano João dos Santos.)

the outside walls as well?" And she said: "Here I have to do it; it is not like in Rocinha. Here, the only ones who don't paint the external walls are those in total deprivation, and I don't want people thinking of me in those terms!" After a while she said: "This is a good thing about the *favela* in Rio—there nobody cares about these things!" This statement reminded me of what Goianiro had told me.

Based on my fieldwork, I came to believe that there is something about living in a *favela* that makes the external appearance of a house less important that it is in other places— whether the neighborhood of Ipanema in Rio, a small town in the state of Ceará, or even Goiânia, my hometown in the interior of Brazil. The reason for people not painting the exterior of their houses doesn't seem to be financial or at least not only financial. Of course with money being limited, people need to make tougher choices; my experience in a *favela*, however, makes me think that painting the exterior of a house comes very low on the list of priorities. The decoration of the interior of the house, including amenities such as a big television, a powerful sound system, or tiles all over the house, have a lot more importance.

In this sense, urban projects that try to improve *favelas* through colorful paint may be operating only on the place where this paint is going: the exterior. The attitude behind not turning red brick into other colors runs deeper, to what it means to live in a *favela*. The color of exterior walls does not seem to confer the same status or have the same value in *favela* life that it usually does in other places. Changing the color of *favelas* in Rio de Janeiro, then, seems to be a preoccupation more for people outside *favelas* than for their own inhabitants. Colored walls can be a sign of increased social status, but not necessarily to the people undergoing the color changes.[9]

9 As I write, in 2010, a few houses in Rocinha have been painted as part of the interventions made by the PAC program, a federal government project to promote the acceleration of economic growth in Brazil. The houses chosen to undergo color changes were along the road that leads to the wealthy neighborhoods of Ipanema and Barra da Tijuca (Auto Estrada Lagoa-Barra).

BLEU
JAUNE
ROUGE
BLEU
JAU
NE
GRIS
VIO
LET
BLEU
BLEU
BLANC
ROUGE
VERT
BLEU
BLEU
GRIS
BLANC
ROUGE
BLANC

PALETTES OF INDIFFERENCE: THE CITY IN THE STUDIO CHARLES A. RILEY II

Charles A. Riley II, PhD, is a professor at the City University of New York, curator-at-large of the Nassau County Museum of Art, and author of twenty-eight books, including *Color Codes: Modern Theories of Color in Philosophy, Painting and Architecture, Literature, Music and Psychology, Art at Lincoln Center,* and *The Jazz Age in France,* as well as an entry on color in the *Oxford Encyclopedia of Aesthetics.*

When the Color Chart exhibition opened to the media on a March morning in 2008, I hustled up the escalator past a dozen other journalists en route to the sunny sixth floor of the Museum of Modern Art, where Donald Judd's 25-foot-long, six-foot-tall monumental sheet-aluminum sculpture in eight bright lacquer tones briefly blocked my way to the galleries. My slower peers were wondering if the MoMA press office would spring for miniature croissants and muffins, but I was in a hurry to see for myself this much-heralded turning point in the aesthetics of a subculture of the art world in which I had been involved since writing an interdisciplinary book of essays on Modern color theory fifteen years earlier. The honor roll of major colorists from the museum's permanent collection (Matisse, Delaunay, Klee, Rothko, Newman, Louis, Frankenthaler) were nowhere to be found. A later, edgier cohort prevailed, among whom Judd, Gerhard Richter, and Ellsworth Kelly presided as éminences grises, with surprise appearances by Bruce Nauman, Richard Serra, and Dan Graham. It culminated in video works by such artists as Angela Bulloch and Cory Arcangel, a hacker too cool to care about ever seeing the whole of his computer-generated video composed of pieces of movies. My face reddened as I rushed from one room to the next, encountering the "new objectivity." The coup de grâce was a suite of photographs Jan Dibbets had taken of the side panels of cars parked on Amsterdam streets, one of a group of works in the show that featured automotive enamel. The wall text read: "The less I cared, the better they came out."[1]

The crowd gathered for the remarks by the curator, Ann Temkin. "What defines color after color theory?" she asked in her introduction. The grids, ladders, and scales presented "store-bought color...after the palette." I spun the revolving doors and headed out into the gray of midtown Manhattan, incensed. What had become of the familiar litany of harmony, cool versus warm, synaesthesia, simultaneous contrast, complementaries? Where was the epochal schism between line and color, the philosophical debate about primaries, even the sexy psychological anxieties over chromophobia and the toxicity of pigments? Goodbye Goethe and his colossally inspiring errors—hello Benjamin Moore. Newly exiled from a chromatic land I never fully understood but dearly loved, I wanted to know who or what had killed color. It turned out that the answer was waiting right outside the door.

Eventually, return trips to the exhibition and a thorough perusal of the catalogue (subtitled *Reinventing Color, 1950 to Today*) revealed the basis for the paradigm shift. So often the job of cultural historian entails attending to language. I had learned color by ear as much as eye, listening during studio interviews to the ways in which artists talked about what color means to them, studying the texts of Seurat, Signac, Matisse, Kandinsky, Albers, and others. This linguistic project focused on the semiotics not just of the hues themselves

1 Cited by Ann Temkin in *Color Chart: Reinventing Color, 1950 to Today* (New York: Museum of Modern Art, 2008), 165.

Jim Lambie (British born, 1964) *Zobop!* (2006). Vinyl tape on floor. Dimensions variable. Installation view, The Museum of Modern Art, New York, 2008. The Museum of Modern Art. Fund for the Twenty-First Century. © 2008 Jim Lambie

2 Briony Fer, "Color Manual," in *Color Chart*, 29.

3 Josef Albers, *Interaction of Color* (New Haven: Yale University Press, 1963), 1.

4 Temkin, "Color Shift," in *Color Chart*, 8.

5 Skeptics (including this writer) point out one important technical difference between digital and analog or painterly color. As with the natural spectrum itself, analog color is continuous, shading gradually from hue to hue, while the discontinuous quality of digital color is caused by its separations determined by pixels, that binary stutter of 0 and 1 that also mars the drawing of a curve by a computer at the fundamental level. Just as Goethe worried over Newton's reduction of color's relational complexity to a dry analytic formula, traditionalists complain that the computational mixtures of digital color fail to succeed the fluid boundaries of paint and ink because red, green, and blue phosphorous dots are its constituent elements and they blend only imperfectly.

(the easy associations of red with communism or Coca-Cola, green with Islam, one blue for Greece and another for the Democrats) but of their effects on artists and viewers. For Kandinsky colors were theatrical characters, while Albers found them untrustworthy obsessions. Nobody I ever met was actually neutral on the topic—they were either chromophobes or chromophiles. The terminological clues to the new art of color in the essays and artists' statements were recurring references to "dead" or "dumb" color, "objectivity," "standardization," and "indifference." In Briony Fer's historically oriented catalogue essay for the exhibition, the message was brutally clear: "Color chart color is color that is relentlessly indifferent to us."[2] Albers, teacher directly or indirectly of many in the show, had become a bête noir, even though on the first page of his classic *Interaction of Color* he had warned: "In order to use color effectively it is necessary to recognize that color deceives continually."[3] The cold absence of subjectivity and expressivity was jarring in an exhibition devoted to what was once one of the most heated emotional elements in the art and design studio. Temkin's eloquent and decisive introduction to the catalogue dismissed the earlier rhetoric: "The color chart could serve as an efficient sign for a kind of color that represented color after the palette, after theory, after mysticism, and all these other considerations that seemed to me anachronistic at the turn of the twenty-first century."[4]

Certain familiar themes emerged in the argument—the influence of machines, chance, quantity, and commerce—each linked to the often overwhelming experience of color in the city. From cars to computers, the mechanical aspect was implicit in the assembly-line production of Andy Warhol's too-numerous screen prints and paint-by-number works, Damien Hirst's monotonous 700-dot paintings, and Richter's exhausting 4,096 panels in one vast grid (even Albers returned to the square an epic 1,000-plus times). The numbers mount vertiginously when the computer appears. There are reportedly 17 million possible color combinations on the latest Mac, succeeding the 256-color palette of the Mac OS9 on which many artists have worked.[5] The scale of these works was also daunting. Richard Serra was an Albers protégé at Yale between 1961 and 1964, hired to color correct the proofs of the first edition of *Interaction of Color* during the summer of 1963. The Serra work in Color Chart was an endless, mind-numbing film of his dirty hand peeling back, one after another, each of the 220 sheets of Color-aid paper used in the Albers class (Color-aid was used by photographers for backgrounds). Serra made the Nauman-esque film in 1970–71 while a visiting artist in New Haven. By reducing Albers's anatomy of color intervals to monotony (the students would beg him to turn off the film), Serra did his level best to dethrone color, which he abandoned in his sculpture in favor of the heavy black and the patinas of Cor-Ten steel. Banality was also the bass note of Dan Graham's serial *Homes for America* (1966–67), a set of dull Polaroids framed with mock sales copy for a housing development in Florida called The Serenade ("the new city," in the artist's words), which offered 2,364 possible color permutations to buyers of the prefab houses to be built on "dead" land, a grim but oddly compelling example of the contextual impact of suburban planning on studio practice.

Color charts rely on the unmixed state of industrial tones in an array that is estranged from the palette or the spectrum, two planar or tabular arrays of relational colors, one individual down to the selections of paints for a

given painting, the other "given' by nature. The charts serve neither making nor matching, to borrow E. H. Gombrich's once-useful distinction.[6] The mass-produced, hermetically "low value" (Judd's term) samples "found" on the commercial chart led to an alarming call for what Frank Stella called "dead" color, taking the negative aesthetic to its limit. That seemed an apt enough metaphor for the most politically charged moment in the show, Walid Raad's *Let's Be Honest, the Weather Helped* (1984–2007), which used Avery dots keyed to the tones found on real ammunition (coded by nationality and source) to mark bullet holes on black and white photographs of Beirut's scarred buildings.

      One of the popular stratagems in Color Chart, adopted from the John Cage playbook (with footnotes to Stéphane Mallarmé and Pierre Boulez), was the acceptance of chance in lieu of choice, a technique for imposing distance from the personal preferences of an artist, bolstering the claim to objectivity via randomness. This is at least in part a response to the urban context outside the studios of most of the artists represented. The charts "engage" (Temkin's term) the gritty geography of such industrial cities as Turin and Glasgow, which join Tokyo, Paris, London, New York, and Los Angeles among the most popular referents. Nobody was better attuned to the city than Cage, who was not represented by a work in the exhibition but makes cameo appearances in the catalogue texts. When he originally invoked chance operations, the empty spaces cleared by the withdrawal of his individual will, those radical silences for which he is best known outside the world of music were created to push back against the urban cacophony that rapidly rushed forward to fill them. His *Roaratorio*

Ellsworth Kelly (American, born 1923) *Colors for a Large Wall* (1951). Oil on canvas. Sixty-four wood panels, overall: 7′ 10 1/2″ x 7′ 10 1/2″ (240 x 240 cm), The Museum of Modern Art, New York. Gift of the artist. © 2008 Ellsworth Kelly.

6 E. H. Gombrich, *Art and Illusion* (Princeton: Princeton University Press, 1972), 29.

(1979), for example, arose from the sense that the oratorio inside the urban cathedral was balanced by the din outside. His marvelously delicate prints and drawings, "urban landscapes" on which little rectilinear "skyscrapers" floated over smoky backgrounds suggested by the pollution hanging over his native Los Angeles or São Paulo, were visual responses to the first work of art he ever acquired, a painting by Mark Tobey, whose "white writing" reminded him of the random etching of the Manhattan concrete sidewalk outside the gallery where he found it (reminiscent of the "pavements grey" in Yeats's most famous poem, "The Lake Isle of Innisfree"). The dance pieces with Merce Cunningham were inspired in part by the movements of passers-by on Sixth Avenue near their loft, where he pondered such problems as global overpopulation. In other words, in every medium and at every moment the aleatory aesthetic that Cage was using owed as much to the city and its crowds as to the contemplative asceticism of the *I Ching*, the source he frequently cited. Within a consideration of the artist, designer, architect, or urban planner as *agent*, the acceptance of chance (or of color choices already in place) is a reminder that much of the color experience in cities is involuntary. You don't like the neon lights of Times Square? "Live with it" is the response when conditions are beyond your control.

Another artist missing from the Color Chart show, presumably because he was too figural (the same principle probably excluded Murakami), was also supremely attuned to the urban pulse of chromaticism, a heroic integrator of the city and his art. James Rosenquist's newly published memoirs include spellbinding descriptions of hanging on scaffolding several stories over Times Square, inches from vast fields of red or yellow that from four blocks away read as the nose of a glamorous movie star hawking cigarettes or whiskey. At the same moment Johns and Rauschenberg were satirically challenging the "shmear" of de Kooning and Kline, Rosenquist was descending from his work on commercial billboards (two coworkers had recently fallen to their deaths) to use discarded, "low-value" paint in his huge works on canvas. Rosenquist also professes indifference:

As I painted large swaths of color on billboards—my nose a few inches from a sea of green or orange—I began to develop my own idiosyncratic vocabulary of color…My chromatic alphabet came from Franco-American spaghetti and Kentucky bourbon. Green became the eyebrows of a kid drinking Coca-Cola; blue was a Chrysler sedan, orange was orange soda and the color of Early Times whiskey… My aesthetic may have come from being too close to what I was painting to know what it was. I didn't give a damn about the images themselves as I was painting them. One billboard would replace another and then I'd paint over it and another one on top of that one. All that interested me was their color and form.[7]

7 James Rosenquist, *Painting Below Zero: Notes on a Life in Art* (New York: Knopf, 2009), 94–95.

Some of the ideas in Color Chart can be traced back to the urban rhapsodies of Leger and Le Corbusier, for example, who also professed nonchalance regarding quality but was a stickler for exactitude. The meticulously produced catalogue (color-correcting those plates on press must have been a tough assignment, no matter how unconcerned one is supposed to be) was a reminder that the specificity and consistency of so many opaque works, their fidelity to the given hue, value, and chroma of the paint or ink "in the can," was as firm a means of control as the vaunted rigor of Albers and his hard-pressed Bauhaus students. Despite

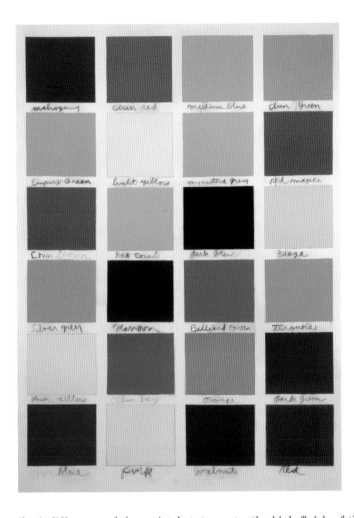

Jim Dine (American, born 1935) *Red Devil Color Chart No. 1* (1963). Oil on canvas, 7' x 60" (213.4 x 152.4 cm), Alice F. and Harris K. Weston. © 2008 Jim Dine/Artists Rights Society (ARS), New York.

the indifference of the artists' statements, the high finish of the predominant monochromes suggests a persistent need for accuracy, control, and aesthetic rigor that similarly made the Modernists such noteworthy alchemists when the autonomy of color emerged as a primary compositional source rather than a secondary quality. The MoMA galleries became a hall of mirrors reflecting an altered relationship between the artist and color dyed in the urban experience of overstimulation. The sheer multiplicity of monochromes and unmixed chips offered quantitative evidence for a large-scale "quotidian sublime" (Temkin's phrase) that reflects the bombardment of the crowd's senses in an urban center. The 31-foot-long Richter is both a scale in the Latinate sense (a ladder of tones) and a tribute to the power of immense spatial presence in contemporary art. Even though he is a giant of contemporary art, the scientific hauteur of the work helped explain in part the antagonism his stained-glass windows in the cathedral of Cologne have encountered.

Taste in this area is volatile. The color wheel spins with alarming velocity, in part due to the volatility of emotions (of which indifference is but one) induced by chromatic vibration. Extreme colorism periodically flames and then fades to formalism. The Fauves, for example glowed for only about four years, about the length of the Blaue Reiter moment, while Color Field painting, which lingers with Helen Frankenthaler and in the extravagant retrospective work of Carroll Dunham and Peter Halley, ceded its popularity and critical acclaim to the advent of the stern blacks, whites, and grays of Minimalism in the 1970s. Music's stylistic periods display a similar brevity—the daring experiments with timbre of Wagner, Liszt, Chopin, Berlioz, and Scriabin were followed by a retreat to Classical transparency until Schoenberg, Webern, and Messaien ventured another liberation of chromaticism as compositional force. Architecture and design have their own periodic efflorescence—the shock of James Stirling's Kermit-the-Frog green or Michael Graves's forest green yields to Taniguchi and Meier and their Belgravian creamy whites. Like strong sun, color except in abrupt doses is almost too much for the eye and mind, perhaps due to a fear of the toxic implications of certain pigments, the type of "chromophobia" that David Batchelor so wittily captured in his slim and timely book, a touchstone of current thinking. Batchelor's work appeared by the Judd just outside the entrance to the exhibition, a curatorial gesture echoed in the frequent footnotes in the catalogue devoted to Batchelor's *Chromophobia*.[8] He has spent most of the last decade stalking London in pursuit of white rectangles (bleached-out advertisements, whitewashed sections of notice boards around which the city's visual traffic circulated) for a series of "monochromes of modern life," some of which are included in this volume. Irresistible blanks inviting the closet graffitist to leave a tag, the series is revelatory in its reminder of the random chromatic excesses of what he calls the "overfull visual field" of the city that surrounds the white space.[9] What will come next? "Dead" color by definition refers to the matte under-painting of the work in progress.

Characterizing the distinction between before and after the major change so graphically presented in Color Chart is a challenge. One way to describe the transition is by adapting a literary distinction applicable to other media such as architecture, design, music, and dance. Although there has always been a dynamic relationship between prose and poetry, Modern literature particularly blurred the categories, thanks to the prose poems of Baudelaire, the roman *fleuve* of Proust, the aural virtuosity of James Joyce and Ezra Pound, who provocatively asserted that poetry should be at least as well written as prose. Much as music can be divided into poetry (Babbitt, Schoenberg) and prose (Cage, Rorem), or architecture (Gehry against Piano), art can also be separated into poetry and prose. The Color Chart crew seems, to me, to be an exemplary group of Postmodern prose stylists by contrast with the poets of color (Kandinsky, Delaunay, Matisse, Van Gogh, the Fauves). The blunt, indexical realism of the urban color chart is, one has to admit finally, as vastly different from the lyrical, psychologically loaded poetry of early abstraction as the prose of an owner's manual from the lyricism of Kandinsky's *Concerning the Spiritual in Art*. The denotation of "writing degree zero" takes the place of connotation as the monochromes in their opacity reflect the detached ennui with which the denizen of the city guards his or her personal space.

This is not entirely novel. As John Gage recounts in his magisterial history of color theory, *Color and Culture*, standardization entered the color world ominously in 1900 when an experimental grid was introduced to Gestalt analysis by the Berlin psychologist Friedrich Schumann. Twelve years later, Wilhelm Ostwald, one of the most renowned figures in the Modern study of color and a Nobel Prize-winning physical chemist and Sunday painter in Riga, was named to the color committee of the Deutsche Werkbund. He was asked to design a scientifically rigorous chart that became the basic map for the study

8 David Batchelor, *Chromophobia* (London: Reaktion Books, 2000).

9 Ann Temkin, *Color Chart*, 180.

of color in Holland (via De Stijl) as well as at the Bauhaus, where an interdisciplinary inclusion of physics, chemistry, physiology, and psychology bolstered the scientific claims. Gage views empiricism as the beginning of the end for the artistic tradition of color, but warns that Albers might have overstated his negative stance: "In this yearning for neutrality, influential as it became, Albers showed most clearly how inadequate his conceptual framework was to account for the power of his paintings."[10] Industrially produced standardization is what so appealed to Le Corbusier, for example, in the 1920s when he promoted his "law of Ripolin," the literal whitewashing of his "machine for living" espoused in a text with rhapsodic footnotes on the standard, universal format for filing cabinets and folders. One of the highlights of the Color Chart exhibition was Sherrie Levine's spectral homage to a 1931 project for wallpaper ("oil paint on rolls" or *Belfarbenanstrich in Rollen*) for Salubra, a Swiss home products company. The historical fidelity of Levine's corner installation was, as always with her verbatim allusions, stunningly precise, testimony to the eighty-year reign of industrially produced color. As Temkin comments, it is not without ambiguity:

Levine's project sets in motion a complex circuitry: an architect who was also a painter made colors based on paintings to use as wall paint, and seventy-five years later an artist returns the colors to paintings. A longtime admirer and sometime producer of monochromes, Levine found a new way to create them within the parameters of her own practice: not simply making monochromes from wall paint but from a historic wall paint that engages the thick tangle of questions that lie at the heart of modernism and its relation to color. She enters into that tangle and emerges with beautiful sets of paintings that allow her to revel in her role as a colorist even as they foreground the ambiguities of such polarities as objective/ subjective and standardized/unique. Levine's work activates the tension between the loss of a faith in originality and the necessity of making something new. It might be too late to base an artistic practice on relational color harmonies, but one can nevertheless celebrate those of the best in the business.[11]

Following Levine's trail of immaculate panels out of that brilliant exhibition was a firm historical reminder that the color chart has long been, like Rosenquist's scaffolding, a perilous platform for objective approaches to a highly subjective area of perception—even the immense intellect of Wittgenstein failed to codify the philosophical analysis of color (a lifelong essay), undone by the unique quality of individual experiences. Physiological and genomic research confirm that no two individuals have precisely identical responses to the same chromatic source, further undermining claims to universality via standardization (and globalization—the "pan" in Pantone). That is why they can never finally kill color. At some point, the chill of the chart succumbs to the warming influence of that Promethean force too dynamic to be confined to its place on a grid without disturbing the memories, associations and emotions of each viewer who dares pass by with studied indifference.

10 John Gage, *Color and Culture: Practice and Meaning from Antiquity to Abstraction* (Boston: Bul Press, 1993), 265.

11 Temkin, *Color Chart*, 205.

URBAN IMAGINARIES, STADTBLIND, AND THE COLORS OF BERLIN: INTERVENING IN THE REALM OF PERCEPTION, INITIATING URBAN TRANSFORMATION

JESSE SHAPINS

Jesse Shapins is a media theorist, documentary artist and urban historian. His scholarly and artistic work has been published in *The New York Times, Wired, Berliner Zeitung,* and *Taiwan Daily News* and been exhibited at MoMA and the Deutsches Architektur Zentrum, among many other venues. He is currently a PhD candidate and an Instructor at the Harvard Graduate School of Design. http://jesseshapins.net

1 Stadtblind was founded in Berlin by myself and German architects and planners Philipp Schwarz and Celia Di Pauli. Since then, the group has expanded its activities to Stuttgart, Innsbruck, New York City, and Cambridge, Massachusetts. See www.stadtblind.org.

2 Andreas Huyssen provides the best definition of the concept of urban imaginaries in the Introduction to his book *Other Cities, Other Worlds: Urban Imaginaries in a Globalizing World* (Durham, NC: Duke University Press, 2009). Other recent literature includes Thomas Bender and Alev Cinar's *Locating the Modern City: Urban Imaginaries* (Minneapolis: University of Minnesota Press, 2007), Gyan Prakesh's *Spaces of the Modern City: Imaginaries, Politics and Everyday Life* (Princeton: Princeton University Press, 2008) and Armando Silva's documenta 11 book *Urban Imaginaries from Latin America* (Ostfildern: Hatje Cantz, 2003).

3 Viktor Shklovsky, "Art as Technique," in *Russian Formalist Criticism: Four Essays,* translated by Lee T. Lemon and Marion J. Reis (Omaha: University of Nebraska Press, 1965), 12.

URBAN IMAGINARIES

Operating since 2002 in the border zones between experimental art, urban design, and ethnographic research, Stadtblind is dedicated to the investigation and transformation of urban life.[1] On a theoretical level, creatively confronting "urban imaginaries" is one of the collective's main concerns. Urban imaginaries are the frameworks of individual and collective consciousness that condition the construction and interpretation of meaning and thus structure active living in the city. Imaginaries are understood as the interface between the immaterial city—the city constantly imagined in the minds of its residents and a global community through popular culture, political agendas, the media, the tourist industry, and the arts—and the lived experience of place. It is the perception of a city, formed and experienced from inside and outside, always in flux and immensely influential. The immediate provinces of urban imaginaries are mental, spiritual, and emotional spaces—the spaces of subjectivity—but their impact can be traced in all facets of urban life.[2]

As a strategy for critically engaging urban imaginaries, Stadtblind developed a color-based method of media making inspired by Russian Formalist critic Viktor Shklovsky's concept of "defamiliarization" [ostranenie]. In his famous 1918 essay "Art as Technique," Shklovsky writes:

Art exists that one may recover the sensation of life; it exists to make one feel things, to make the stone *stony*. The purpose of art is to impart the sensation of things as they are perceived and not as they are known. The technique of art is to make objects 'unfamiliar,' to make forms difficult, to increase the difficulty and length of perception because the process of perception is an aesthetic end in itself and must be prolonged.[3]

For Shklovsky, art is not exclusively a mode of expression (as the Romantic ideal assumed), but instead a tactical technique for producing new forms of knowledge through the unique capabilities of the aesthetic faculties. As such, the central domain in which art intervenes is the realm of perception, that space between social context, individual consciousness, and sensorial experience—precisely the same sphere and constellation of forces that produce urban imaginaries.

146

THE COLORS OF BERLIN

Stadtblind's initial project was *The Colors of Berlin*, an exhibition premiered in Berlin in 2003 and published by Prestel in 2005.[4] Targeting the lacunae in the representation and perception of the city, we developed the project under the paradoxical premise: "Too often Berlin is seen blindly [*Zu oft wird Berlin blind betrachtet*]." In this ever-progressing work, we have modified the form of a classic Pantone color-fan to create a database-driven platform that contains five interrelated elements: color blocks, an image, a theme, a text, and a map.

The choice of the color-fan was not to highlight the visual vibrancy of Berlin but instead to serve as a means toward reframing perception. The two colors below every picture give the work its emotional and polemical element. The color tones are drawn directly from the pictures themselves and are intended to intensify and complexify the images, aiding viewers to see these often mundane objects, scenes, and spaces with new eyes and feelings. A photograph of a standard brown doorknob is easily ignored. However, reframed through *The Colors of Berlin*, this everyday element takes on a new life and is no longer seen blindly. The choice of colors is not scientific nor algorithmic but in every instance intensely subjective, foregrounding the viewer's agency in constructing meaning and perception in the city. The colors also assure the work a degree of energy, fun, and accessibility, thereby opening the project to multiple audiences.

The sources of our images are from nearly every corner of the city: the border in the east by Hohen-Schönhausen, the backyards of single-family homes in Hermsdorf, Mies's Neue Nationalgalerie, the banks of Teufelssee in Wilmersdorf, the main residential arteries of Neukölln. Collectively, we traversed the city for more than two years, building a database of thousands of images.

Our text selection is as diverse as the locations of our photographs. We have quotations from such classic Berlin commentators as August Endell and Wim Wenders, citations from the daily newspapers *Berliner Morgenpost* and *die tageszeitung*, statistical information, and personal observations. In an age when the central form of communication is the rapid consumption of images, we find the insertion of texts necessary to slow the viewer/reader. The exact location where the picture was taken is marked with a black circle on a cutout from the Berlin map. This localization is essential to our documentary process and lends every image a crucial specificity.

The themes outline some of the most basic, everyday aspects of urban life in any city: sitting, eating, vehicles, façades, the ground. This thematic structure is the organizing principle of the work, allowing us to highlight the diversity of the city by presenting series that illustrate contrasts and continuities. It is the combination of the image, text, and map that make each card or page specific to Berlin.

We attempt to evoke "lived experiences" by displaying the many traces that daily activity leaves behind in the urban landscape. These traces may be fleeting, such as a puddle, or the more consistent presence of such essential everyday urban utensils as trash cans, benches, and trailers. But it is precisely this focus on life in the city that forms the basis of our practice; architecture for us is "spatial scaffolding [*eine räumliche Gerust*]," the backdrop against which urban life transpires. Our approach to the city rejects pure aestheticism in favor of attention to the way urban space is used and inhabited. Such an approach is echoed by the words of anthropologist and architectural critic James Holston

Color card photography and design by Stadtblind.

4 Celia di Pauli, Philipp Schwarz, Jesse Shapins. *Die Farben Berlins / The Colors of Berlin.* München: Prestel Verlag, 2005.

KULTUR · *CULTURE*

5 James Holston, "Spaces of Insurgent Citizenship," in *Cities and Citizenship*, edited by James Holston (Durham: Duke University Press, 1999), 166.

when he writes in "Spaces of Insurgent Citizenship," "The crucial question for us to consider…is how to include the ethnographic present in planning, that is, the possibilities for change encountered in existing social conditions."[5]

Color, of course, has a long history within design. Most often, it is approached as an issue of ornament and beauty. In contrast, *The Colors of Berlin* suggests using color not as an end in itself but a means for reimagining and re-interpreting the city. Color can be deployed as a heuristic device for challenging conventional perception. In a sense, such an approach shares surprising affinities with the color experiments of Itten, Albers, and others at the Bauhaus. Color was crucial to the curriculum of the visual fundamentals course, like texture, shape, material, and other qualities that the masters deemed to be essential, universal categories for design. The aim was, on one level, to understand the properties of color and how to use them effectively in diverse design practices (whether painting or architecture). However, on a more substantial level, the visual fundamentals course was based on a belief in the education of seeing. The aim of the Bauhaus colors and *The Colors of Berlin* is a second-order refiguring of the artist's general perceptual capacities, a renewal of sensory experience that translates not only to design with color but also to a more fundamental defamiliarization of the world around us.

EINSAMKEIT · *LONELINESS*

TOURIST INDUSTRY

One of *The Colors of Berlin*'s most consistent reference points is the tourist industry. Tourism in Berlin feeds off the city's two dominant urban imaginaries: Berlin as construction site and Berlin as historical landscape. Berlin's top tourist destinations are Checkpoint Charlie, the Brandenburg Gate, Potsdamer Platz, the Jewish Museum, the Reichstag, Museumsinsel, and the Hackesche Höfe. Tertiary tourist destinations might include the "bohemian flair" surrounding Kollwitzplatz in Prenzlauer Berg, shopping on the Ku'Damm and around the Gedächtniskirche, the Kulturforum, the fabricated medieval alleys of the Nikolaiviertel, or a trip to the top of the TV Tower. Almost no major tourist sites are outside of Mitte, and none are outside of the Ringbahn.

The power of tourism rests not only in the experience of a city that is presented to visitors. The tourist industry and its apparatus also have a tremendous impact on the residents of a city. The touristic approach to a city tends to reduce a place to a collection of isolated monuments and districts, blending out everything in between. In the interest of increasing the touristic attractiveness of a city, city planning policy attempts to develop a city that fits the dominant touristic image and focuses on blockbuster events and monumental building projects. These chosen "highlights" receive the attention and investment of the city planning office. That which seemingly does not fit into the touristic image of the city is, for all practical purposes, forgotten.

Stadtblind's response to this relationship between tourism and urban development has been to adopt the mass-oriented strategies and language of the tourist industry, but to focus on places outside of the normal tourist program. With this intent we initiated the project by running a gallery in Wedding from January to August 2003. We see the work *The Colors of Berlin* as a type of "guidebook" to Berlin. However, instead of the classic tourist sites, the seemingly banal scenes and details of lesser-known inner-city districts and the vast periphery are mapped out for potential tours. Moreoever, the colors are to be understood in dialogue with the practices of the tourist industry and its facile appeal to conventional notions of beauty. The colors, often perceived in a positive manner, are a means of generating immediate accessibility and clarity, and their aesthetic language borrows from the fields of popular advertising and marketing. But unlike a traditional ad, once one looks closer, it is not a product that is seen, but instead an urban detail or perspective that is often overlooked.

CONCLUSION

In *Invisible Cities*, Italo Calvino presents this fictional conversation between Marco Polo and Kublai Khan:

Marco Polo describes a bridge, stone by stone. "But which is the stone that supports the bridge?" Kublai Khan asks. "The bridge is not supported by one stone or another," Marco answers, "but by the line of the arch that they form." Kublai Khan remains silent, reflecting. Then he adds: "Why do you speak to me of the stones? It is only the arch that matters to me." Polo answers: "Without stones there is no arch."[6]

We believe that choosing to focus on the traces of everyday life in the city is akin to paying attention to all the stones that constitute an arch. A city is not constituted by a sum of its monuments, a collection of its "highlights," but by the combination of all of its details. Our ambition is to generate such a sensitivity to the city of Berlin. It was precisely this inability to confront the complex actualities of Berlin that doomed the city planning policies of the 1990s to failure. The Berlin that city authorities imagined was drastically out of touch with the Berlin that actually existed or that realistically could develop in merely ten years' time. One of the most serious problems facing Berlin today is a lack of critical self-reflection. More than presenting answers, *The Colors of Berlin* asks questions. Less a direct representation of our version of Berlin's "reality," *The Colors of Berlin* should be seen as a metaphor for a method of critically examining the city.

For a change in Berlin to truly take place, a change in mentality is necessary. Intervention in the fields of the city's urban imaginaries is crucial. If we want to change the city, we must challenge our forms of perception. How we perceive determines the decisions we make—in other words, it determines how we act. Berlin will always be disappointed with itself if it only sees itself in relation to Paris, London, or New York. Berlin, because of its singular history as capital of the Third Reich, capital of the German Democratic Republic, "Showcase of the West [*Schaufenster des Westens*]," and site of the Berlin Wall, will never achieve "normality." In fact, accepting the whole range of everyday phenomena that these historical events have instigated in the city, the core of Berlin's abnormality, is the essential first step toward a better future. Our hope is that *The Colors of Berlin* can be a small provocation to seeing the city in a different way.

6 Italo Calvino, *Invisible Cities*, translated by William Weaver (New York: Harcourt Brace, 1978), 82.

STATION · *STATION*

Berlin, Stadt, Schönheit, Metropole – ein Jonglieren also mit vier Unbekannten, zeitweiligen Entleerungen. Vielleicht sollte man es genau darauf ankommen lassen. Daß Vorverständnisse dieser Art an der Wirklichen Stadt zu Makulatur werden, genau das ist es, was man Berlin allemal noch zutrauen kann. Diese Wahrheitsfähigkeit ist vielleicht das, was in Berlin an Schönheits Stelle steht.

Berlin, city, beauty, metropolis—a juggling, that is, with four unknowns that are also occasionally empty. Perhaps one should simply be prepared to risk it. That preliminary understandings of this kind disintegrate in the face of the real city is precisely what one can expect of Berlin. This ability to be true is perhaps what takes the place of beauty in Berlin.

Dieter Hoffmann-Axthelm. »Berlin: Schönheit der Stadt.« In: *Kursbuch. Berlin. Metropole.* Berlin: Rowohlt, 1999. S. 85.

Ausschnitt aus Blatt 424 der Karte von Berlin 1:10 000 Ausgabe 2000
Vervielfältigt mit Erlaubnis der Senatsverwaltung für Stadtentwicklung von Berlin vom 19. Mai 2003

READING THE COLORS OF MACAO
JIANMING SONG, YIN DI (TRANSLATED BY YIFAN LI)

Jian Ming Song is Deputy Director and Professor at the China Academy of Art, and Director of the Color Research Center. Song is Vice-President of China Fashion & Color Association, Director of the Chinese Artists Association, Vice-President of the Study of Chinese Architectural Culture, Institute of Higher Education Design Education Committee, Director of Asia Fashion Association, Member of AEC, and Deputy Director of Hangzhou Government's decision-making advisory committee.

Yin Di is a professor at Zhejiang Science-Tech University, Art and Design School, and Design Director of the Color Research Center at the China Academy of Art.

Yifan Li is a designer at the Color Research Center at the China Academy of Art.

1 Jean-Philippe Lenclos and Dominique Lenclos, *Colors of the World: The Geography of Color* (New York and London: W. W. Norton and Company, 2004).

Macao is colorful. From the point of view of French color scholar Jean Philippe Lenclos urban landscape colors are a result of geo-cultural forces.[1] Indeed, over the past 400 years Macao has undergone tremendous change through the juxtaposition of Chinese and Portuguese cultures, as well as several man-made and natural disasters. Maybe that is part of the reason Macao's urban landscape is so full of color.

Throughout our research on Macao's colors, we used video, photography, transcripts, color comparison, and sampling, among other methods, to record the colors of the city. Our research group took more than 20,000 photographs according to geographical classification and established a library. In later work at the China Academy of Art's Color Research Center, we chose typical streets for color analysis. We also restored dozens of typical street scenes. Meanwhile, we classified the architecture in accordance with the age, style, shape, and tone, with the aim of recording and understanding the elements of urban landscape color: their hue, brightness, color mode, texture, and material. In addition, we made a color analysis of building components to reveal the Macanese understanding of decorative colors and way of expression.

We introduced the idea of "frozen symphony" for the layout of the colors in Macao. The city's several subcenter and district zones were understood as the various movements in this symphony. Each area can often be subdivided into many blocks. Regardless of the levels of partition, the color change can be interpreted as an ingredient of the vocal part in this melody. This symphony is structured along five levels.

The first, is the historic colors of Macao, through color comparison and physical color sampling, we sum up Macao's color pedigree of historic buildings and traditional architecture. The second is the color of modern buildings located in the old areas. They are relatively close to historic buildings or distributed in the streets and alleys of the central city, and are often six or seven floors, in a modern style. The third level is the color in neighborhoods, mostly residential buildings and cottages. Colors are often applied by locals and the quality and materiality of colors are poor. The forth level is the color of commercial buildings, almost all of these business-related constructions are small shops. The fifth level is the color of large-scale buildings for the gaming industry and tourism. Macao's gaming industry has long-standing prestige, and the casino buildings have exaggerated forms and florid color. Meanwhile, a large number of casinos have adopted the most expensive materials in an extravagant style. Colors are generally dark gray, gold, and warm red.

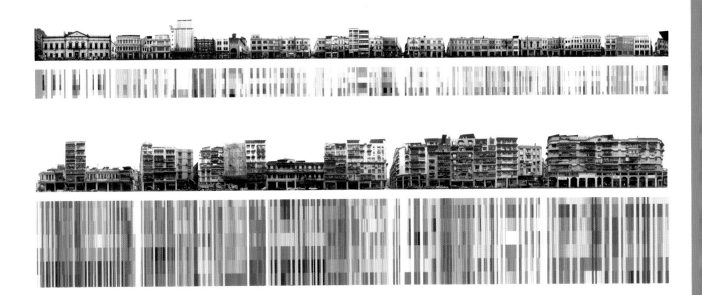

As color scholars, we are concerned about the composition of Macao's urban colors as a foundation on which to base design strategy and guidelines for urban color planning. There may be a conflict between the demands of building owners and the goals of color planning. Macao has a strong sense of democracy; therefore we need to find norms that can keep a balance between flexibility and the need to control. We need research on urban color management and construction. Color is presented through a visual form; otherwise, it cannot be expressed, even through nice statements and scientific methods. Therefore, it is important to create a system of chromatography and illustrative plates that can control and manage urban color planning. Urban color planning, design, and construction is complex and challenging work.

Xin Ma Road South and He Bian Xin Road East building elevation color reduction and color melody analysis.

Technical advisor:
Ding Zong Yu
Bin Bin Huang

Group leader:
Jian Ming Song
Wei Ming Wu

Deputy leader:
Da Cheng Lu
Yin Di

Technical advisor:
Din Zong Yu
Bin Bin Huang

Group Members:
Ding Ding
Jian Chong Zao
Zi Yu Chen
Ting Ting Yue
Shen Qun Tan
Bin Sun
Jie Zhang
Wen Jia He
Yifan Li

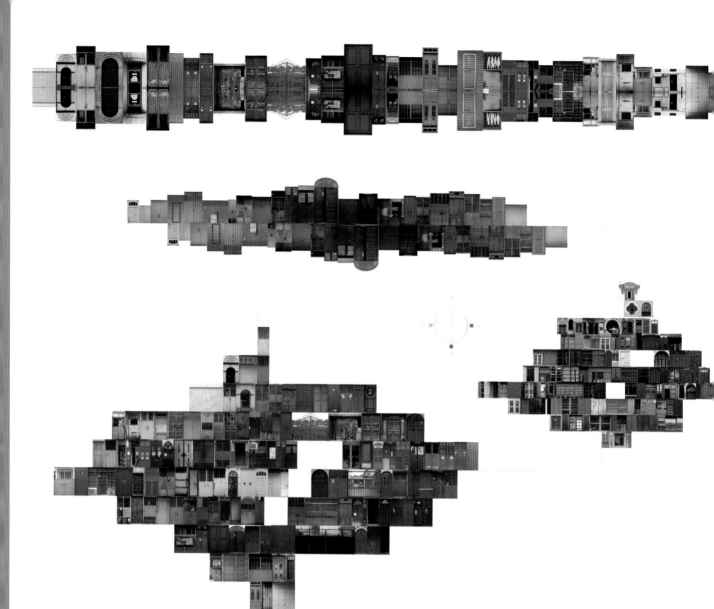

Analyses of color use on doors and windows
in Macao.
Locations of historic buildings in Macao.

Color spectrum chart of historic buildings where the dominant and secondary colors are recorded.

FROM RUSKIN TO PLEASANTVILLE: COLOR AS AN INSTRUMENT OF SOCIAL (DIS) AGREEMENT SUSAN NIGRA SNYDER & GEORGE E. THOMAS

Susan Nigra Snyder, an architect, is a partner in Civic**Visions** and teaches in the Urban Studies program at the University of Pennsylvania. Professional work focuses on transformation of towns and institutions to create places responsive to contemporary lifestyles; research and writing focus on the forces of consumption on urban form.

George E. Thomas, Ph.D., an historian, is a partner in Civic**Visions** and teaches in the Urban Studies program at the University of Pennsylvania. Professional work focuses on creating contemporary places that juxtapose new designs with historic fabric. Author of *Frank Furness: The Complete Works, William L. Price: From Arts and Crafts to Modern Architecture, Building America's First University,* and *Buildings of the United States: Philadelphia and Eastern Pennsylvania.*

1 Excerpt from the script (http://www.imsdb.com/scripts/Pleasantville.html) for PLEASANTVILLE: A Fairytale by Gary Ross. The movie Pleasantville: Nothing is as Simple as Black and White (1998) was written and directed by Gary Ross.

Bud Parker and William Johnson, you have been charged with desecration of a public building and the intentional use of prohibited paint colors in violation of the Pleasantville Code of Conduct and laws of common decency. Do you admit that on the night of May 1, you did consciously and willfully apply the following FORBIDDEN colors to the Pleasantville Town Hall:
(beat)
Red, Pink, Vermillion, Puce, Chartreuse, Umber, Blue, Aqua, Ox Blood, Green, Peach, Crimson, Yellow, Olive and Magenta.[1]

When 1990s' teenagers magically enter Pleasantville, a 1950s' television family drama similar to Father Knows Best, they confront a black-and-white world where colors they know from before landing in the television show are forbidden by the Code of Conduct. In Pleasantville color, whether on people or buildings, is considered "desecration." Whether "FORBIDDEN" or not conforming to "laws of common decency," either in a fictional place or in the real battles in modern historic districts and community associations, the choice of color is a window into a cultural battle that has been waged in many guises. Color choice is about far more than design, composition, aesthetics, pleasure, beauty, or ugliness. These are performative aspects that don't explain the deeply felt antagonisms that cultural battles elicit. The Pleasantville hearing isn't about what looks good or bad. Bud and William are charged with desecration because their act of using prohibited paint colors challenged the dominant hegemony of Pleasantville. Just look at the magenta and you know that change has arrived: the old guys are not in charge anymore, and they are afraid.

Color choice, like all cultural choices, is important because of what the choice communicates about how we express our identity. Choices are acts of consumption that express our relationships to categories of culture and thereby communicate social relations.[2] In contrast to the fixed nature of premodern culture, modern culture is constantly being redefined as battles are fought over who (or what group) has the power to make their choices matter and fix the meaning of that choice.[3] Except in the most enduring traditional societies where change is glacial and content is inherited, social agreement is an ongoing battle. In *In Not Being Seen Dead*, Mary Douglas favors hostility as a key motivating force in making cultural choices. Choices are not neutral. They announce cultural affiliations. To Douglas choice is against another group, hence the phrase, "I'd rather be dead than . . ." means that if one group gives in to another's choice, they lose their identity. Mutual hostility maintains stability.[4]

The battle fought in Pleasantville isn't about color; it is about power. Mary Douglas asks us to forget about utility, how something works, what it looks like, and instead to think about what it tells about social relationships.[5] Our interest in color choice is not just about correlating it to the cultural group that it represents but also understanding what the choices mean. From the battles over color, we can begin to understand cultural forces and operative worldviews.

EARLY COLOR: FROM SPECIFICITY TO UBIQUITY

One of the pleasures in driving through Great Britain and Ireland is reaching the villages that are sufficiently beyond the suburban edge of the great cities, where they become distinct places clearly different from the homogenized world of contemporary life. Rough-laid stone and thatched roofs characterize certain villages in Ireland; in Buckinghamshire, there is the vivid orange-red brick that Jordans village shares with the region around Exeter in an array of buildings from markets and churches to the rows of houses bordering streets; and who can forget the black-and-white speckled flint buildings of the old villages of East Anglia? Each of these places live in our memory because of the strong visual unity of their essential aspect, their color.

These villages are unified not by a design code like a New Urbanist village but rather because they are products of the vernacular, premodern world. As a consequence, their buildings reflect indigenous construction systems that evolved over centuries, using materials drawn from the immediate vicinity. It is this local character that we remember. As long as buildings were made from local materials using techniques handed down from generation to generation, each place was unified and consistent in form and color. Although early New England wood houses often varied in color, their pigments were earth tones, siennas, umbers, lamp black, and oxblood—colors that were local in origin. In a word, these places are highly specific, characterized as they are by local material and building practice.

Modern ubiquity began to triumph over vernacular specificity in the nineteenth century as two forces began to break down this unity. First was the rise in status of new groups, who chose to express their separate identities as political subgroups. The choice of architectural style became one such means, but was initially reserved for the super-wealthy who had the resources to commission architects. Identity was expressed in the political subgroup split. Whig-moderns represented what we call Regency with the sleek forms of John Soane, while the old elites draped their new country seats in the more conservative Rome-lite of the brothers Adam. But because most of these expressions of group identity

2 Mary Douglas and Byron Isherwood, *The World of Goods* (New York: Basic Books, 1979).

3 Ibid. 62–63.

4 Mary Douglas, *Thought Styles Critical Essays on Good Taste* (London: Sage, 1996), 82.

5 Douglas and Isherwood, *The World of Goods*, 43–47, 59–63.

Irish Village; John Vickary House, Newport RI, 1770; Greek Revival, Kennebunkport, ME; John Riddell Architectural Designs for Modern Country Residences; Kingscote Newport RI.

Colonial Revival Turns White, c. 1880; Stockton Row Cape May NJ 1971: Colonial Revival White applied to Victorian; Stockton Row Cape May NJ 1997: Return to California Version of Victorian Color.

Oatmeal Architecture Las Vegas NV 2003; Oatmeal Architecture Las Vegas NV 2000, photo by Susan Nigra Snyder and Steven Izenour.
All other images courtesy of George E. Thomas.

were still built of the local masonry, the resulting color continued to trump stylistic detail. It required the connoisseur to read the subtle tweaks of classical systems that connoted the different group identities.

The Greek Revival began at the end of the eighteenth century as an act of elite connoisseurship that incorporated new information about the Greek orders as depicted in Stuart and Revett's *Antiquities of Athens* (1762 ff.). Once again, because most of these façades were built of local stone, they maintained the local color. The controversy over Lord Elgin's removal from Greece of the Parthenon pediment sculptures and their subsequent purchase by the British government in 1816 made the Greek Revival into one of the first modern mass culture episodes. Almost overnight it found expression in buildings, furniture, and dress, capturing the buzz of the moment, the rise of democracies, western hostility to the Turkish takeover of Greece, and the poetry of Keats and Byron.

In its new guise as a mass phenomenon, the Greek Revival spread rapidly because it could be reduced to a minimal design strategy that was based on the incorrect but universal notion of the purity and whiteness of Greek architecture. Because the Greek Revival could be suggested using stone, stucco, or even just paint (depending on the budget), it soon became a favorite of developers who realized that a couple of slabs of stone or even planks of wood could connect their project to the style of the day—and by extension, to elite culture. Technology played a role as well. With the invention of cheap methods of producing white lead for paint, with its capacity to resist insects, mold, and rot, the Greek Revival style conspired to paint much of the western world white.

A second force that arose simultaneously was the construction of ever cheaper transportation systems. In the era of the horse and wagon, masonry moved but short distances. When the iron horse replaced nature's horse, masonry could be moved long distances for relatively low cost. Stones known for their beauty were shipped across ever greater distances, and in the process the unity of place was destroyed and replaced with the variety of choice that characterizes the modern building era.

By the middle of the nineteenth century, style and transportation formed the junction of possibility. New styles replaced old and made yesterday's mode look quickly dated in an endless tide of movements, each with a beginning, a peak, and a decline. The pendulum-swing theory of color choices can be explained as each new generation rose to power, expressed their distinct identity, and advanced their taste: first mid-nineteenth-century tans and earth tones; then Victorian polychromy; and later Beaux-Arts "city beautiful" monochromy for public buildings and simultaneous colonial revival white for homes (which persisted into the 1960s); countered by 1920s art deco with varied color; reversed by International Modern monochromy; and finally with the postmodern pattern and color.[6]

6 Pendulum-swing theory is discussed in Douglas, *Thought Styles*, 77–79.

But architectural color is about more than which group has the power to control the narrative. It also encapsulates cultural forces that are at the root of how architecture is perceived. In the United States, for example, democratic feelings reached a high pitch in the 1820s as the country neared its fiftieth anniversary and in turn made the Greek Revival and its white color a national phenomenon, reaching from Maine to Georgia and west to the frontier. Columned porticoes in white-painted wood, stucco, or stone linked houses, churches, public buildings, and banks to the collective culture and national identity of the new nation. By 1850, the Greek Revival was under attack by architectural writers and critics. What had happened?

The change was precipitated by the criticism of John Ruskin, whose *Seven Lamps of Architecture* sought to correct architectural expression from flights of baroque and classical fancy cheapened to mass-produced classical elements that appeared on every urban church. Ruskin instead sought the true principles of design, rooted in the Gothic, which he believed to be the only style appropriate to a Christian nation. Ruskin's theoretical frame advanced in *The Seven Lamps of Architecture* held that process and materials were valuable insofar as they were expressed truthfully. "Truth" of course is a loaded concept that, mixed with power and identity, authenticity and cost, is the fulcrum of what we recognize as the high and low architectural divide that dominated the century before the 1960s.

Truth also became the weapon that initiated the color wars of the mid-nineteenth-century United States. As at the end of the eighteenth century in Britain, self-created wealth gave new groups the opportunity to vie for elite status. What better way to put the new financial and industrial plutocrats in their place than denying them the value of their Greek porticoes? In the United States this was accomplished by Andrew Jackson Downing, who, despite being named for the renegade Tennessee president, was a staunch advocate of traditional elite values. Downing's *The Architecture of Country Houses* established the ground rules of midcentury cultural combat. Downing linked his writing to Ruskin's with the encyclopedic claim that "all beauty must be based on truth" which in turn recalls John Keats's "Beauty is truth, truth beauty,—that is all Ye know on earth, and all ye need to know."[7]

7 John Keats, *Ode to a Grecian Urn* (1819).

Downing's central topic was the artistic, country villa that was the ornament of the new wealthy lifestyle. He attacked the Greek Revival on the grounds of color, rather than its cultural connection to the political values of the nation: "The greater number of all country houses in the United States have been hitherto painted white – partly because white-lead is supposed to be a better preservative than other colors ... and partly from its giving an appearance of especial newness to a house, which, with many persons is in itself a recommendation." Downing then added the cudgel of taste to the whip of truth: "No person of taste, who gives the subject the least consideration, is, however, guilty of the mistake of painting or coloring country houses white" because "it is too glaring and conspicuous" and because "it does not harmonize with the country."[8] He concluded with a prescription: "We ought properly to employ modified shades, taken from the colors of the materials of which houses are constructed."[9] To make certain this point was understood, he added that the goal was the "unity of color in the house and the country around it."[10] In other words, the narrative of old money and the landholding classes was reified over the new narratives (Greek Revival, and by extension white) that represented the new money. Downing's conclusions became the basis for the pastoral character of the elite midcentury country houses that represented true status as exemplified in land ownership and not in the expression of great wealth, which Downing felt was inimical to American democracy. The color palette of the countryside again signified that the old elites controlled the narrative of what was "tasteful."[11]

8 Andrew Jackson Downing, *The Architecture of Country Houses* (New York: D. Appleton and Co., 1800), 198–199.

9 Ibid., 201.

10 Ibid., 202.

11 For the color palette of the era, see John Riddell *Architectural Designs for Model*

At the end of the nineteenth century, Thorstein Veblen applied anthropological investigative techniques to the modern elite in *Theory of the Leisure Class*. There he posited a simple means test for cultural significance in chapter 6, entitled "The Pecuniary Canons of Taste." Simply put, Veblen proposed that if something was expensive or even looked expensive, it was best. Ruskin's values were converted into the currency of the day, but the core idea remained: if truth was what mattered and it was more costly, and could not be afforded by all, so be it. The elites would have the valued art as a marker of their own importance and the poor would not. Class and culture were merged in the pyramid of taste.

COMMERCE INTO CULTURE

If the natural earth-tone palette meant "good taste" and associated those who choose these colors with wealth (preferably inherited wealth), what can be said about the vibrant colors forbidden in Pleasantville? While part of nature, the pigments were products of the scientific revolution of the nineteenth century, drawn from coal tar instead of ground earth and often termed "artificial." If, as Ruskin and Downing suggest, we see expressions of taste as markers of class, then the Pleasantville palette marks "bad taste" and presumably a lower social status. In *Distinction: A Social Critique of the Judgment of Taste*, Pierre Bourdieu, writing in 1979 reminds us that "the capacity to see (voir) is the function of knowledge (savoir)."[12] The code of cultural competence—a mix of education and social origin—enables us to respond aesthetically with prior knowledge of the meaning encoded. To see aesthetically is to understand the cultural code. Without the cultural code, we respond only to the sensible properties without comprehending meaning beyond an emotional response. Bourdieu explains how cultural competence fulfills the function of legitimizing social differences.[13] Thus cultural incompetence is expressed when the only response to a color palette is the feeling it elicits (e.g., gray tones of stone are "cold" and "drab," while yellow, pink, and magenta equal "warm" and "happy"). But if the nuances and derivation of the earth-tone palette in nineteenth-century architecture can be explained, then cultural competence is established.

When cultural competence is seen in dialectics of high-low brow or good-bad taste, it reflects the centralized order of society organized as a fixed hierarchy with elite, traditional culture in charge. Into the 1960s, this order was paralleled in the communication/transportation systems and urban form of the Industrial Age. Top-down control goes along with landline telephone systems, train routes aimed at centralized cities, and fixed social/cultural/taste distinctions. Repercussions of the underlying upheaval precipitated by WWII culminated in the 1960s' destruction of the dominant hegemony. This occurred in multiple arenas, signaling the beginning of a new decentralized order that appeared in spatial patterns, communications, and challenges to authority. The transition was marked by uncoordinated choices that blurred and pushed boundaries: the autonomy of the automobile and suburbanization began to erode the centralized form of the city, and the proliferation of the new television media changed how we communicated; Warhol challenged the boundaries of commerce and art; Venturi, Scott Brown, and Izenour used their study of Las Vegas to explore the changing form of the automobile-generated architecture/urbanism

Country Residences (Lippincott and Co, 1862). Citations for Downing are the 1850 edition, republished by Dover in 1969.

12 Pierre Bourdieu, *Distinction: A Social Critique of the Judgment of Taste* (Cambridge: Harvard University Press, 1979), 2.

13 Ibid., 7.

14 John Seabrook, *Nobrow: The Culture of Marketing, The Marketing of Culture* (New York: Vintage Books, 2000), 64–72. Tom Wolfe in *The Painted Word* (New York: Farrar, Straus and Giroux, 1975) divided the world into the 400 in "Cultureburg" who shaped the whole cultural frame of modernism while the rest of the world was looking elsewhere.

15 Seabrook, *Nobrow,* 92–94.

Hierarchical Culture diagram.

Buzz Culture diagram

(diagrams by Susan Nigra Snyder).

to include signs, ordinary buildings, and the automobile strip. By the beginning of the twenty-first century the old dominant hegemony that had defined good taste and culture had been displaced.

Such battles help us understand the arenas in which the new culture is being shaped. In 2000 John Seabrook chronicled his observations of a new cultural landscape in *Nobrow: The Culture of Marketing, The Marketing of Culture.* There he described the shift from what he terms "townhouse culture" (the traditional cultural hierarchy described by high, middle and mass culture) to "megastore" culture (the new cultural order described by identity, subculture, and mainstream culture). Seabrook noted that the dominant hegemony that once controlled the cultural arena had been displaced by what he calls the "Buzz"—the mix of media outlets that had become the new authority.[14]

The new order is characterized by fluidity and ever-changing dynamics flashing across our media screens that is not controlled by any one group. Cultural power today can begin in an individual identity that gathers acceptance as others join in agreement to become a subculture. The subculture rises to the mainstream culture via the media Buzz. For example a kid starts a garage band that becomes a local indie rock group that catapults to the mainstream at the Grammys. But as any kid will tell you, the minute a subculture goes mainstream it is abandoned in search of a new unique subculture, keeping the fluidity of the system in motion. This cultural order is open to anyone and increasingly democratic as the media outlets become more grassroots and less corporate. In this system the traditional elite culture hasn't disappeared, it is now merely one of the subcultures in play.

Unlike traditional culture, Buzz culture makes no distinction between culture and commerce, between price and value. In our classroom, the wood-grain laminate desks that meant fake, cheap, non-Ruskinian and drew the ire of design students as recently as a generation ago are now irrelevant as cultural markers. Traditional culture's internal social agreements placed culture in opposition to anything in the commercial realm where it was presumably corrupted by monetary agendas or considered déclassé. But, just as becoming a player in mainstream culture is open to any individual, the subject of what is culture is open to any source, and the most vibrant sources are arising from the commercial arena, not the academy.[15]

HISTORICAL PAINT COLORS VERSUS CELEBRITY/BRANDED COLORS

The means by which paint colors are sold reveals the tension between commerce and high culture. The currency of traditional culture is inheritance, authenticity, uniqueness, and quality; Buzz culture values choice, identity, celebrity, and experience. Historic paint colors validate ancestral homes, tradition, and the taste culture approved by the elite subculture, whereas the celebrity/branded colors exemplify the authority and power of the media-fueled Buzz. Consider the target audiences for "Valspar®" proud to be the only paint brand authenticated by the National Trust for Historic Preservation" and the celebrity paints of Laura Ashley, Ralph Lauren, and Martha Stewart. Disney Color is perhaps the most obvious example of merging brand identity into color choices. The Disney brand is best seen in gender-specific colors palettes. For boys there is "Disney Pixar: The World of Cars"; for 'tween girls, "Disney High School Musical"; for 'tween boys, "Disney Pirates of the Caribbean." In a reverse of Seabrook's Buzz bottom-up movement, Disney's mainstream movies become subcultures and eventually the identity children express in their room colors. For the elite sub-culture that values color as art, there are the full spectrum paint colors created by Donald Kaufman, who states: "I am a collaborative artist, the middleman between architects and designers and paint colors."[16] While all of these choices are subsumed into the commercial world of branding, the nuances of choice, identity, and how this reveals underlying values remain.

16 http://www.donaldkaufmancolor.com/

HISTORICAL GROUPS/TASTE POLICE BRIGADES /GATED COMMUNITIES

In the urban arena, battles over color are now fought before review boards that were formed so that upholders of traditional culture could retain power through rules and jurisdictional review. In 1997, when African-American shop owners Michelle and Barry Burton opened a new shop, "Mellonhead," in Philadelphia's old-elite community of Chestnut Hill they painted their storefront in bright col-ors. They were visited by Myrna Pope, head of the Aesthetics Committee, who "handed Michelle Burton a Finneran & Haley brochure showing the Authentic Colors of Historic Philadelphia, as approved by the National Park Service and Chestnut Hill's aesthetic committee and strongly suggested repainting."[17] The battle that ensued entwined race and taste with color and control. Pope argued that a store selling high-end art did not need bright colors:

17 Diana Marder, "A Matter of Aesthetic Standards / A Brighter Look Is Meeting Resistance in Chestnut Hill," *Philadelphia Inquirer*, December 6, 1997.

"Bright neon colors," Pope said, "are usually a sign that the economy is on the decline." To the press she added, the Burtons' color scheme "works beauti-fully in the southern climates, but it doesn't work in the northern climates."

"When you look at low-cost retail in various parts of the U.S., you tend to have very sharp colors—colors that you find in the Caribbean and in parts of Miami, and with that come low-end products," Pope said. "In order to sell high-end retail products, it's best to choose a conservative palette."[18]

18 Ibid.

Pope later tangled with a fellow member of the Aesthetics Committee who had installed a colorful façade for his new toy store:

"The O'Donnell family is one of the patriarchal families of Chestnut Hill," Pope said. "And you expect more from people like that."[19]

19 Ibid.

The Aesthetic Committee's conservative color palettes were a thin-ly veiled metaphor for the white elites with ancestral homes who held power. Anyone who stepped outside these bounds or belonged to another cultural/race/taste group threatened the social agreement for homogeneity in the community. The message is: conform or leave. The Burtons' store no longer exists in Chestnut Hill, but the O'Donnell family's toy store sign remains. All too often historical commissions use similar arguments for the same purposes.

New gated communities that have no claim to history or taste of elite families often control exterior color not to reify one group over an-other but to modulate choice within a limited range to maintain property val-ues. Uncertainty, the enemy of real estate values, is avoided by controlling any choice that might deviate from the normative masking identity differences. In Summerlin, a master-planned community in Las Vegas, Design Review Committees are part of the corporate management structure. Like Historical and Aesthetics Committees in older communities, they seek to assure "the con-tinuity of character which helps preserve the property appearance and seeks

20 Summerlin North Community Association Design Guidelines and Standards, August 31, 1994; updated November 2005, p. 5, Purpose. Real Property Management Group Inc. manages community governance documents for multiple communities in the Las Vegas area: http://www.rpmginc.com.

21 Gary Ross, *Pleasantville* (1998), reviewed by Edward Johnson-Ott. http://www.imdb.com/Reviews/149/14904

to protect the overall value of every property"[20] Most choices are limited to variations of what might be termed "oatmeal architecture"—a bland palette of shades of tan with accent color in earth tones. In the fast-changing commercial world, the ubiquity of oatmeal architecture reifies a bland, soulless, corporate world and is as controlled as Pleasantville. Gary Ross, the writer and director of Pleasantville, commented, "This movie is about the fact that personal repression gives rise to larger political oppression That when we're afraid of certain things in ourselves or we're afraid of change, we project those fears on to other things, and a lot of very ugly social situations can develop."[21] Again, control of color choice offers a window into underlying agendas and tensions in society.

NEW FRONTIERS/OLD BATTLES

In spite of the shift to a more fluid, dynamic cultural system, color battles are still animated by the canons of "good taste," whether defined by Ruskin, old elites, a community design review committee, or the new mantra of authenticity. As society becomes more atomized and anyone can be empowered by a voice on the web to create a subculture, ideologies have become the next arena where cultural battles are waged. New cultural forces, values and world views were predicted in the prescient 1975 novel, *Ecotopia*, which depicts a fictional utopia driven by ideology.

"The orchards, fields and fences looked healthy and surprisingly well cared for, almost like those of western Europe. Yet how dingy and unprosperous the farm buildings looked, compared to the white-painted farms or Iowa or New England! The Ecotopians must be positively allergic to paint. They build with rock, adobe, weathered board—apparently almost anything that comes to hand, and they lack the aesthetic sense that would lead them to give such materials a coat of concealing paint. They would apparently rather cover a house with vines or bushes than paint it."[22]

22 Ernest Callenbach, *Ecotopia: The Notebooks and Reports of William Weston* (New York: Bantam, 1975), 10.

The next frontier may not be in choice of paint color but in the rejection of applied color—a return to the natural mode of the nineteenth century but not for reasons of Truth or Honesty. Instead the ecological zealot values creating a sustainable environment free of toxic chemicals. Brown is the new green. At the same time technology offers a new counter as building façades comprised of media walls that project building-size LED videos can be figurative or abstract from the commercial or art world and can be any color. The Greenpix. Zero Energy Media wall by architect Simone Giostra in Beijing uses a photovoltaic laminate to capture solar energy to power the wall. It projects videos coloring the entire environment with dynamic changing colors and images.[23] Façades have collapsed into signs, into videos, into art, into commerce—all energy-friendly. Color choice is no longer fixed but reflects a state of being capable of satisfying any palette at any time. Suffice it to say, in the Nobrow ideologically driven identity world that we now occupy, the old elites and the Ecotopians, the electronic slices and yet unnamed subcultures that will surely arise will continue to harbor a hostility for each other. The battles over color will persist.

23 Carolina A. Miranda, http://tmagazine.blogs.nytimes.com/2008/06/25/oversize-art-the-energy-wall-of-china/ June 25, 2008

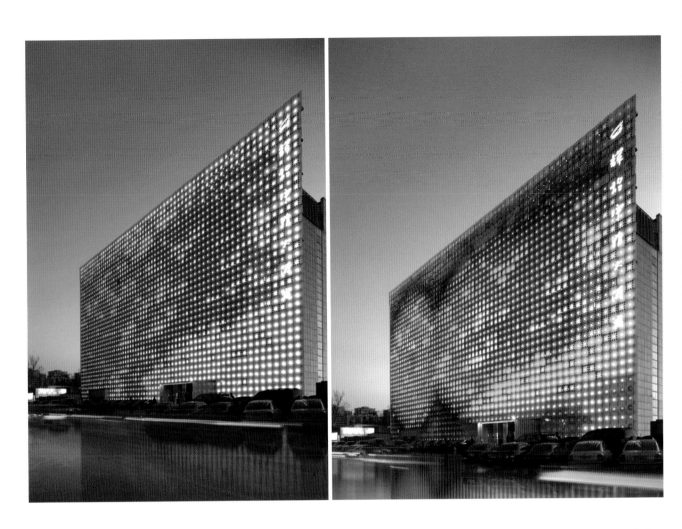

GreenPix—Zero Energy Media Wall. Nighttime photos showing different content projected on the wall (© Simone Giostra- ARUP-Ruogu).

ON NOT PERCEIVING URBAN COLOR
JOHN R. STILGOE

Author of many books, John R. Stilgoe is Orchard Professor in the History of Landscape at Harvard Graduate School of Design.

Barkentine *Morning Star* at the wharf, 1884. Photography by Nathaniel L. Stebbins. Courtesy of Historic New England. (RS# 18002)

1 Scant scholarship exists concerning how the erection of a new building alters perception of the color of adjacent ones.

2 In fairness to many otherwise educated observers, few other than painters knew (or know) how blocks of color appear when closely juxtaposed; see Howard Fisher, *Color in Art* (Cambridge, MA: Fogg Museum, 1974).

3 I base this assertion on a comprehensive content analysis of manufacturer advertising between 1934 and 1974 undertaken as part of an in-progress work on landscape perception; see also Ralph M. Evans: *Eye, Film, and Camera in Color Photography* (New York: John Wiley, 1959).

4 Or because no one knew how to write about it: see A. Maerz and M. Rea Paul, *A Dictionary of Color* (New York: McGraw-Hill, 1930).

5 Giovanni Brino and Franco Rosso, *Colore e citta: Il piano del colore di Torino, 1800-1850* (Trin: Idea, 1980) offers a useful example. In his *Builders' Architectural Drawing* (Chicago: Drake, 1904), Frederick T. Hodgson explained the draftsman's code that indicated sewers and drains in Prussian blue, granite in purple madder and pale India ink, electric-bell wires in yellow, "York and Soft Stone" in sepia, new brickwork in Roman ochre, and so on, with a particularly convoluted color scheme for concrete involving sepia *or* indigo *or* Payne's grey.

6 One reason scholars know so little about American perception involves the narrowness of the post-1900 public-school curriculum: wealthy, thoughtful parents educated children

Period perception of urban form vexes historians. Often structures and entire neighborhoods change dramatically over time, and retrospective inquirers face frustrating contemporaneous sources.[1] Written description proves oblique and maddening: educated writers often failed to remark on the proportion, scale, and especially color of structures, their skewed comments suggesting some inchoate mix of biased observation and half-conscious occlusion.[2] Monochrome photography further occluded the accurate notice paid only by rare painters and strengthened shape-based vocabulary against that grounded in color: the late 1930s' proliferation of color film paradoxically withered color vocabulary acuity, especially since film-manufacturer manuals emphasized non-urban subjects.[3] Urban color did not exist, not because architects and builders did not create it but because almost no one realized it.[4] Not there—a nothing not there, a nothing almost no one bothered to record since the mind's eye saw through it only to form—color drifted deeper into perceptual obscurity.

Certainly archeologists know the colors of period buildings: material-history scholars have many subtle tools to reveal such.[5] What scholars lack is even rudimentary glimpses of what earlier generations saw.[6] Paintings and colored engravings of whaling offer a striking parallel: almost never does one find the least depiction of blood or the oily, bloody water so evident in modern photographs of harpooning and flensing, a lack suggesting some powerful if unspoken artistic code.[7] Codes and expectations undoubtedly governed image-making as they do still.[8] Today anyone listening actively at the south doors of Pennsylvania Station in New York hears children exclaim at the lack of "tall buildings" as they exit and see only the massive but low-rise McKim, Mead & White–designed post office.[9] But as Stanley Milgram demonstrated conclusively in 1971, city dwellers perceive urban form differently than visitors: his seminal work suggests that not seeing urban color may be learned extremely subtly.[10] Not remembering color may be learned too.[11] But perhaps not seeing color is fundamentally doctrinal, a lingering after-effect of Victorian-era moralism defining color as fundamentally sinful and indeed "ethnic" in ways British Empire savants understood as distinctly infe rior, subversive, and certainly not "sober."[12]

Period urban photographs perpetuate dichotomous illusion. Images of port cities especially reward sustained scrutiny. Readers of William H. Bunting's *Boston: Portrait of a Port* infrequently realize the lack of wind obvious in many photographs: water surfaces often indicate the flat calm that mid-nineteenth-century photographers so valued. In-port stillness prompted ship-masters to dry sails in the all-amidships positions marine painters hagiographied centuries earlier: many harbor photographs now too casually understood as "ships under sail" depict sails rigged only to dry. Calm enabled post-1860s pho-tographers huddled behind tripod-mounted, slow-shutter view cameras to make

in extracurricular ways using the series by William G. Whitford, Edna B. Like, and William S. Gray, *Art Stories* (Chicago: Scott, Foresman, 1934); Book Two, for example, is about first-class cars on long-distance trains.

7 The New Bedford Whaling Museum holds many paintings and a copy of almost every known engraving: to my knowledge, none depicts the oily bloodiness so apparent in its collection of color photographs.

8 Educated American adults still claim to see indigo in the standard-array prism colors, but the color exists only because Isaac Newton worried that six colors might indicate the workings of Satan: see also Johann Wolfgang von Goethe, *Theory of Colours* [1810], trans. Charles Lock Eastlake (London: Murray, 1840) and Johannes Itten, *The Elements of Color* (New York: Van Nostrand, 1970) for alternatives to Newtonian color theory.

9 Over decades the author has listened actively to tourists leaving Penn Station and walking into Times Square (which is definitely not square).

10 Milgram, "Experience of Living in Cities," *Science* 167 (March 13, 1970), 1461–1468: when it appeared, this seminal article prompted me to consciously examine differences in urban perception, not only among different cohorts of people but among different cities; now, forty years later, I am at work on a monograph concerning those differences.

11 See, for example, Winston Churchill, *Painting as a Pastime* (New York: Cornerstone, 1950), 30.

12 The extent to which the Victorian "reform of manners" still affects educated westerners lies beyond the scope of this essay; but see, for example, Stephen Tomkins, *William Wilberforce: A Biography* (New York: Oxford University Press, 2007), Anne Stott, *Hannah More: The First Victorian* (New York: Oxford University Press, 2003), and Philip Davis, *The Victorians, 1830–1880* (New York: Oxford University Press, 2002).

13 W. H. Bunting, *Portrait of a Port: Boston, 1852–1914* Cambridge, MA: Harvard University Press, 1971), xv.

14 Earle G. Shettleworth, Jr., and W. H. Bunting, *An Eye for the Coast: The Maritime and Monhegan Island Photographs of Eric Hudson* (Gardiner, ME: Tilbury House, 1998).

slow-emulsion (ISO 2 or 3 in contemporary measurement) exposures without worrying about multiple moving vessels blocking views of context and each other, or waves or shivering sails rendering as blur. Sundays permitted photographers to work without interruption, but the images now beguile and trick: observers typically fail to note Sabbath inactivity. "I think that one's obvious reaction when observing old photographs is simply to measure the scenes against the present," Bunting asserts. "It is just as important to measure them against their own heritage. To the people in the photographs, and to the photographers, our present was an unimaginable abstraction."[13] Contemporaneous color endures as occluded abstraction too: never does the contemporary viewer muse about the color variation causing difference in tone and never does the observer imagine what the monochrome photograph abstracted then from its real-world subject. Only rarely do inquirers compare photographs with paintings.

In *An Eye for the Coast: The Maritime and Monhegan Island Photographs of Eric Hudson*, Bunting and Earle G. Shettleworth emphasize that painters discovering handheld cameras in the late 1880s distinguished consciously between capacities of paint and monochrome negative film, especially in port-city work. Hudson knew not only the painterly tradition but how to make successful a bifurcated career painting and photographing ships in both urban and rural locales. In Venice, Boston, and especially New York, he recorded the urban context of ships, barges, and small boats in ways markedly different than those he employed to frame images near Monhegan and other Maine-coast islands. Hand-held cameras enabled him to work in improvisational ways impossible with slow-plate, tripod-mounted view cameras: he could record vessels moving in rising wind and waves. He understood color differently in urban ports than in small fishing harbors.[14] Tiny harbors thronged with anchored vessels seemed more urban than the widely scattered houses on the treeless slopes above the ports: urban form rode to anchor, and owners had painted their sloops and schooners brightly, in marked contrast to unpainted, weathered terrestrial structures.[15]

At the start of the twenty-first century, period port-city photographs gull even meditative viewers. Monochrome images trick observers into equating buildings with ships, not so much in terms of form but of color. An astute scrutinizer of urban Boston discovers that in summer the *USS Constitution* remains one of the tallest forms in the city. With its topmasts set up, Old Ironsides suggests not only what height meant in early nineteenth-century Boston but what even taller late-nineteenth-century sailing ships meant in an urban context often designed to accommodate them. The MBTA viaduct adjacent to the Charles River Basin lock includes a drawbridge so that sailing ships might enter the lock beyond and proceed up river until blocked by Longfellow Bridge. Travelers found true urban verticality only in port cities, even with ships absent.[16] But almost never does anyone realize that the ships boasted bold, often vibrant color schemes unlike those of almost any building. Color remains as absent from the contemporary imaginative view as it remains absent from the period monochrome image.[17]

In 1905 Joseph Conrad analyzed juxtapositions of bright-painted sailing ships and soot-grimed urban structure, studying at length the wrenching incongruities of the London docks. A sailing ship "with a landscape of green hills and charming bays opening around her anchorage" remains stately even when surrounded by lighters, he asserted in *The Mirror of the Sea*, but when docked next to begrimed warehouses becomes brutalized. "It is only then that the odious, rectangular shadows of walls and roofs fall upon her decks, with showers of soot." Conrad enumerated the indecencies of coal smoke, a second cousin to the black dust that smothered sailing ships unloading coal in London, a blackening more permanent than shadow. Ships arrived from sea clean, almost bleached, and with their bright paint refreshed on standing orders from ship owners. Conrad emphasized that one such ship might have been a staggering vision to city dwellers, but in the 1870s vessels stretched around the docklands a quarter mile abreast at a time,[18] Fifty ships "used to overhang in a serried rank the muddy pavement by the side of New South Dock," he recalled, "as if assembled there for an exhibition, not of a great industry, but of a great art." Some "just out of dry-dock with their paint glistening freshly," others in from the sea: "their colours were grey, black, dark green, with a narrow strip of yellow moulding defining their sheer, or with a row of painted ports." But even such parti-colored vessels emerged from many ports smothered in "the infernal gritty night of a cloud of coal-dust," something requiring stormy days at sea to put right. London and other general-cargo ports proved cleaner than colliery ones, but "the dust and ashes of the London atmosphere" transformed overnight clean, brightly painted sailing vessels and later, steamships.[19] Shadowed in rectilinear shade, then begrimed, especially in mist and light rain they lost color and individual identity as they fused into monochrome urban structure.[20]

The mere presence of sailing ships in the centers of many cities remains alien to many historians of urban form who perforce ignore the great blocks of bold, often primary color. Conrad marveled at Antwerp, Nantes, Bordeaux, and Rouen, where stores, cafés, and even opera houses directly abutted wharves in ways most unlike London and Amsterdam, whose docklands lay far from elites.[21] In 1933 Alexander Bone (another former merchant ship officer) ruminated on ships running their bowsprits far into residential neighborhoods, "high and dry, amid the backyard washings of London's sailor town," and like Conrad understood ships as iridescent interruptions in grime. Coal smoke soiled any building even as carpenters and masons completed it, and foiled the efforts of building painters and artists alike. *Bowsprit Ashore* opens with Bone noticing a photograph of a bowsprit belonging to his first ship: like Conrad, who could remark acutely on the olive color of hurricane clouds, Bone loved form, light, and color, none of which he understood as especially germane to any description of London.[22]

In the 1920s H. M. Tomlinson probed the ways light, odor, and color combined to shape understanding of home cities and far-distant ports: his *Gifts of Fortune and Hints for Those About to Travel* recognizes that coal grime distinguishes all British cities from his first-visited foreign one, Oran. London smelled of coal smoke and the hot grease of steam tractors prowling its streets: such smells conjure visions of it no matter how far away Tomlinson sailed, and all prove invariably gray. Structural grayness merely stage-sets the wet, gray weather foreigners associate with London: "the wind will begin to back. We are not at once aware of the reason for it, but the colours fade from the earth and from one's spirit. The light dims." As he steamed into the Indian Ocean, Tomlinson teased out the intricacies of the British inability to dissect the grayness of London and other coastal cities and to consciously know it as a fundamental context of British travel perceptions and of a worldview colonials suspected. He valued and acknowledged perpetuating the old language of de-

15 "Openness" became a specific concept in American urban reform as early as 1850, when Sylvester Judd argued for it in *Richard Edney and the Governor's Family: A Rus-Urban Tale* (Boston: Phillips, 1850), especially pp. 322–324. Putting that concept in the context of a crowded harbor proves difficult nowadays, especially if the historian must assume the ships to be colorful and the "density" (to use Judd's term) monochrome.

16 At least until the skyscraper era began in Chicago.

17 This is a powerful theme as late as Peter Barlow's *Marine Photography* (New York: Motor Boating, 1973). The scope of this article does not allow me to introduce my ongoing research into the differences between architectural, marine architectural, and landscape architectural photography after 1915.

18 Abreast, not bow-to-stern. The sheer mass of docked sailing ships, especially in London but also in New York, now proves awkward to analyze as a constituent element of urban form. Conrad assumed readers knew the 36–foot beam [width] of the narrow clipper *Cutty Sark* (launched 1869) and could thus imagine how many such ships needed to be docked side by side to occupy 1,200 feet of dock-space frontage.

19 Joseph Conrad, *The Mirror of the Sea* [1905] (New York: Doubleday, 1938), 116–117, 129–130, 111.

20 William McFee explores a similar phenomenon, although in the harbor of Salonika. See his *More Harbours of Memory* (Garden City, NY: Doubleday, 1934), especially pp. 26-28.

21 *Mirror of the Sea*, pp. 107, 48.

22 Alexander H. Bone, *Bowsprit Ashore* (Garden City, NY: Doubleday, 1933), xix. Conrad, *Mirror*, 79.

23 H. M. Tomlinson, *Gifts of Fortune and Hints for Those About to Travel* (New York: Harper, 1926), pp. 43, 232.

24 H. M. Tomlinson, *Out of Soundings* (London: Heinemann, 1931), 177: on the impacts of cinema and broadcast radio, see especially pp. 115–117, 144–145.

25 Contemporary students no longer imagine the smells of cities, perhaps especially horse manure and tobacco.

26 The perceptions of Britons (and Americans) arriving by sea in brightly lit harbors (especially in the Mediterranean and Caribbean) reward scrutiny but lies far beyond the scope of this essay. For a period introduction, see Charles. J. Makin, *With Pen and Camera in Three Continents* (London: Tribune, 1913).

27 Marine camouflage offers a stunning introduction into what mariners from different countries notice at sea. For an introduction, see John Lovell, "Camouflage and Cubism," *Art Express* I (November–December, 1981), 23–29 and Scott Gerwehr, "Cross-Cultural Variation in Denial and Deception," *Defense Intelligence Journal* 15 (May 2006), 51–80.

28 This is a peculiarly powerful argument once one understands that in Hebrew the name Adam means at root "red" and "alive." See Manlio Brusatin *A History of Colors*, trans. Robert H. Hopcke and Paul Schwart (London: Shambhala, 1991), 23.

29 Trans. R. J. Hollingdale, eds: Maudemarie Clark and Brian Leiter (Cambridge: Cambridge University Press, 1997), sec. 426–427, 433. The foci of such art lies beyond the scope of this essay but here Nietzsche appears to predict the post-1920s division between painting and popular illustration, cinema, and radio-broadcast music.

scription in an era of roll-film photography and cinematography and wondered if anyone noticed architectural color.[23] "There is an avenue of old trees leading up to the house in which the full day is but a greenish twilight," he wrote in *Out of Soundings* [1931] of a South of France estate. "When the house is seen in sunlight beyond the framing end of the avenue, its front, of Caen limestone, looking to the south, seems self-luminous and of the placid shine and colour of a newly-risen harvest moon." But he argued that realizing such places, especially the greenish twilight cast by trees, became more difficult and less common each day, as monochrome motion pictures captivated and then skewed the perception of ordinary Britons, whose other senses often proved immune to modernization. The tobacco shop seemed "a good substitute for sunny weather," and the smell of tobacco implied that some certainties endured from the era before World War I.[24] London smelled of good tobacco on rare sunny days, of coal smoke and hot grease on most others, and everywhere in the tropics Tomlinson envisioned gray days when he smelled the common smells of burning coal and steam engines.[25] Monochrome motion pictures only exacerbated the British way of seeing in gray, through gray, and to gray, especially in cities.[26]

Not seeing urban color consciously, not realizing it, not reifying it, exists as part of a larger philosophical conundrum that nowadays belies global-village cheeriness and consequently puzzles many shrinking-planet advocates. Cultures perceive color differently, and often realize (or fail to realize) some color at all.[27] Philosophers probe past Conrad and Tomlinson and encounter calamities like the storms presaged by olive-green sky.

"How different nature must have appeared to the Greeks if, as we have to admit, their eyes were blind to blue and green, and instead of the former saw deep brown, instead of the latter yellow (so that they used the same word, for example, to describe the colour of dark hair, that of the cornflower, and that of the southern sea)," Friedrich Nietzsche averred in his 1881 *Daybreak: Thoughts on the Prejudices of Morality*, "and again the same word for the colour of the greenest plants and that of the human skin, honey, and yellow resins." Having accepted contemporaneous archeological reports as buttressing classical scholarship, he determined that "their greatest painters reproduced their world using only black, white, red and yellow," and concluded that the ancient Greeks saw nature through a lens of human-body colors which made all nature the emanation of humanoid gods and demigods.[28] But then Nietzsche shifted aim. "Every thinker paints his world in fewer colours than *are actually there*, and is blind to certain individual colors," he insisted. "And even today many an individual works himself out of a partial colourblindness into a richer seeing and distinguishing: in which process, however, he not only discovers new enjoyments but is also *obliged to give up and relinquish* some of his earlier ones." Nietzsche understood modern color awareness as paralleling modern landscape architecture, arguing that "rococo horticulture arose from the feeling 'nature is ugly, savage, boring—come! Let us beautify it!'" Designed landscape became (at least for some) a "deception of the eyes," a new-constructed whole deflecting attention from the beauty of wilderness and city and a paradigm of the beautification he predicted would happen to science as its inquiries became a new entertainment subject. Artistic realism involved happiness, he concluded, and "the kind of beauty we can most easily grasp and enjoy" would shape the art that modern westerners would value most highly.[29] His argument proved prescient.

In the early 1970s, cultural color perception became a treacherous subject as global politics and trade, especially distribution of motion pictures and television programming, embroiled scholars in intractable issues.[30] In 1972, for example, Toshihiko Izutsu undertook to explain the cultural forces producing "the negative attitude toward colour" which "is in fact characteristic of the Far Eastern aesthetic experience." He focused on Chinese and Japanese brush-and-ink painting, arguing that "in this monochromic world of artistic creation, the inexhaustible profusion and intricacy of the forms and colours of Nature is reduced to an extremely simplified and austere scheme of black outlines and a few discrete touches of washes of ink here and there, sometimes in glistening black, sometimes watered down to vaporous grey." But such painting fails to represent the fierce Japanese love of color that ebbs and flows over centuries, the love reaching its highest mark in the Momoyama Period (1573–1615). Warrior leaders built castles with interiors painted in "crimson, purple, lapis, emerald, and blue on backgrounds of pure gold," what he calls "a flowery mosaic of rich colours" utterly unrepresented in the brush-and-ink painting of the same period. Izutsu argues that the painting exists in a separate conceptual continuum of experience: thus it matters more to (and perhaps should be viewed only by) those who have had disciplined experience of natural and constructed color.[31] Especially, he remarks on the importance of experiencing "tinted maple leaves" in order to value their rendering in brush-and-ink monochrome, and then to understand that black best represents those frost-tinged leaves manifesting themselves as red. Although each color harbors within it all other colors, only black accurately represents each in all, and while the maple leaves will be another color very soon the painting endures across time.[32]

Maple trees work strongly in Japanese and North American visual culture and distinguish both from that of Britain, which lacks maples. British forests have few trees that turn red with the frost, and autumn produces rural and forested landscapes marked by yellows and browns (especially the khaki colors of the oaks and beeches) punctuated by the gold of birches. Across much of North America the maple fundamentally alters the seasonal color of forest: its leaves define not only much Canadian understanding of landscape, periodicity, and even nationhood (the maple leaf being the national symbol) but a striking amount of New England selfhood.[33] While New Englanders value maples in part for their variegated post-frost color range, only rarely does the leafless maple now strike viewers as something very like a ship's mast and spars seen through many other bare masts. In their leafless form many deciduous species evoke (or once evoked) sailing ships in dock, sails furled or stowed away, bare masts against the sky, masts and spars seen through masts and spars and other maritime verticality.[34] Landsmen arriving by land at prosperous coastal cities once saw "forests of masts" above abutting buildings and bowsprits overhanging harbor-frontage streets as spreading maple limbs once overhung rural roads.[35] Such landsmen had typically walked from rural through suburban landscape into urban form, passing through zones of color and form nowadays difficult to reconstruct as perceptual forces, let alone as colored objects.

Travelers (pedestrian and equestrian) moved through regions dominated by domesticated plants, and understood the color and shape of plants to indicate type of crops and condition and season. Farmhouses, barns, and other agricultural structures tended to be unpainted (and thus the color of weathering

30 A handful of American manufacturers had been embroiled in the subject since the 1910s. See, for example, American Colortype Company, *Business Uses for Color Photography* (Chicago: The Company, 1911).

31 By extrapolation, perhaps, the colored whaling engravings should be viewed only by those accustomed to bloodshed; the monochrome ones prove suitable for any viewer.

32 Toshihiko Izutsu, "The Elimination of Colour in Far Eastern Art and Philosophy" [1972], *Color Symbolism: Six Excerpts from the Eranos Yearbook 1972* (Dallas: Spring, 1977), 167-195.

33 Over decades I have learned that Harvard University students know the maple leaf as the national symbol of Canada, but almost never know its color.

34 Augsut Endell, *Zauberland des sichtbaren* (Berlin-Westend: Verlag der gartenschönheit, 1928) proves useful in this regard.
35 E. Keble Chatterton, *Fore and Aft* (London: Seeley, Service, 1912), 117.

36 In *Borderland: Origins of the American Suburb, 1820–1939* (New Haven: Yale University Press, 1988), I argue that scholars typically imagine suburbs as perceived by people leaving cities despite migration patterns demonstrating that vast numbers saw suburbs before entering urban form.

37 Smaller vessels in nineteenth-century harbors often freighted building stone, like the brownstone brought to Manhattan by Hudson River sloops and small schooners operating from the Connecticut coast.

38 Spires tended to be leaded, and thus gray.

39 Pamela W. Hawkes, "Economical Painting: The Tools and Techniques Used in Exterior Painting in the 19th Century," *The Technology of Historic American Buildings: Studies of the Materials, Craft Processes, and the Mechanization of Building Construction,* ed. H. Ward Jandl (Washington, D.C.: Foundation for Preservation Technology, 1983), 189–220. This excellent essay analyzes the expense of painting all kinds of buildings.

40 See my *Metropolitan Corridor: Railroads and the American Scene* (New Haven: Yale University Press, 1983), 17–48.

41 See, for example, *Architectural Brickwork* [1878], ed. David Jenkins (Secaucus, NJ: Wellfleet, 1990).

42 The kaleidoscope of color along South Street in Manhattan has not yet received the historical attention it deserves. For passengers, the ocean voyage began in a liminal zone of bright, chaotic color.

43 The lack of mature trees in urban cities and especially along waterfronts has received little scholarly attention. Typically urban builders felled most trees in land-clearing operations (or for fuel) and did not plant even shade trees in part because insurance companies thought trees communicated fire among buildings. But mature trees threatened windows, scraped façades, and tended to fall over in great storms; even today, few cities lack 100-foot-tall trees outside of great parks. The immense trees that suburbanites unthinkingly accept are rare in urban form.

wood) or painted in a simple palette of house white and barn red. Urban zones boasted only more white-painted houses and a preponderance of unpainted commercial and industrial structures, often with roofs and sides clad in long-lasting white cedar shingles.[36] More important buildings stood in brick or stone, the latter built of locally quarried stone because moving stone overland proved extremely expensive.[37] With the exception of church spires, few buildings stood more than two-and-a-half stories and until the freight-elevator era, even in dense cities few stood more than four.[38] Until the 1920s, then, most travelers arrived in cities through roughly demarcated zones of dispersed low built form typically colored in "earth" tones, with the exception of white-painted houses.[39] Newcomers emerging at street level from underground railroad terminals might stare about in surprise, but even then they tended to boggle at the size of the Manhattan post office across the street from Pennsylvania Station but not note its gray tones.[40] At the core of cities, local brick and stone formed the palette: experimentation with patterning brick did little to alleviate sameness immediately masked by grime and soot.[41] Only when arriving at inner harbors and at dockside did newcomers note the immense forms of ship's masts, the curving shape of hulls, and above all, the bold and gleaming paint as combining to make the massed docked ships different from the near-monochrome urban form immediately adjacent.[42]

Those arriving by boat disembarked near city centers usually lacking mature trees.[43] They remarked on only the near-seamless, earth- or grime-colored environment before them if they remarked on anything at all. Terrestrial color lay beyond, in forests, woodlots, and agricultural fields, and landsmen and seamen alike noticed it and remarked on it perhaps because such color originated in divinity, not sinfulness.

Even the educated nowadays forget the early nineteenth-century transformation of British (and then American) culture engineered by William Wilberforce and other politicians and by Hannah More (among other moralists) who created what is today designated Victorian morality and is still the unnamed Victorian aesthetic. They argued for sobriety and seriousness, dismissed color as frivolous if not worse, and they valued form over color in distinctly imperialist ways: in his 1879 *Modern Chromatics*, Ogden N. Rood wrote easily about the "colour-education of the race." The blacks, whites, and grays of Victorian morality (and Victorian fashion), according to Rood, explain why "buildings are painted with various sober tints."[44] Bold, vibrant colors belong to a suspect world beyond urban control, and perhaps particularly to the sea and to ships: As Goethe remarked as early as 1810, the little black dress makes women appear smaller than light-colored ones, but the triumph of black/white/gray bourgeois moralism and attire cast the bright-colored clothing of southern Europe into scandal and invisibility.[45]

Any study of urban color perception might analyze terra-cotta, the fired earth tiles available by 1900 in multiple colors, often in very bright glazes intended to punctuate the stuttering end of Victorian narrowness. By 1925 the Ludowici-Celadon Company in Chicago furnished roofing tile and other shapes in olive, emerald, Brookville and dull green, a range of yellows, blues, and browns, along with more traditional red, black, and Imperial Spanish.[46] Between the early 1890s (largely due to the example of the 1893 Columbian Exposition and the subsequent use of deep-yellow terra cotta by McKim, Mead & White) and the early 1930s, younger architects and daring corporate clients rejoiced in the striking beauty of terra-cotta color.[47] But terra-cotta surfaces appealed to everyone on another level: the glazed surfaces cleaned themselves in rain, something of extraordinary significance in cities burning soft coal, especially London.[48] After the long interruption caused by the Depression and World War II, architects and clients favored much less expensive and more modern structures built of concrete, steel, plate glass, and chrome-plated metal and aluminum. But those new structures rose in large part because cities no longer heated with soft coal and had become markedly cleaner, something of great importance to a rising generation of young women office workers anxious to wear pastels and other colors against neutral backdrops.[49] By the early 1970s, Milgram understood the subtleties of urban perceptual learning, including changed attitudes involving the moralism of colorful clothing, but urban historians studiously ignore the late-1920s architectural fascination with terra-cotta.

Although spatial perception (at least for navigating officers) abruptly changes when mariners shift from Mercator-projection charts (where the rhumb line depicts a magnetic course) to coastal charts (representing a "flat" scaled depiction of coastline and harbors), perhaps color perception does (or did) too.[50] Air travel discombobulated generations raised to value Mercator-projection maps: as early as 1930 experts worried that airline travel might distort children's world–views as sharply as viewing motion pictures, and by 1943 geographers realized that peacetime air routes would wreck school-room and college-classroom cartographical understanding.[51] But after the early-1970s burst of scholarly activity involving cross-cultural color perception, scholars have ignored the awkward issues involving period and contemporary perception of urban color just as public-school curricula studiously ignores post-1940s non-Mercator mapping. Marine preservationists noted as early as 1990 that period painting demonstrates that seventeenth- and eighteenth-century ships and small boats boasted extremely bright colors (red, yellow, blue, orange, and bright green especially) lost to "conservative and sober" ones in the Victorian era.[52] Anglo-American color perception shifted massively by the close of that era, causing any inquirer to wonder if the coloration of so many modern buildings endures as an after-effect of the Victorian sobriety, piety, and moralism that still governs men's formal and everyday work attire and much of the everyday wardrobe of educated, modest women. Black-tie and the little black dress take their antecedents in an era in which Britons and Americans turned from color as though color involved frivolity and worse. Today some of the most brightly colored urban form lies docked far up Chelsea Creek in a part of the city architects rarely visit.

BALDWIN COOLIDGE, Phot.

44 (New York: Appleton, 1879), 307.

45 Johann Wolfgang von Goethe, *Theory of Colours* [1810], trans. Charles Lock Eastlake (Cambridge, MA: MIT Press, 1970), pp. 6, 27–28, 327 and passim. Eastlake translated the book into English in 1840, as the trajectory of Victorian-era moral reform sharpened.

46 *Roofing Tiles* (Chicago: Ludowici-Celadon Co., 1925), 1.

47 See, for example, Virginia Guest Ferriday, *Last of the Handmade Buildings: Glazed Terra Cotta in Downtown Portland* (Portland: Mark, 1984), especially pp. 2–7.

48 Paul N. Hasluck, *Terra Cotta Work* (London: Cassell, 1905) makes this argument throughout. See also Robert C. Mack, "The Manufacture and Use of Architectural Terra Cotta in the United States," *Technology of Historic American Buildings*, 117–151.

49 At the end of the 1920s, architectural innovation (especially in terra-cotta color) and fashion commingled in ways that excited many observers. Most of the February, 1930 issue of *Fortune* reflects an extraordinary energy withered by 1932 and not apparent again until the middle 1960s. Neutral buildings enable the urban street to become a stage-set for women wearing colorful clothing. The neutral-painted office enabled IBM to experiment with bright-colored electric typewriters and other equipment used only by women employees.

50 See, for example, John Q. Stewart, "The Use and Abuse of Map Projections," *Geographical Review* 33 (October 1943), 589–604 and Peabody Gardner, *Ready About: Sailing Adventures Down East* (New York: Barnes, 1959), especially pp. 129, 160–161.

51 Clarence D. Chamberlin, "Shall We Let Our Children Fly?" *Parents' Magazine* 5 (January 1930), 14–16 is a useful introduction. See also "The Geography of Post-War Air Routes," *Geographical Journal* CIII (March 1944), 89–100.

52 Maynard Bray, "Painting for Decoration," *WoodenBoat* 93 (March/April, 1990), 42–50.

T-Wharf, Boston, Mass., ca. 1885. Photograph by Baldwin Coolidge. Courtesy of Historic New England. (RS# 001753)

THE COLORS OF WATER: HYDROLOGY AND HUMAN EXPERIENCE AT THE TAJ MAHAL JAMES L. WESCOAT JR.

James Wescoat, Aga Khan Professor of Architecture at MIT, is a landscape historian of Mughal gardens in South Asia, an environmental geographer focusing on water management and policy, and a conservationist who has worked on Indo-Islamic sites in India and Pakistan. His research has concentrated on water systems in South Asia and the US from the site to river basin scales.

Fig. 1: This satellite image of the Taj Mahal was collected on Oct 17, 2009 by GeoEye-1. GeoEye-1 is in a sun synchronous orbit 423 miles above the earth.

 GeoEye

1 Ebba Koch, "The Mughal Waterfront Garden," in *Gardens in the Time of the Great Muslim Empires: Theory and Design* edited by Attilio Petruccioli (Leiden: E.J. Brill, 1997), 140–60.

2 David L. Haberman, *River of Love in an Age of Pollution: The Yamuna River of Northern India* (Berkeley: University of California Press, 2006).

3 C. Singh, "Early 18th Century Painted City Maps on Cloth," in *Facets of Indian Art*, edited by Robert Skelton (London: Victoria and Albert Museum, 1986), 185–192.

4 Ebba Koch, *The Complete Taj Mahal* (London: Thames & Hudson, 2006).

5 Wayne E. Begley and Z.A. Desai, *Taj Mahal: The Illumined Tomb: An Anthology of Seventeenth-Century Mughal and European Documentary Sources* (Cambridge, MA: Aga Khan Program for Islamic Architecture, 1989).

6 James L. Wescoat Jr., "Landscape Heritage Conservation in Agra: An Historical-Geographic Perspective,"*in Taj Mahal Heritage Conservation*

THE TAJ MAHAL AND RIVER YAMUNA

Far from being colorless, water mirrors the mood of the landscapes through which it flows in a full spectrum of colors. This is nowhere more evident than at the Taj Mahal, constructed by the Mughal ruler Shah Jahan in the mid-seventeenth century in the city of Agra along the river Yamuna.[1] The Yamuna has been a sacred goddess for many in India.[2] Her primary color is green, while her brother Yama, god of death, is associated with black. The Yamuna originates in Himalayan snow and ice fields, flowing through partially forested piedmont hills out onto the irrigated plains. Massive canals date back to Sultanate times (fourteenth century BCE), but the scale of river diversions above Delhi escalated dramatically in the nineteenth and twentieth centuries, leaving little in the river but wastewater return flows in all but the monsoon months of the year. Even these waters are now withdrawn to supply Agra, which in turn discharges largely untreated wastewater back into the channel that flows downstream to its confluence with the Ganges and legendary Saraswati River at the city of Allahabad or Prayag.

Historical maps and modern satellite imagery help reveal the context, layout, and colors of the Taj Mahal complex (Fig. 1).[3] Its white marble tomb was built along the Yamuna River terrace, which was lined on both sides by walled rectangular gardens of the Mughal nobility (Fig. 2). In Mughal times, visitors to the Taj Mahal arrived at a square marketplace known as Taj Ganj, where they could bathe and prepare to enter the forecourt (*jilu khana*) of the tomb-garden.[4] They entered a massive red sandstone gate with white and black marble inlay inscriptions from the Quran, into a square, lushly planted garden divided into quadrants from broad water channels that emanate from a raised white marble pool in the center of the garden. The axial channels and abundant plantings lead to the white marble-clad plinth and tomb of the Taj Mahal. From the plinth, one sees the recently restored Moonlight Garden (*Mahtab bagh*) directly across the river, with the Yamuna flowing between the Taj Mahal and Moonlight Garden in a manner that evokes passages of the Quran that describe the paradise that awaits the faithful on the day of judgment as "gardens underneath which rivers flow" (e.g. *Sura 3:136 passim*).[5] The long record of conservation projects and controversies related to the Taj Mahal landscape range from embankments to excavation of piping and replacement of fountains.[6] Conventional approaches to waterworks conservation have been eclectic and fragmented, based mainly on the materials to be conserved (e.g., brick, stone, metals, etc.).[7] More recent approaches strive to integrate the conservation of waterworks, water resources, water livelihoods, and meanings.[8] As a further contribution along those lines, it may be useful to think systematically and imaginatively about the colors of water.[9]

Fig. 2, Sites along the Yamuna River near Agra.

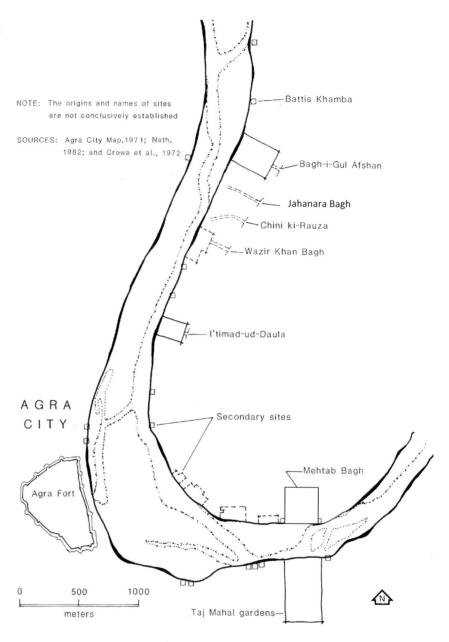

NOTE: The origins and names of sites are not conclusively established

SOURCES: Agra City Map, 1971; Nath, 1982; and Crowe et al., 1972

Battis Khamba

Bagh-i-Gul Afshan

Jahanara Bagh

Chini ki-Rauza

Wazir Khan Bagh

I'timad-ud-Daula

AGRA CITY

Secondary sites

Mehtab Bagh

Agra Fort

0   500   1000

meters

Taj Mahal gardens

Fig. 3 and Fig. 4

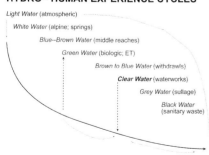

HYDRO - HUMAN EXPERIENCE CYCLES

Light Water (atmospheric)

White Water (alpine; springs)

Blue--Brown Water (middle reaches)

Green Water (biologic; ET)

Brown to Blue Water (withdrawls)

Clear Water (waterworks)

Grey Water (sullage)

Black Water (sanitary waste)

In contrast with color wheels and color charts, the spatial framework proposed here maps color terms onto a cross-sectional diagram of the hydrologic cycle—from atmospheric waters to white waters and successive reuses of water by plants, animals, soils, and humans, culminating in return flows to the oceans and atmosphere (Fig. 3, Table 1).

TABLE 1. HYDROLOGY AND HUMAN EXPERIENCE

Light water – atmospheric waters
White water – cascading, aerated headwaters
Blue water – upper reaches of rivers and tributaries
Brown water – middle and lower reaches of rivers
Green water –- water in plants, soil, and animals
Clear water – water in channels, pools, and fountains
Gray water – stormwater runoff from urbanized areas
Black water – sanitary sewers and wastewaters

Some of these color terms are derived from cultural and architectural practices, while others have acquired currency in modern water management (e.g., gray water, green water, blue water, and black water).[10] These sources come together in fascinating intersections of color theory, color science, and hydrologic optics, both in South Asia and more widely.[11] One of the strengths of this approach is that most societies employ a relatively small number of water and color terms (three to twelve) for a large number of visually distinguishable colors (roughly 7 million).[12]

THE COLORS OF HYDROLOGY AND HUMAN EXPERIENCE

This section applies the model presented in figure 3 to landscape experience at the Taj Mahal complex. It begins with water in the atmosphere—alternately viewed as pure "light water," or polluted "yellowing water"[13]—and traces its flows through the riverscapes of Agra—leading to the "black waters" of urban sewage and culminating in the light waters of evapotranspiration and purification.

1. *Light Water.* We begin with water in the atmosphere, which is especially important at the Taj Mahal for its atmospheric aesthetics, as well as for chemical weathering of marble surfaces (Fig. 4). The most common color distinction in most societies is between lightness and darkness, related to the cycle of the day. Indeed, the Taj Mahal was known in Mughal times as the *Illumined Tomb (rauza i-munavara)*, which reflected its associations with light *(nur)*.[14] Even apparently clear skies contain moisture in the form of humidity, defined as the amount of water vapor the atmosphere holds, or can hold, at a given temperature. Atmospheric humidity is not always visible, but it is experienced and can be managed at the microclimatic level by shade trees, irrigation, breezes, and riverfront views. Psychologically it is affected by fountains, blooms, fragrances, bird life—all of which depend on water.

The India Meteorological Department collects humidity and comfort-index data that has relevance for the experience of the Taj Mahal, while the Ministry of Environment and Forests collects the air-quality data relevant for its management. Air pollution emission of SO_2 and particulates cause marble to yellow and weather. Atmospheric haze, generated in part by water vapor, affects

Plan, edited by Amita Sinha et al. (Lucknow and Urbana: University of Illinois, Department of Landscape Architecture, 2000), 4–9.

7 James L. Wescoat Jr., "Waterworks and Landscape Design at the Mahtab Bagh," in *The Moonlight Garden*, edited by Elizabeth B. Moynihan (Washington, DC: Arthur M. Sackler Gallery, 2000), 59–78; and James L. Wescoat Jr., "Water in Garden Archaeology," in *Handbook of Garden Archaeology*, edited by Aicha Malek (Paris, forthcoming, 2011).

8 James L. Wescoat Jr., "Waterscapes and Water Conserving Design," *LA! Journal of Landscape Architecture* (India), 25 (2009).

9 A short essay on this approach was published in James L. Wescoat Jr., "The Taj Mahal in Its Yamuna River Context," *A+D Architecture and Design* (India), special issue on the Taj Mahal (December 2003): 80–83; James L. Wescoat Jr., "Beneath Which Rivers Flow: Water, Geographic Imagination, and Sustainable Landscape Design," in *Landscapes of Water: History, Innovation and Sustainable Design*, edited by U. Fratino et al. (Bari: Uniongrafica Corcelli Editrice 1, 2002), 13–34.

10 As Erika Friedl has shown in the Luristan province of Iran, there are subtle variations in the pragmatics of color terms, i.e., variations that depend upon use, e.g., for wool dying, foods, beads, and animals. Erika Friedl, "Colors and Culture Change in Southwest Iran," *Language in Society* 8 (1979): 51–68; and Ram Nath, *Colour Decoration in Mughal Architecture* (Bombay, D. B. Taraporevala Sons, 1970). M. Falkenmark and J. Rockström, "The New Blue and Green Water Paradigm: Breaking New Ground for Water Resources Planning and Management," *Journal of Water Resources Planning and Management* 132, no. 3 (2006): 129–132.

11 Brent Berlin and Paul Kay, *Basic Color Terms: Their Universality and Evolution* (Berkeley: University of California Press, 1969); R.J. Davies-Colley, W.N.Vant, and D.G. Smith, *Colour and Clarity of Natural Waters* (New York: Ellis Horwood, 1993); R.W. Preisendorfer, *Hydrologic Optics*, 6 vols. (Honolulu: U.S. Department of Commerce, National Oceanic and Atmospheric Administration, Environmental Research

visibility and is managed in Agra by decrees of the Supreme Court of India (as the U.S. government oversees air quality in the Grand Canyon National Park in the USA). Fog, by comparison, is a common winter phenomenon in Agra that has an ethereal effect, which carries us to the next color (Fig. 5).

2. *White Water.* White is the presence of all colors, a phenomenon central to the experience and meaning of the Taj Mahal. Clouds and monsoon rainfall have enormous visual significance, as when the dome of the Taj Mahal was compared with clouds, milk, and sugar in Mughal times (Fig. 6).[15] Whitecaps are rare today on the river Yamuna, but they were common features in Mughal paintings that depicted the power of the river in flood, and an evocation of the mountain streams of the earliest Mughal gardens in Central Asia and Afghanistan.

Today, as in Mughal times, rain and runoff cause the extensive white surfaces of the Taj Mahal complex to glisten. Unfortunately, the axial channels have mistakenly been painted blue in a gesture to modern taste. Their original white color was central to the garden's meaning, for white is the color of grief in South Asia. Court poets wrote that Shah Jahan's grief caused his hair and beard to turn white, that he wore white clothes, and shed rivers of tears. The only exception was a verse in which, "tears of blood pour[ed] ceaselessly from the eye," a common poetic association between blood and water.[16] But there is more to it. Ebba Koch argues that the combination of red sandstone and white marble in Mughal architecture constituted a "color dualism" that shifted over time from predominantly red sandstone structures with white marble details in the late sixteenth century to the largely marble architecture with red paving and auxiliary buildings at places like the Taj Mahal in the early seventeenth century.[17] Koch interprets these stone color patterns in relation to caste hierarchy as well as color symbolism in India: Brahmin (white, priestly) and Kshatriya (red, warrior), which share the Sanskrit term *varna* (color or caste).

3. *Blue to Brown Water.* The mistakenly blue channels of the Taj Mahal gardens today return us to the skies and river channel at Agra. Mughal paintings often depicted both features in blue hues. Poets compared the sky to a polished mirror, as when the poet Qudsi reminded his listeners that, "The sky's very appearance is inconstant. Its azure color hardly endures for a moment."[18] Similarly, the river's color changes throughout the day and year, from blue to green, yellow, and brown, reflecting the Taj Mahal tomb in myriad ways that stir one's imagination (Fig. 7). What do these reflections convey? Do they evoke the story of Solomon and Bilqis (Queen of Sheba), who mistook a polished floor for water in Islamic and Jewish mystical traditions,[19] the turbulent mixing of purity and pollution? These stories come to mind as one ferries across the river to work, as children swim, and as farmers cultivate vegetables on exposed sand flats.

4. *Green Water.* The river Yamuna irrigates tens of thousands of hectares. In Mughal times it supported a profusion of floodplain vegetation and fauna in Agra that is difficult to imagine today. It is only when monsoon rains fall that we gain a sense of the green condition of water at the Taj Mahal, in which rain is intercepted by trees, washing dust off their leaves, cooling leaf temperatures, reducing plant water stress, and increasing transpiration back into the atmosphere (Fig. 8). Tree cover in the Taj Mahal garden and surroundings has varied enormously over the centuries, from dense multistoried plantings of the late eighteenth century to colonial orchards and Victorian ornamental designs of the nineteenth century. Monsoon rains still sustain these green waters that are

Fig. 5 and Fig. 6

Laboratories, 1976); Andre Morel and Howard R. Gordan, Report of the Working Group on Water Color," *Boundary Layer Meteorology* 18 (1980): 343–355; and Delwin T. Lindsey and Angela M. Brown, "Universality of Color Names," *Proceedings of the National Academy of Sciences* 103 (2006): 16608–16613.

12 Berlin and Kay, *Basic Color Terms.*

13 P. Goyal and M. P.Singh, "The Long-Term Concentration of Sulfur Dioxide at Taj Mahal Due to the Mathura Uttar Pradesh India Refinery," *Atmospheric Environment, Part B Urban Atmosphere* 24:3 (1990): 407–412.

14 Begley and Desai, *The Illumined Tomb.*

15 Ibid., 84.

16 Ibid., 35.

17 Ebba Koch, *The Complete Taj Mahal* (London: Thames & Hudson, 2007), 214–217.

18 Begley and Desai, *The Illumined Tomb*, 35.

19 Wescoat, "Waterworks and Landscape Design," 71–72.

a postcolonial amalgam of exotic flowering trees; carefully edged, shortly mown Calcutta dub grass lawns (also known as Bermuda grass, *Cynodon dactylon);* and annual bedding plants. The supplemental irrigation that supports these exotic plantings is undergoing a transition from flood irrigation to automated sprinklers, trying to sustain bright green lawns in a region that has natural cycles of dormant yellow grass and that now suffers severe water shortages. This trend recalls the poet Qudsi's verse that, "In this garden, not a single green leaf grows, which the autumnal wind does not cause to yellow and wither."[20] But before turning to the colors of death and decay, one may return briefly to the ideals of clarity and purity in the Taj Mahal garden waterworks.

20 Begley and Desai, *The Illumined Tomb*, 35.

     5. Clear Water. After experiencing the waters of the sky, river, and vegetation of Agra, we arrive at the architectural waterworks originally designed for the Taj Mahal tomb-garden complex, set within their broader hydrologic context. They are indeed white-flowing, transient symbols of grief that direct one's path to the tomb, and more than that. A chain of twenty-five fountains runs down the center of each major channel, producing concentric ripples that extend to the channel edge and refract with one another and the sunlight that strikes them (Fig. 9). When the fountains go quiet, the channels become perfectly clear. At an angle, they reflect the true colors of surrounding trees and passersby, whose profusely colored clothes envelop the flowing waters of human bodies moving through the main artery of the garden (Fig. 10). Halfway down the central axis, one arrives at the elevated white marble pool. Five tall marble fountains spray water above the pool's surface, lapping the white marble lotus-carved edge in a way that combines white, bright, light, and green water in one surface. Another rectangular tank in front of the mosque, just west of the tomb, holds clear waters for ablution. These experiences of clear waters prompt us to ask where they lead, which takes us back to the irrigated garden and river Yamuna.

     6. Gray Water. Many of the Taj Mahal's water channels and ablution tanks spilled out into the gardens, irrigating groves of trees and swaths of ground-cover with what today is called gray water. Carved stone drains carry effluent into cisterns and overflow channels that return ultimately to the Yamuna River (Fig. 11). Gray-water reuse, like rainwater harvesting, is advancing rapidly in India and world-wide.[21] When designed to avoid contamination of potable water, it has enormous potential to extend the supplies of water-scarce metropolitan regions like Agra. Gray is also the color of shadows that reach over the garden in the evening when excess moisture slowly drains out from the soil, where its successive reuse has supported insects, plants, and animals toward the river Yamuna and its aquifer.

     7. Black Water. Gray water reuse is often pre empted by contamination from sanitary wastewater, known today as black water. Human and animal waste has had both ecological value and health dangers in every era. Its volume was minuscule in Mughal times (even in Agra, the largest city in Mughal India), compared to the present-day population and use of flush toilets. Sanitary wastewater degrades the Yamuna terribly, especially during the dry season; and while various treatment projects are under way, they face enormous challenges (Fig. 12). Black waters are not just sewage in the modern sense, they are the waters of Yama, death.

     The hydrologic cycle and human experience do not end in darkness. The Taj Mahal is compared with the light of morning that renews the cycle of life, death, and reflection on the path to paradise. The colors of water remind us

Fig. 13

that these qualities of water are immanent in every drop of water, changeable at every moment in space and time, as a grand chromatic system of creation.

LESSONS FROM, AND FOR, THE TAJ MAHAL

This essay has sought to take us from a perspective on red sandstone and white marble water channels to a more comprehensive hydrologic and experiential perspective on color in the waterscape. Clouds that rained tears of grief at the death of Mumtaz Mahal in 1631 formed a "pool of tears [that] became a mirror of his [Shah Jahan's] heart and mind," and the torrents that carried them away, in the words of the court poet Kalim.[22] Mughal poets remind us that, "the water that causes your seeds to flourish shall eventually wash away your house," like "a violet garden on the bank of the river of calamity, having manifested itself to the gaze of people in the garb of mourners."[23] The Taj Mahal's "pictures on the water of white marble have a remarkably durable ...and watery luster," as "pictures of semi-precious flowers, written on the water of the white marble sarcophagus," or "dewdrops engraved upon crystal," with their "red and yellow flowers, dispel the heart's grief."[24]

These verses on colors of water in the Taj Mahal and river Yamuna landscape have relevance for their conservation. Conservation of natural resources is inherently entwined with conservation of the built environment. There are many conservation design lessons to be drawn from atmospheric water harvesting, blue-stream ideals, green plantings, gray- and black-water reuse— as well as cautionary tales of excessive use and pollution. Much remains to be done, and undone, as in the case of the blue-water channels where white was envisioned.

Color offers a complex figurative model for waterscape conservation that extends beyond the capacity of societies to describe it in other terms, especially at places such as the Taj Mahal (Fig. 13). Mughal painting reminds us that water experience encompasses the full spectrum of aesthetic emotions (*rasa*), each one characterized by its own color and mood. Past and present, they have addressed the processes of hydrology and human experience, so much so that a "colors of water model" may contribute to the conservation of complex ecological, economic, and cultural forces in the landscape.

22 Begley and Desai, *The Illumined Tomb*, 33.

23 Ibid., 30.

24 Ibid., 83.

Harvard University
Graduate School of Design

Tenured Professor

Geography and Urbanism

A senior faculty position is available for a preeminent international scholar in the cultural, economic, ecological, and spatial geographies of urbanization at the Harvard Graduate School of Design. We are interested in including geography and urban theory more broadly in our curriculum and in research initiatives in the school's planning, urban design, and doctoral programs across disciplines, as well as in the school's other fields of architecture and landscape architecture. The appointment will be made at the level of Professor and is a full-time tenured position with responsibilities for teaching, research, and administration; we expect the successful candidate to play an important role in the school's advanced and doctoral programs. Candidates should have a PhD or equivalent, an internationally respected publication record, and, preferably, experience in teaching in the context of a graduate professional school and in working with colleagues and students in the fields of design and planning.

Applications will be considered starting immediately (and can continue to be submitted into the new year). Interested candidates should submit a c.v. and a statement of interest to: Mike McGrath, Director of Faculty Planning, Harvard University Graduate School of Design, 48 Quincy Street, Cambridge, MA 02138, Tel: 617-495-5409, Fax: 617-495-9026, E-mail: mmcgrath@gsd.harvard.edu.